Lecture Notes in Artificial Intelligence   3123

Edited by J. G. Carbonell and J. Siekmann

Subseries of Lecture Notes in Computer Science

Anja Belz   Roger Evans   Paul Piwek (Eds.)

Natural
Language Generation

Third International Conference, INLG 2004
Brockenhurst, UK, July 14-16, 2004
Proceedings

 Springer

Series Editors

Jaime G. Carbonell, Carnegie Mellon University, Pittsburgh, PA, USA
Jörg Siekmann, University of Saarland, Saarbrücken, Germany

Volume Editors

Anja Belz
Roger Evans
Paul Piwek
University of Brighton, Information Technology Research Institute
Lewes Road, Brighton BN2 4GJ, UK
E-mail: {Anja.Belz,Roger.Evans,Paul.Piwek}@itri.brighton.ac.uk

Library of Congress Control Number: 2004108214

CR Subject Classification (1998): I.2.7, I.2, F.4.3

ISSN 0302-9743
ISBN 3-540-22340-1 Springer-Verlag Berlin Heidelberg New York

Springer-Verlag is a part of Springer Science+Business Media

springeronline.com

© Springer-Verlag Berlin Heidelberg 2004
Printed in Germany

Typesetting: Camera-ready by author, data conversion by Boller Mediendesign
Printed on acid-free paper   SPIN: 11017578   06/3142   5 4 3 2 1 0

Preface

The Third International Conference on Natural Language Generation (INLG 2004) was held from 14th to 16th July 2004 at Careys Manor, Brockenhurst, UK. Supported by the Association for Computational Linguistics Special Interest Group on Generation, the conference continued a twenty-year tradition of biennial international meetings on research into natural language generation. Recent conference venues have included Mitzpe Ramon, Israel (INLG 2000) and New York, USA (INLG 2002). It was our pleasure to invite the thriving and friendly NLG research community to the beautiful New Forest in the south of England for INLG 2004.

INLG is the leading international conference in the field of natural language generation. It provides a forum for the presentation and discussion of original research on all aspects of the generation of language, including psychological modelling of human language production as well as computational approaches to the automatic generation of language. This volume includes a paper by the keynote speaker, Ardi Roelofs of the Max Planck Institute for Psycholinguistics and the F.C. Donders Centre for Cognitive Neuroimaging, 18 regular papers reporting the latest research results and directions, and 4 student papers describing doctoral work in progress. These papers reveal a particular concentration of current research effort on statistical and machine learning methods, on referring expressions, and on variation in surface realisation. The papers were selected from 46 submissions from all over the world (27 from Europe, 13 from North America, 6 from elsewhere), which were subjected to a rigorous double-blind reviewing process undertaken by our hard-working programme committee. In addition, the conference had a poster session giving a snapshot of ongoing research projects in the field (published as ITRI technical report No. ITRI-04-01).

As always, the conference and this volume of proceedings are the result of the combined efforts of many people. First and foremost we would like to thank all the authors who submitted papers, and the Programme Committee who helped us to put together an excellent conference programme. In addition, we thank everyone who helped us put the conference together, especially the ITRI administrative team, staff at Careys Manor Hotel, and members of the SIGGEN and ACL boards, especially Owen Rambow and Kathy McCoy. Finally we thank all the staff and students at ITRI, and in the wider generation community, for their advice, support and participation in INLG 2004.

July 2004   Anja Belz, Roger Evans and Paul Piwek

Organisation

INLG 2004 was organised by the Information Technology Research Institute, University of Brighton, UK, on behalf of the Association for Computational Linguistics Special Interest Group on Generation (ACL SIGGEN).

Co-chairs

Anja Belz, ITRI, Brighton
Roger Evans, ITRI, Brighton
Paul Piwek, ITRI, Brighton

Administration

Domino Moore, ITRI, Brighton
Martyn Haddock, ITRI, Brighton
Petra Tank, ITRI, Brighton
Amy Neale, ITRI, Brighton

ACL SIGGEN Liaison

Owen Rambow, Columbia
Kathy McCoy, Delaware

Programme Committee

Anja Belz, ITRI, University of Brighton, UK (Co-chair)
Roger Evans, ITRI, University of Brighton, UK (Co-chair)
Paul Piwek, ITRI, University of Brighton, UK (Co-chair)
Ion Androutsopoulos, Athens University of Economics and Business, Greece
Srinivas Bangalore, AT&T, USA
Regina Barzilay, CSAIL, MIT, USA
John Bateman, Bremen University, Germany
Tilman Becker, DFKI, Germany
Sandra Carberry, CIS, University of Delaware, USA
Alison Cawsey, CEE, Heriot Watt University, UK
Robert Dale, Maquarie University, Australia
Kees van Deemter, ITRI, University of Brighton, UK
Michael Elhadad, Ben-Gurion University of the Negev, Israel
Barbara di Eugenio, Computer Science, University of Illinois at Chicago, USA
Nancy Green, University of North Carolina at Greensboro, USA

Table of Contents

Keynote Paper

Regular Papers

Student Papers

The Seduced Speaker: Modeling of Cognitive Control

Ardi Roelofs

Max Planck Institute for Psycholinguistics, F.C. Donders Centre for Cognitive Neuroimaging, and Nijmegen Institute for Cognition and Information, Wundtlaan 1, 6525 XD, Nijmegen, the Netherlands
ardi@mpi.nl
http://www.mpi.nl/world/persons/profession/ardi.html

Abstract. Although humans are the ultimate "natural language generators", the area of psycholinguistic modeling has been somewhat underrepresented in recent approaches to Natural Language Generation in computer science. To draw attention to the area and illustrate its potential relevance to Natural Language Generation, I provide an overview of recent work on psycholinguistic modeling of language production together with some key empirical findings, state-of-the-art experimental techniques, and their historical roots. The techniques include analyses of speech-error corpora, chronometric analyses, eyetracking, and neuroimaging. The overview is built around the issue of cognitive control in natural language generation, concentrating on the production of single words, which is an essential ingredient of the generation of larger utterances. Most of the work exploited the fact that human speakers are good but not perfect at resisting temptation, which has provided some critical clues about the nature of the underlying system.

1 Introduction

Unlike most Natural Language Generation programs that run on serial, digital computers, human speakers are occasionally distracted while performing a natural language generation task. "I can resist everything except temptation" (p. 5), a play character of Oscar Wilde [1] once said, and this difficulty in resisting temptation holds for most people. Distractibility seems to be the price paid for the parallelism of the human brain. One of the key tasks of the human cognitive system is to select one appropriate action at any given moment and to focus the machinery of planning and movement on that action. Selectivity of attention is required for the coherent control of action. At the same time, the system needs to remain open to events that may happen outside the focus of attention (e.g., to detect possible danger in the background). The opposing forces of the need to focus and the need to remain open make the human system distractible. This raises the issue of cognitive control.

In speaking, the distractibility of the human cognitive system is revealed by speech errors and delays in initiating articulation. The distractibility is also evident from the eye movements that speakers make. By examining speech errors,

A. Belz et al. (Eds.): INLG 2004, LNAI 3123, pp. 1–10, 2004.

delays, and eye movements, researchers have discovered much about the cognitive foundations of speaking. Computer models have been developed that account for the kinds of speech errors that occur and their relative frequencies, and also for the eye movements and the exact duration of the delays caused by distraction. Furthermore, much has been discovered about the brain areas that are involved in speaking. Computer models can even predict the time course of the increase in blood flow to certain brain areas required for speech production. I provide an overview of work in psycholinguistics that tried to shed light on the human language generation system using evidence from speech-error corpora, chronometric experiments, eyetracking, and neuroimaging. The overview is built around the issue of cognitive control in natural language generation. It concentrates on the production of single words, which is an essential component of the generation of larger utterances. Nearly all of the work that is reviewed exploited the fact that human speakers are good but not perfect at resisting temptation, which has provided important evidence about the nature of the underlying system.

2   What Speech Errors Say About Speaking

A slip of the tongue or speech error is an unintended, nonhabitual deviation from a speech plan. Meringer and Mayer [2] were among the first to draw attention to speech errors as a data source that might illuminate the mechanisms underlying speech production. In 1895, they published a large corpus of German speech errors along with a theoretical analysis. They made several seminal observations. First, they discovered that slips of the tongue are typically meaning-based or form-based. The substitution of "dog" for "cat" is a meaning-based error and the substitution "cap" for "cat" is a form-based one. The distinction suggests that words are planned at a conceptual level and at a form level. Second, they observed that there is often a form-relation in meaning-based errors (e.g., "calf" for "cat"), suggesting that the planning levels do not operate completely independently, although this is still a hotly debated issue [3]. Third, they observed that contextual errors may be anticipations (e.g., "*l*eading list" for "reading list"), perseverations (e.g., "beef n*ee*dle" for "beef noodle"), exchanges (e.g., "*fl*ow *sn*urries" for "snow flurries"), or blends (e.g., "clear" combining "close" and "near").

Although speech error analyses continued to be carried out during the next half century, there was a real revival of interest in the late 1960s. In 1973, Fromkin [4] edited an influential book on speech errors that included an appendix with part of her own speech error corpus. Another important corpus was collected during the early 1970s at MIT by Garrett and colleagues. Garrett [5] discovered that word exchanges such as the exchange of *roof* and *list* in "we completely forgot to add the *list* to the *roof*" tend to involve elements from different phrases and of the same syntactic category, here noun. By contrast, segment exchanges such as "she is a real *r*ack *p*at" for "pack rat" are likely to involve elements from the same phrase and they do not respect lexical category. Garrett explained this finding by assuming a level of syntactic planning (at which the lexical exchanges occur) that is different from the level of form planning (at which the segment exchanges occur). Garrett argued that the speech errors also provide support for a distinct morphological planning level.

Some morphemic errors appear to happen at the syntactic level, whereas others arise at the form level. For example, in "how many *pies* does it take to make an *apple*?", the interacting stems (i.e., *pie* and *apple*) belong to the same syntactic category and come from distinct phrases. Note that the plurality of *apple* is realized on *pie*, which suggests that a number parameter is set. The distributional properties of these morpheme exchanges are similar to those of whole-word exchanges. This suggests that these morpheme errors and whole-word errors occur at the same level of planning. They seem to occur when lexical items in a developing syntactic structure trade places. Similarly, errors such as "I'd *hear* one if I *knew* it" for "I'd *know* one if I *heard* it" suggest that syntactically specified lexical representations may trade places independently of their concrete morphophonological specifications. By contrast, the exchanging morphemes in an error such as "*slicely thinn*ed" for "thinly sliced" belong to different syntactic categories and come from the same phrase, which is also characteristic of segment exchanges. This suggests that this second type of morpheme error and segment errors occur at the same level of planning, namely the level at which morphemes and segments are retrieved and the morphophonological form of the utterance is constructed.

On the basis of his speech error analyses, Garrett [5] proposed an unimplemented model of speech production that distinguished between conceptual, syntactic, morphological, phonological, and phonetic levels of speech planning. Ten years later, Dell [6] developed the first computer model of memory retrieval in sentence production, instantiating several of Garrett's insights. Following a long associationist tradition that began with Aristotle [7], Dell convincingly argued that our word memory is organized as an associative network that is accessed by spreading activation. The network contains nodes for conceptual, syntactic, morphological, phonological, and phonetic information about words. In retrieving information for concepts to be verbally expressed, activation spreads from the corresponding concept nodes to associated nodes in the network. After fixed periods of time, the highest activated lexical, morpheme, phoneme, and phonetic nodes are selected. Dell's associative network model of word memory provided quantitative accounts of the major facts about speech errors: the kinds of errors that occur, their relative frequencies, and the constraints on their form and occurrence. On the account, errors occur when, because of noise in the system or influences outside the intended utterance (distraction), another node in the network than the target one is the most highly activated node and becomes erroneously selected.

3   What Response Times Say About Speaking

The first person to measure (in milliseconds) speech production latencies – the time between stimulus onset and the initiation of a verbal response – was Donders [8]. Until Donders' work in the 1860s, most scientists had assumed that the mental operations involved in responding to a stimulus occur instantaneously. Donders designed a subtraction technique to time the different mental processes that the brain goes through when faced with different tasks. His chronometric work demonstrated a simple principle: The time it takes to perform a task depends on the number and types of mental stages involved. With this observation, he laid the foundation of a research programme that is still extremely productive today: the componential processing analysis of human task performance. At the end of his seminal article on the measurement of mental processing times [8], Donders reports that "distraction during the appearance of the stimulus is always punished with prolongation of the process" (p. 428). This observation is interesting in the light of later research developments exploiting distraction, in particular, the work of Stroop in the 1930s. Surprisingly, it was only in the 1990s that speech error and chronometric analyses became equal partners in the study of speaking. Most of the chronometric work that has been done addressed the production of single words or simple phrases. This seems to be due to the fact that it is awfully difficult to investigate the generation of more complex utterances (sentences and discourse) in controlled experimental settings. Still, the investigation of word production has provided some key insights into the algorithms that underlie human language generation. The first computer model of word production built on chronometric evidence is WEAVER++ [9] [10] [11]. This model recognizes the key insights from the speech error analyses, but it was specifically designed to provide a unifying account of the increasing body of chronometric data.

Like Dell's model, WEAVER++ assumes that word planning involves the retrieval of information from an associative network through spreading activation. In addition, WEAVER++ assumes that the associations are labeled, because a mere associative link between two nodes in a network tells nothing about the relation between the entities represented. For example, the concept RED(X) is strongly associated with both GREEN(X) and FIRE(X), but the relationship between RED(X) and GREEN(X) is very different from the relationship between RED(X) and FIRE(X). The importance of representing the relation between entities symbolically was first recognized by Selz [7] in the early 1900s. Labeled links have become a central part of semantic networks in computer science since the seminal work of Quillian in the late 1960s.

To explain even the simplest forms of language generation, like single word production, it is not enough to assume an associative memory and spreading activation. Natural language is a very flexible tool that can be used to achieve various goals. Around 1900, Watt, Ach, and Külpe of the Würzburg school [7], as well as Selz [7], called attention to the importance of understanding the directedness of action in general and verbal action in particular (the problem of cognitive control is also referred to in the literature as the problem of attentional, executive, or willed control.) They convincingly argued that the various associative models that had been developed during the past two millennia failed to explain the directedness of thought and action. Plato already drew attention

to the problem, which he characterized in *Phaedrus* as the problem of a chari-
oteer attempting to manage a number of horses pulling in different directions.
Until recently, this aspect of natural language generation was neglected in psycholinguistic research on word production. The directedness of natural language
generation has, in its simplest form, perhaps been most intensively studied by
using the "gold standard" of attentional measures, the color-word Stroop task
[12] and picture-word analogs of it. The Stroop task is one of the most widely
used tasks in academic and applied psychology, reviewed by MacLeod [13]. In
the classic, color-word version of the task, speakers name the ink color of color
words (one basic task variant) or they read the color words aloud (another basic
task variant). In performing the Stroop task, speakers are slower naming the ink
colors of incongruent color words (e.g., the word BLUE in red ink) than of a
series of Xs. Word reading times are unaffected by incongruent ink colors. The
correct naming of the colors of incongruent color words shows that goals keep
verbal actions on track in the face of distraction, albeit with a temporal cost.

Issues of cognitive control were already explored in the early days of experimental psychology (between 1870-1920) by Cattell, Donders, James, and Wundt,
who saw all his work on response times as studies of volition [14]. However, no
progress was made in understanding the mechanisms of control. Associationist
and behaviorist theories accounted for action selection by postulating associations between stimuli and responses (e.g., Müller in the early 1900s [7], and later
Watson and Skinner). However, if all our actions were determined exclusively by
stimulus-response associations, goals could not determine which action to make
because the strongest association would automatically determine the response.
Watt and Ach of the Würzburg school [7] extended the idea of stimulus-response
associations to associations between stimuli and an internally represented task
goal ("Aufgabe"), on the one hand, and responses, on the other. Later theoretical
developments are descendants of this idea.

On the view that currently dominates the attention and performance literature, which was anticipated by Müller [7] and recently implemented in the
GRAIN computer model by Botvinick and colleagues [15], goals associatively
bias the activation of one response pathway (e.g., for color naming) rather than
another (e.g., for oral reading). On another view, implemented in WEAVER++
[16], attentional control arises from explicit, symbolic reference to goals, accomplished by condition-action rules. WEAVER++'s associative network is accessed
by spreading activation while the condition-action rules determine what is done
with the activated lexical information depending on the task. When a goal symbol (e.g., indicating to name the color) is placed in working memory, attention is
focused on those rules that include the goal among their conditions (e.g., those
for color naming rather than reading). Words are planned by incrementally extending verbal goals. Lexical nodes are selected for concept nodes, morpheme
nodes for lexical nodes, segment nodes for morpheme nodes, and phonetic syllable program nodes for syllabified segment nodes, whereby the syllabification
of segments proceeds incrementally from the beginning of a word to its end.

The idea of incrementality in natural language generation was first proposed by Wundt [14].

WEAVER++'s combination of a spreading activation network with a parallel system of goal-factored condition-action rules yields a simple but powerful and efficient device for selecting one line of action among the available options. The crucial role of spreading activation in the model is to provide a relevance heuristic. Spreading activation serves to solve the "frame problem" that confronts any cognitive system. In making decisions, a cognitive system can, in principle, draw on all the information available, but the amount may be indefinitely large in that everything may potentially be relevant. The frame problem is how to get at the relevant information and when to stop thinking and start acting. Spreading activation is a parallel mechanism for making relevant information available and triggering relevant computations, following the heuristic that information associated with the current information is likely of direct relevance too. Triggering condition-action rules by spreading activation prevents the problem of all rules having to test their conditions at any one moment in time. Only the rules that are linked to a sufficiently activated piece of associative memory become evaluated. For example, in naming a color, no more than a dozen or so condition-action rules test their conditions rather than all rules in a speaking lexicon of some 30,000 words. Moreover, because condition-action rules may be triggered by the activation of elements outside the current focus of attention, the system remains open to what happens in the background.

The idea of goal-referenced control originated with Selz [7] and it flourished in the work of Newell and Simon, Anderson and colleagues [17], and others, on higher-level cognitive processes like problem solving (e.g., playing chess, proving logic theorems, and solving puzzles such as the Tower of Hanoi), where associative models generally failed. However, due to the traditional partitioning of experimental psychology into cognition, perception, and action, with little communication across the boundaries, goal-referenced control models have had little impact in the perception-action literature, because they generally did not aim at fine-grained modeling of the temporal structure of human information processing in the attention and performance tradition. Only recently, goal-referenced control made successful strides into the attention and performance literature. For example, there are now successful models for fine-grained aspects of visual attention, dual-task performance [17], and Stroop [16]. It seems that we are on the verge of a unified account of the control of cognition, perception, and action.

4   What Eye Movements Say About Speaking

In the second half of the nineteenth century, well before the modern era of cognitive and brain sciences, Donders and Wundt studied eye movements and constructed mechanical models for them. Whereas before those days the eyes used to be poetically called a window to the soul, Wundt took gazes to be a window into the operation of the attention system. As Wundt [14] reasoned in his *Outlines of psychology*, visual acuity is best at the point of fixation. Therefore, to bring aspects of the visual world in the focus of attention, eye fixations are directed to those visual aspects that are of most interest. This makes a shift of gaze an overt sign of the allocation of attention, as later studies confirmed, although at times visual attention and eye movements can be dissociated. According to Wundt [14] "the successive movement of attention over a number of objects is a discontinuous process made up of a number of separate acts of apperception following one another" (p. 212).

Whereas it has long been assumed that we look at aspects of the visual world just as long as is needed to identify them and that response factors play no role, recent research suggested that when we want to verbally describe the visual aspects, the gaze durations depend on the time to plan the corresponding words [18]. In naming objects, Wundt's "successive movement of attention over a number of objects" has been shown to be determined by word planning. For example, when speakers are asked to name two objects in a row, they look longer at first-to-be-named objects with disyllabic than with monosyllabic names even when the object recognition times do not differ [18]. The effect of the number of syllables suggests that the shift of gaze from one object to another is initiated only after the phonological form of the name for the object has been encoded.

Dissociations between vocal response latencies and gaze shifts suggest that the signal to move the eyes is the completion of (a critical part of) planning the phonological form of the vocal response rather than a flag that a signal to begin a vocal response has been sent out to the articulatory system. Response latencies and gaze durations can be dissociated in that gaze durations may reflect the phonological length (e.g., number of syllables) of the utterance even when response latencies do not [19]. Speakers were instructed to describe colored left and right objects (e.g., a big red scooter and a ball) in a simple or in a complex way. They either had to respond with "the scooter and the ball" or "the *big red* scooter and the ball". The gaze durations for the left object (the scooter) were much shorter for the simple utterances than for the complex utterances. However, the vocal response latencies did not differ between the two utterance types. Furthermore, the shift of gaze to the right object was initiated before articulation onset for the simple utterances, but after articulation onset for the complex utterances. This suggests that the shift of gaze, but not the onset of articulation, is triggered by the completion of phonological encoding of the first object name. It seems that the attention required for planning the vocal response prevents the eyes to move before the object name has been planned. Because the planning takes longer with disyllabic than with monosyllabic names, the attention shift, and consequently the gaze shift, occurs later with two syllables than with one syllable.

Recent research from my own laboratory showed that Stroop-like interference is reflected in the gaze durations of speakers during object naming. Speakers were presented with picture-word stimuli. They either named the picture, named the word, or categorized the word, and shifted their gaze to a left- or right-pointing arrow to manually indicate its direction. Eye movements were monitored. Overall, there was a close correspondence between the magnitude of the distractor effects on the latencies of vocal responding, the gaze shifts, and the manual responding. This further supports the idea that the eyes are only free to move elsewhere when the verbal action goal is achieved.

The evidence from eyetracking suggests that in generating multiple-word utterances, speakers are not operating in a maximally incremental way. For example, in naming two objects in a row, they do not perform a lexical selection for the second object before they have planned the phonological form of the first object name. Moreover, the evidence suggests that a major reason why speakers fixate objects until having planned their names is that word planning requires attention. This conclusion agrees with recent evidence from dual-task performance by Ferreira and Pashler [20], which suggests that individuals cannot select a word for production and select a manual response at exactly the same moment in time. Ferreira and Pashler argued that all selections in word planning require attention. However, that does not need to be the case. If only one task goal (e.g., vocal responding or manual responding) can be in the focus of attention at any one moment in time, goal-referenced control predicts that one cannot perform selections for two tasks concurrently, even when they are automatized. This would explain the available data without assuming that attention is required for all individual selections in word planning. Instead, if selections are made with explicit reference to the task goal, word planning requires attention until (a critical aspect of) the word form is planned, as empirically observed.

5   What Brain Activity Says About Speaking

Currently, Donders' [8] subtraction technique developed for the temporal aspects of mental processes is widely applied to their spatial aspects – their correlates in the human brain. In his seminal article on response times, Donders [8] remarked that "as in all organs, the blood undergoes a change as a consequence of the nourishment of the brain" (p. 412). One "discovers in comparing the incoming and outflowing blood that oxygen has been consumed" (p. 412). This insight, together with the subtractive method designed by Donders, constitutes the basis of the two most widely used modern functional neuroimaging techniques, PET (positron emission tomography) and fMRI (functional magnetic resonance imaging).

Recent neuroimaging and electrophysiological studies have shed light on the neural correlates of speaking. The techniques include PET, fMRI, MEG (magnetoencephalography), and LRP (lateralized readiness potential) analyses. Indefrey and Levelt [21] performed a meta-analysis of 82 neuroimaging studies in the literature, which anatomically localized the word planning system in the brain. As can be expected from the classic neuropsychology literature and most later studies, the system is basically located in the left hemisphere (for most people). Visual and conceptual processing appear to involve the occipital, ventrotemporal, and anterior frontal regions of the brain. The middle part of the left middle temporal gyrus seems to be involved in lexical selection. Next, activation spreads to Wernicke's area, where the phonological code of the word seems to be retrieved. Activation is then transmitted to Broca's area for post-lexical phonological processing such as syllabification. Finally, phonetic encoding takes place, with possible contributions of the supplementary motor area and the cerebellum, while the sensorimotor areas are involved in articulation.

Recent neuroimaging studies also revealed that an extensive network of brain areas is involved in the attentional control of word planning. For example, color-word Stroop performance engages the anterior cingulate and dorsolateral prefrontal cortices, both subserving attentional control, the left lingual gyrus for color processing, the left extrastriate cortex for visual word-form processing, and the left-perisylvian language areas including the areas of Broca and Wernicke [22]. Whereas evidence suggests that the dorsolateral prefrontal cortex serves to maintain the goals in working memory, no consensus exists as to whether anterior cingulate activation reflects the presence of conflict [15] or goal-referenced control [16] [22]. The latter view is in line with Paus' [23] characterization of the anterior cingulate cortex as the brain area where "motor control, drive and cognition interface" and Simon's [24] characterization of attention as the principal link between cognition and motivation. For action control, it is not enough to have goals in working memory, but one should be motivated to attain them. Extensive projections from the thalamus and brainstem nuclei to the anterior cingulate suggest a role for drive and arousal. Extensive reciprocal connections between the anterior cingulate and dorsolateral prefrontal cortices suggest a role for working memory. The motor areas of the cingulate sulcus densely project to the spinal cord and motor cortex, which suggests a role of the anterior cingulate in motor control. The motor areas seem to contain subregions controlling vocal responses, manual responses, and eye movements [23]. Goal-referenced control was supported by successful WEAVER++ simulations of the hemodynamic response in the anterior cingulate during Stroop task performance [22].

Condition-action rules are sometimes criticized for being not brain-like in their computation. However, it is important to realize that the rules mean nothing more than the operations that they specify. Crucial for the issue of neural plausibility is whether we can exclude that the brain performs such if-then operations, and the criticisms do not bring forward evidence for that. On the contrary, there is increasing evidence that the human brain, in particular prefrontal cortex, supports the use of abstract rules [25].

6   Final Remarks

I provided an overview of recent work on psycholinguistic modeling of language production together with some key empirical findings and state-of-the-art experimental techniques, including analyses of speech-error corpora, chronometric analyses, eyetracking, and neuroimaging. Most of the work examined the production of single words. Sentence and discourse generation has received much less attention. We are still far away from a complete understanding of the ultimate natural language generator.

References

1. Wilde, O.: Lady Windermere's fan. Dover Publications, Mineola (1893/1998)
2. Meringer, R., Mayer, K.: Versprechen und Verlesen. Goschenscher-Verlag, Stuttgart (1895)
3. Roelofs, A.: Error biases in spoken word planning and monitoring by aphasic and nonaphasic speakers: Comment on Rapp and Goldrick (2000). Psych. Rev. 111 (2004) 561–572
4. Fromkin, V.A. (ed.): Speech errors as linguistic evidence. Mouton, The Hague (1973)
5. Garrett, M.F.: The analysis of sentence production. In: Bower, G.H. (ed.): The psychology of learning and motivation. Academic Press, New York (1975) 133–177
6. Dell, G.S.: A spreading-activation theory of retrieval in sentence production. Psych. Rev. 93 (1986) 283–321
7. Mandler, J.M., Mandler, G. (eds.): Thinking: From association to Gestalt. Wiley, New York (1964)
8. Donders, F.C.: On the speed of mental processes. Acta Psych. 30 (1868/1969) 412–431
9. Roelofs, A.: A spreading-activation theory of lemma retrieval in speaking. Cogn. 42 (1992) 107–142
10. Roelofs, A.: The WEAVER model of word-form encoding in speech production. Cogn. 64 (1997) 249–284
11. Levelt, W.J.M, Roelofs, A., Meyer, A.S.: A theory of lexical access in speech production. Behav. Brain Sci. 22 (1999) 1–38
12. Stroop, J.R.: Studies of interference in serial verbal reactions. J. Exp. Psych. 18 (1935) 643–662
13. MacLeod, C.M.: Half a century of research on the Stroop effect: An integrative review. Psych. Bull. 109 (1991) 163–203
14. Wundt, W.: Outlines of psychology. Engelmann, Leipzig (1897)
15. Botvinick, M.M., Braver, T.S. , Barch, D.M., Carter, C.S., Cohen, J.D.: Conflict monitoring and cognitive control. Psych. Rev. 108 (2001) 624–652
16. Roelofs, A.: Goal-referenced selection of verbal action: Modeling attentional control in the Stroop task. Psych. Rev. 110 (2003) 88–125
17. Anderson, J.R., Lebiere, C. (eds.): The atomic components of thought. Erlbaum, London (1998)
18. Meyer, A.S., Roelofs, A., Levelt, W.J.M.: Word length effects in object naming: The role of a response criterion. J. Mem. Lang. 48 (2003) 131–147
19. Levelt, W.J.M., Meyer, A. S.: Word for word: Multiple lexical access in speech production. Europ. J. Cogn. Psych. 12 (2000) 433–452
20. Ferreira, V., Pashler, H.: Central bottleneck influences on the processing stages of word production. J. Exp. Psych.: Learn. Mem. Cogn. 28 (2002) 1187–1199
21. Indefrey, P. Levelt, W.J.M.: The spatial and temporal signatures of word production components. Cogn. 92 (2004) 101–144
22. Roelofs, A., Hagoort, P.: Control of language use: Cognitive modeling of the hemodynamics of Stroop task performance. Cogn. Brain Res. 15 (2002) 85–97
23. Paus, T.: Primate anterior cingulate cortex: Where motor control, drive and cognition interface. Nature Rev. Neurosci. 2 (2001) 417–424
24. Simon, H.A.: Motivational and emotional controls of cognition. Psych. Rev. 74 (1967) 29–39
25. Miller, E.K.: The prefrontal cortex and cognitive control. Nature Rev. Neurosci. 1 (2000) 59–65

Generating Intensional Answers in Intelligent Question Answering Systems

Farah Benamara

Institut de Recherches en Informatique de Toulouse, IRIT,
118 route de Narbonne, 31062 Toulouse Cedex, France.
benamara@irit.fr

Abstract. In this paper, we present a logic-based model for an accurate generation of intensional responses within a cooperative question-answering framework. We develop several categories of intensional forms and a variable-depth intensional calculus that allows for the generation of intensional responses at the best level of abstraction. Finally, we show that it is possible to generate such NL responses on a template basis.

1 Introduction

Data generalization, statistics summarization and generalized rule extraction are essential techniques for intelligent query answering. These techniques, generally called intensional query answering (IQA), tend to abstract over possibly long enumerations of extensional answers in order to provide responses, in general at the highest level of abstraction. In addition, the intensional character of these answers may give hints to users about the structure of the knowledge base and of the domain knowledge and can help to clear up misconceptions. Most of the previous studies on IQA focused on generating intensional answers (IA) at a single level of abstraction using integrity constraints and/or rules of the database without any access to the extensional answer set (see [4] and [3] for a general overview). In addition, in most of these systems, there is no NL generation.

Our approach is substantially different from these approaches: the set of potential generalizers is directly derived via an intensional calculus from the set of direct responses to the question. Recently, [2] used a similar approach by applying data mining techniques for IQA at multiple levels of abstraction in a relational database environment. The originality of our work lies around three major points : (1) the use of the question focus (extracted while parsing the NL question) paired with a rich ontological description of the domain. The goal is to select and rank the set of relevant concepts to be generalized, (2) the definition of a *variable-depth intensional calculus* based on a cooperative know how component that determines, via a supervisor, the best level of abstraction for the response, using a conceptual metric, and (3) the NL generation of IA since we think that responses, expressed as explanations and justifications, should make explicit, in some way the underlying intensional calculus that led to the answer.

In the following sections, we first present a general typology of IA. Then, we show how ontological information coupled with the question focus can help to

A. Belz et al. (Eds.): INLG 2004, LNAI 3123, pp. 11–20, 2004.

provide IA at different levels of abstraction. Finally, we give some aspects of how IA are dynamically generated in natural language using a template based approach [6]. Results are integrated and evaluated within the WEBCOOP project, an intelligent, cooperative question-answering system.

2   A Typology of Intensional Answers

To have a more accurate perception of how intensionality is realized in man-man communication, we collected a corpus of 350 French FAQ (Frequently Asked Question) pairs found in a number of web sites dedicated to a large public, among which, most notably: tourism, health and education. The analysis of this corpus and a synthesis of various studies in the IQA field, allow us to structure and to classify intensional answers according to the type of knowledge and inference schemas involved. We distinguish the following five main categories. Examples given below are annotated in order (1) to identify the underlying types of knowledge and intensional inferential mechanisms used to produce the response (fragments in bold font) and (2) to analyze lexical choices and lexical variations, between the terms used in the question and those used in the response (fragments in italics). We indicate, between brackets, for each of these categories, how often they occur in the corpus.

1. *Introduction of higher level concepts* (5%) in the answer [2] is a simple substitution of some low level data in the answer by corresponding super concepts, at an appropriate level w.r.t. the user model, based on the query intent analysis. For example, if the question : "who is Tom?" is asked to a relational database, instead of responding "Tom is a junior student born in Vancouver on July 1977", the following intensional answer (IA) can be given "*Tom is* an **undergraduate** *student, born in* **Canada** in **1977**".

2. *Data reorganization* (26%) aims at e.g. sorting the extensional answer set according to specific criteria generally inferred from question elements. An IA for the question "give me hotels near Nice airport" can be "*list of hotels* **sorted according to the their distance w.r.t the airport**".

3. *generalization/exception* (43%) can be realized by mechanisms that infer generalizers from concepts or rules that better summarize the given answer set [4]. A term, judged as particularly relevant can be chosen as generalizer, even if its extension is larger than the answer set. Then, exceptions, provided they are limited, can be listed. The generalization can be done using statistical information (e.g. aggregation [5]) or by choosing higher concepts in an ontology [2]. For example, a possible IA for: "which country can I visit without any visa formalities" is : *you can visit* **all the countries of the EEC except the UK and Norway**. This category is the most important of our classification.

4. *quantification* (21%) where the relative size of the answer set w.r.t. the size of the objects denoted by the focus is expressed by means of quantifiers such as *a few, some, a majority, most*. For example, a possible IA for "does all country cottages have swimming pools", can be : *no, only* **a few** *country*

cottages have a swimming pool. This approach is also valid for other forms of quantification operating on various semantic domains, such as time, where markers can be *rarely, frequently, etc.*

5. *correlation* is a type of IA observed in 5% of our corpus. It is generated when a relation can be derived from two or more elements in the question. For example, "how many cooks and guides do we have for our excursion?" has the following response : **this depends on the number of people in our group**, *(...)*.

In a large number of situations, we observe that some of the above 5 categories can co-occur in a single response. In this paper, we focus on formal aspects of the content determination of IA that belong to categories 2, 3 and 4 cited above as well as on their NLG realizations.

3   Content Determination

3.1   Knowledge Representation in WEBCOOP

WEBCOOP has two main sources of information: (1) general knowledge and domain knowledge represented by means of a deductive knowledge base that includes facts, rules and integrity constraints and (2) a large set of relevant paragraphs that responds to the question keywords, indexed using logical formulae. Our system being a direct QA system, it does not have any user model.

The first source includes basic knowledge (e.g. countries, distances between towns), and ontological knowledge. Ontologies are organized around concepts where each concept node is associated with its specific lexicalizations and properties. For example, the concept `hotel` has the specific properties `night-rate` and `nb-of-rooms`. Values associated with scalar properties allow for sorts which is useful for category (2) above. The aim is to sort concepts according to specified dimensions. We have at the moment about 1000 concepts in our domain ontology.

Indexed texts are represented by the pair: text(F, http) where F is a first-order formula that represents some knowledge extracted from a web page with address http [9]. For example, if we index texts about airport transportations in various countries, we can have:
$text(route(50) \land to(50, cointrin) \land bymeansof(50, Y) \land train(Y) \land airport(cointrin) \land$
$localisation(cointrin, in(geneva)),$ *www.gva.ch*).

3.2   Query Representation and Evaluation

The parse of a query allows to identify: the type of the query (yes/no, entity, definition ,etc.) [10], the question focus and the semantic representation of the query in first-order logic (conjunctive formula). For example, the question:
Q1: *what are the means of transportation to go to Geneva airport,*
has the following logical representation:
$(entity, means\_of\_transportation(Y),$
$route(X) \land to(X, Z) \land bymeansof(X, Y) \land means\_of\_transportation(Y) \land$
$airportof(Z, geneva)).$

For the moment, we mainly focus on boolean and entity questions possibly including fuzzy expressions. Evaluating a query is realized in two different ways:

- from the deductive knowledge base, in that case, responses are variable instances or,
- from the indexed text base, and in that case, responses are paragraphes formulae which unify with the query logical form. Roughly, unification proceeds as follows. Let Q (conjunction of terms q_i) be the question formula and F(conjunction of f_j) be a formula indexing a text. F is a response to Q iff for all q_i there is an f_j such that:
  - q_i unifies with f_j or
  - q_i subsumes f_j, via the ontology (e.g. means_of_transportation(Y) subsumes tramway(Y)), or
  - q_i rewrites, via rules of the knowledge base, into a conjunction of f_j, e.g.: $airportof(Z, geneva)$ rewrites into: $airport(Z) \wedge localization(Z, in(geneva))$.

In the rest of the paper, we assume that queries are consistent with the knowledge base and that the set of extensional answers for each query is large enough (more than 8 answers) so that IA can be generated.

3.3   An Algorithm for the Content Determination of IA

Given the set of extensional answers to a question, which are, in most cases formulas, as explained above, content determination of an IA is defined as follows: (1) search in the answer set or in a related node in the ontology, for the adequate element to be generalized, then (2) find the best level of abstraction for the answer, possibly including a list of exceptions. An intensional supervisor (section 3.4) manages the different operations, including non-determinism (*variable depth intensionality*) using a conceptual metric. The resulting intensional answers cover the extensional set of direct answers.

The content determination process begins by searching, in the answer set, a relevant generalized element. It is important to note, that our algorithm identifies and eliminates those predicates in the response that are not relevant for the abstraction task, e.g. predicates that have the same instantiations in the response logical formula, or predicates that do not have any entry in the domain ontology such as hotel names.

The algorithm that searches for the best elements to generalize is as follows:

1. **the generalizer is the question focus.** Check if the list of extensional answers includes a term that can be generalized or sorted using the question focus. For example, the question Q1 above can have the following IA : *all public transportation and taxis go to Geneva airport* where the extensional answers, e.g. buses, trolleys and trains, are generalized using the type of the question focus *means_of_transportation*. Else

2. **the generalizer is a property of the focus in the question.** Search in the question for a property associated with the focus that has variable values in the answer set. For example, the list of answers to the question :
$hotel(X) \wedge localization(X, [atborderof(Y), in(monaco)]) \wedge sea(Y) \wedge city(monaco)$
(*what are the hotels at the border of the sea in Monaco*) cannot be generalized using the focus $hotel(X)$ which corresponds to hotel names and is therefore eliminated, as described above. The property *localisation* of the concept hotel is selected because all extensional answers include the distance of the hotel to the sea, (distance which is an instance of the semantics of atborderof(Y)). A possible IA is then the list of hotels in Monaco sorted according to their increasing distance to the sea. Else,

3. **the generalizer is a property of the focus in the ontology.** Search in the ontology for a property related to the focus on which a generalization can be made. For example, if we ask for *hotels in Cannes with a swimming pool*, represented by the formula :
$hotel(X) \wedge localization(X, in(cannes)) \wedge equipment(X, Y) \wedge swimmingpool(Y)$,
no possible generalizer can be found neither on the focus X, nor on its properties, localization and equipment. So a possible IA is : "3 stars and 4 stars hotels in Cannes have a swimming pool" where the generalization is realized on the property 'hotel category' associated with the concept hotel. Else,

4. **no IA can be generated.** The answer list is simply enumerated without any intensional treatment.

Given the element in the response on which intensional calculus operates, the next stage is to find the best level of abstraction. Considering the set of instances of this element in the answer set, generalization proceeds by grouping instances by generalizable subsets w.r.t. the ontology. This procedure may be repeated until a single generalizer is found, if it exists, possibly with a few exceptions. Let us take an example. Suppose the following fragment of a transportation ontology such as described in the following figure.

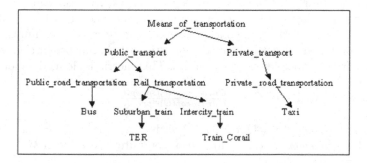

Fig. 1. A fragment of the transportation ontology

Suppose again, that the question : "what are the means of transportation to go to Geneva airport" has the following extensional answers set: trains, buses and taxis. According to the ontology described in 1, this question has the following response set [1] :

1. IA1: all intercity and all suburban trains of Geneva, taxis and buses go to the airport,
2. IA2: all rail transportations, buses and taxis of Geneva go the airport,
3. IA3: most public transportations and taxis of Geneva go to the airport,
4. IA4: most means of transportation of Geneva go to the airport.

IA1 to IA3 are possible generalizations, IA4 is correct, but not very informative because of its proximity to the query[2]. The quantification *most* is introduced in the answers IA3 and IA4 because the quantification *all* makes the underlying answers wrong.

It is then necessary to select responses at the best level of abstraction. [7] performs a syntactic check on the response set that selects only those IA that are not logically subsumed by any others (e.g. IA3 above). They also used another criterion which aims at limiting the set of interesting IA only to answers which share the same vocabulary defined by the user in his question in term of concepts, properties and constants. These techniques are simple and not adequate for our purpose since, first, the choice of the best level of abstraction is automatically performed and, second, we want to give to users the possibility of choosing the type of intensional answer which is the most appropriate for them. This is, in our sense, more cooperative, provided the system is not very verbose.

3.4   A Supervisor for Intensional Calculus

In our case, a supervisor manages both the abstraction level and the display of the elaborated IA. In WEBCOOP, we have a *variable depth intensional calculus* which allows for computing the degree of intensionality in responses in terms of the abstraction level of generalizers in the ontology. The choice of the best level of abstraction is based on a conceptual metric $M(C, C')$ that determines the ontological proximity between two concepts C and C'. Considering the form of our ontology, roughly, our similarity metric considers the sum of the distance in the ontology between the two concept C and C' in terms of the number of arcs traversed combined with the inverse proportion of shared properties, w.r.t the total number of properties on these nodes. This metric is defined as follows :

$$M(C, C') = NbArc(C, C') + \frac{Card(prop(C) \cup prop(C'))}{Card(prop(C) \cap prop(C'))}$$

Suppose $ResponseSet = \{IA_1, ..., IA_n\}$ with : $IA_i = all\ Gen_1\ and...and\ all\ Gen_j$ For each $IA_i \in ResponseSet$, the supervisor computes the value of $M(Gen_a, Gen_b)$

[1] We only give the most relevant answers
[2] The query itself is often the only IA of the retrieved set of values of which the user is aware [4]

$(1 \leq a \leq j, 1 \leq b \leq j$ and $a \neq b)$ which corresponds to the conceptual distance between the generalizers Gen_k. If this metric shows an important distance between concepts, then it is more appropriate to stay at the current level of abstraction. Otherwise, it is best to replace two similar concepts by their immediate mother concept in the ontology, and recursively for the other $Gen_{k'}$. If we go back to the example in the last section, the supervisor computes, for the response IA2, the metric M(bus, taxi), M(rail_transportation, taxi) and M(rail_transportation, bus). After the computation of the metric associated to responses IA1, IA3 and IA4, this strategy allows to choose the IA2 as the best summary.

The organization of the response display is as follows. The retrieved intensional answers are structured in two parts. First, the generation of an IA of category 3 and 4 (cf section 2) and then the generation of IAs of category 2 which corresponds to a sorted (if responses can be sorted) list of the retrieved extensional answers according to different criteria, identified as sortable (section 3). This strategy avoids the problem of having to guess the user's intent. This second part is best viewed as the expression of the cooperative know-how of the system. For the moment, the maximum number of IA given in the second part is fixed up to three which seems to be a manageable number of possibilities. If the number of ordering criteria, for a given concept or property in the ontology, is more than three then the system arbitrarily chooses three of them. This choice still under evaluation.

IA are displayed in our system WEBCOOP using an hyperlink presentation that allows the user to view either the intensional definition of the generalized classes or their extensional enumeration. Because the user is familiar with the query language he or she is using, we try to keep in the natural language responses, as much as possible, the same syntactic structure and lexicalizations as in the question. The following figure illustrates how intensional answers are displayed in WEBCOOP, as explained above.

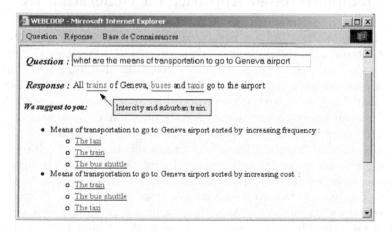

Fig. 2. An example of intensional answers in WEBCOOP

Table 1. Some Basic Generation Templates for the Intensional Schemas

IA Schema	Generation Templates
Generali-zation	**(1) The generalizer is a concept** $(lexicalisation(quantf)$ $\underline{\text{Lexicalisation(GEN))}}^{+}$ R **(2) The generalizer is a property** $(lexicalisation(quantf)$ $\underline{\text{lexicalisation(Concept)Lexicalisation(GEN))}}^{+}$ R **Example:** tous les hôtels 3 étoiles et tous les hôtels 4 étoiles ont des piscines à Cannes. (all 3 stars and all 4 stars hotels in Cannes have swimming pool)
Generaliza-tion/ Exception	**(1) The generalizer is a concept** $(lexicalisation(quantf)$ $\underline{\text{Lexicalisation(GEN))}}^{+}$ $(sauf$ $\underline{\text{lexicalisation(Excep))}}^{+}$ R **Example:** Vous pouvez voyager dans tous les pays de la communauté Européenne sauf la Norvège et le Royaum Uni (You can travel in all the countries of the EEC execpt the UK and Norway) **(2) The generalizer is a property** $(lexicalisation(quantf)$ lexicalisation(Concept) $\underline{\text{Lexicalisation(GEN))}}^{+}$ $(sauf$ $\underline{\text{lexicalisation(Excep))}}^{+}$ R
Data Sorting	**Increasing sorting :** R *classé par ordre croissant de* lexicalisation(SortingCriteria) : $\underline{\text{(lexicalisation(ExtenResponse))}}^{+}$ **Example:** liste des aéroports proches d'Albi classés par ordre croissant de distance par rapport à Albi : Carcassonne, Toulouse, Montpellier (nearest cities to Albi, ordered by increasing distance from Albi: Carcassonne, Toulouse, Montpellier)

4   A Template-Based Approach for Generating IA

Let us now show how IAs are generated in natural language. We found that, for each intensional procedure, it is possible to define a small set of generic and underspecified natural language templates that somewhat suggest the inferences performed by the intentional calculus in accessible terms so that the user understands that the system is trying to respond as appropriately as possible to his query. Underspecified elements depend on the question, on local semantic factors and on the type of solutions elaborated. Their generation relies on ontological knowledge, general linguistic knowledge (e.g. semantics of prepositions [1]) and lexicalisation and aggregation functions. Templates have been induced from a number of question-response pairs found in different large public domains on the web. Our goal is to have templates as generic as possible. Responses have been normalized, trying not to loose their accuracy, in order to get stereotyped response forms usable in NL generation frameworks. A large portion of the template is presented as an hyperlink to the user, as illustrated in the example of the previous section. This avoids, to a large extent, to manage the general structure of the response [8], and leaves open navigation possibilities to the user. We define for each inference schema a set of semantically equivalent templates. Each paraphrase involves different lexicalizations and argument organizations and results in a slightly different global meaning. For the moment, in WEBCOOP we have 28 templates among which we have 9 basic templates for generating intensional answers. Due to space limitations, we only give a few generation templates.

Table 1 above presents some generation templates for French for each type of intensional schema cited in the previous section. Let *GEN* be the concept or the property that generalizes the extensional answer set, *Excep* be the concept or the individual that corresponds to a list of exceptions, and R, the logical formula that corresponds to the remainder of the query. We define the function lexicalisation(C) that produces an adequate NL fragment expressing the concept C. The set of possible lexicalisations for a given concept is defined in the domain ontology or, alternatively, in the lexicon. Underspecified fragments are in italics, underlined portions are generated as hyperlinks. A template fragment of the form (fragment)$^+$, indicates that that fragment occurs in the generated response at least one time. The variable *quantf* stands for one of the following quantifiers : *all, some, a majority, a few, etc.*

5   Conclusion and Perspectives

On the basis of [4], IQA can be evaluated according to three main features : (1) intensional only (pure) versus intensional/extensional (mixed) ; (2) independence from the database instances versus dependence and (3) completeness of the characterization of the extensional answers. Our approach is mixed, dependent and complete since our algorithm computes all non redundant IAs. Our method is based on the question focus and a rich ontological description of the domain in order to select a set of relevant concepts to be generalized. We proposed in this paper the notion of *variable depth intensional calculus* which allows for the generation of intensional answers at the best level of abstraction. A supervisor guides this process using a conceptual metric and manages the response display by structuring IAs in two parts, allowing for a mixed and graded generation of IAs based on different criteria. Finally, a number of NL templates have been defined in order to explain the underlying inferential mechanisms that led to the answer. This work has several future directions among which we plan to :

- integrate integrity constraints in the intensional calculus,
- investigate other metrics in order to enhace the system capabilities for choosing the best level of abstraction,
- introduce a user model for the selection of the best response,
- finally enhance NLG templates and evaluate their linguistic and their cognitive adequacy w.r.t the end users. This kind of evaluation aims at studying how users react to having multiple types of intensional responses displayed.

We also think that this work can be transposed to other domains than question answering where intensionality is useful, like, e.g. automatic summarization.

Acknowledgement. I thank anonymous reviewers that contribute to improve this work. This project is partly supported by the CNRS TCAN program.

References

1. E.Cannesson, P. Saint-Dizier. Defining and Representing preposition Senses: a preliminary analysis. In ACL02-WSD, Philadelphia. July 2002.
2. S.C. Yoon and E. K. Park. An Approach to Intensional Query Answering at Multiple Abstraction Levels Using Data Mining Approaches. Proceedings of the 32th Hawaii conference on System Sciences, 1999.
3. Zhengxin Chen. Computational Intelligence for Decision Support. CRC Press 1999.
4. A. Motro. Intensional Answers to Database Queries IEEE Transactions on Knowledge and Data Engineering, volume 6 number 3. pages 444-454, 1994.
5. C.D. Shum and R. Muntz. An Information-Theoretic Study on Aggregate Responses. In Proceedings of the 14th VLDB Conference, pages 479-490, 1988.
6. E. Reiter, NLG versus Templates. In Proceedings of 7th European Workshop on Natural Language Generation, Leiden, The Netherlands, 1995
7. L. Cholvy and R. Demolombe. Querying a Rule Base. Expert Database Conf, pages 477-485. 1986.
8. R. Dale and J. Oberlander and M. Milosavljevic and A. Knott. Integrating Natural Language Generation and Hypertext to Produce Dynamic Documents, Interacting with Computers 11(2), pages 109-135.1998.
9. F. Benamara and P. Saint-Dizier. Knowledge Extraction from the WEB: an Experiment and an Analysis of its Portability, Vivek Journal, volume 15, number 1, pages 3-15, 2003.
10. F. Benamara and P. Saint-Dizier. WEBCOOP: a Cooperative Question-Answering System on the Web. EACL project notes, Budapest, Hongary, April 2003.

Salience-Driven Text Planning

Christian Chiarcos and Manfred Stede

University of Potsdam
Dept. of Linguistics
Applied Computational Linguistics
D-14415 Potsdam
Germany
chiarcos|stede@ling.uni-potsdam.de

Abstract. We present an algorithm for hierarchical text planning of paragraphs involving object descriptions, comparisons and recommendations. Building on previous work on bottom-up text planning and user-tailored text generation, we develop a numerical model of 'propositional salience' to capture both speaker's intentions and local coherence in a single framework for generating complex discourse structures.

1 Introduction: Comparisons and Recommendations

We present a new approach to text planning that is implemented in the POLIBOX generator [14]. The paper first summarizes the idea of POLIBOX and discusses peculiarities of the text genre, which lead us to develop a new approach to text planning that combines top-down schema application with bottom-up planning, and uses a numerical model of *salience* for making decisions on text structure (and also later on during linearization, but sentence planning is not covered in this paper). Section 2 motivates our use of 'salience', Section 3 explains the text planner, and Section 4 compares our approach to earlier research.

POLIBOX is a hypertext generator that was inspired by ILEX [10] and similar systems, but moves beyond them in some interesting ways. It implements the scenario of clients (e.g., students) inquiring about a textbook suitable for their current needs. The subject matter realized in our prototype is computational linguistics; a database with information on 25 CL texts is the basis for the generator. The users specify topics they want to see covered by the book, the language, the programming language used, and some other attributes. POLIBOX determines a number of books that match the requirements, usually to different degrees, and generates a description of the first, accompanied by hyperlinks to further titles. When the user selects a link, a text on this new title is generated, which contains explicit comparisons to the book that has been presented before. Hence, all but the first book description pay attention not only to the "target features" specified by the user, but also to the prior descriptions, as stored in the discourse history. Furthermore, the generator may decide that one book is a clear favourite and actively recommend this one.

A. Belz et al. (Eds.): INLG 2004, LNAI 3123, pp. 21–30, 2004.

Technically, POLIBOX implements a version of the standard NLG pipeline model. We concentrate here on the text planning stage, assuming that the content selection module has already determined some suitable books and a ranking among them (according to degree of match).

As indicated, the texts combine portions serving different discourse purposes: *describe* an object, *compare* an object to another (or to the target specification provided by the user), *evaluate* one object with respect to another. This mixture is typical for discourses that inform about products and possibly involve recommendations on choosing one rather than another. Due to this multi-faceted nature, no single text planning strategy is appropriate to produce an entire paragraph. In evaluations, there are rhetorical moves involved that could be produced top-down by schemata or by planning, but this is less useful for descriptions and comparisons — the former being more or less independent of intentions, the latter leading into complexity problems. Since the number of possible feature combinations is exponential in the number of features an item has, our schemata (or plan operators) would have to be quite complex to cover a sufficient number of possible combinations. On the other hand, the use of less explicit schemata restricts the flexibility of generated texts. In descriptions and comparisons, the most important characteristic of good text is *local* coherence: the information should be presented such that the focus of attention moves smoothly from one object or attribute to another.

To illustrate the problem of creating text in this framework, here is one that manages to be *cohesive* in the sense that clauses are nicely connected, but it is not optimally *coherent*, because the chosen arrangement of information does not make the overall purpose of the text particularly clear.

> The book NICETITLE by FAMOUSAUTHOR uses Lisp, as you desire. It is like the previous one in that it covers chart parsing. Unfortunately, it is much older than you have asked for. It differs from PREVIOUSTITLE in that it is quite a bit shorter. NICETITLE matches your request for a book in German, which the previous book didn't. NICETITLE resembles the previous book in the number of exercises.

2   Background: Salience in Text and Text Planning

Our approach combines two communicative principles whose universality seems to be a commonly shared assumption in functional linguistics.[1]

Adjacency Pieces of information that are closely related are expected to be presented together.

Importance More important information will be presented more prominently than less important information.

---

[1] Both principles are motivated by iconicity. On their impact on syntax see, for example, Givón [4, p. 44 and 75]. Further, similar assumptions are inherent to theories of discourse structure such as RST [7], where they are underlying the adjacency constraint of rhetorical relations and the concept of nuclearity.

In the following, we introduce the notion of 'propositional salience' to formalize terms like "relatedness" and "importance" as used above. Thereafter, we propose some domain-specific heuristic measures of propositional salience and show how to apply these to our bottom-up algorithm.

The notion of *salience* is usually defined as degree of prominence or attention an entity is assigned at a point in time when producing or comprehending a discourse. This idea can be extended to *propositional* salience: the degree of prominence a proposition receives in a given context. We distinguish two different granularities of context: *Local* context is established by the immediately preceding proposition, whereas *global* context includes all descriptions generated so far, plus the user model, i.e., the portion of extra-linguistic context that clearly influences the relevance of a proposition.

Thus, local propositional salience is a relation between two propositions. For text planning, it is used in deciding whether they should be neighbours in the rhetorical tree or not. In contrast, global propositional salience is a section-dependent feature of a proposition, i.e. measured within its paragraph (here: one paragraph is the set of sentences dealing with one single book).

Our text planner ensures that global salience is reflected on the one hand by *nuclearity assignments* of coherence relations, and on the other hand by the depth of embedding in the rhetorical tree. (The factors contributing to global salience will be explained in Section 3.2.) Local salience influences text planning by an optimization function that looks for the best local neighbourhood of propositions. The original usage of *salience* for discourse referents closely resembles the discrete model of *familiarity* by Prince [12]. When we now apply it to propositions, an equivalent can be seen in the concept of *grounding* of a discourse unit, as used by Traum [15]. In Traum's model, grounding of an utterance depends on the possible ways of relating it to a restricted set of discourse units 'on top of the stack'. Similarly, we treat a proposition as locally salient if there is a 'thematical' relation connecting it with another proposition uttered before — see Section 3.2.

3 Salience-Driven Text Planning

3.1 Content Selection and Goal Determination

In POLIBOX, when a book has been chosen for presentation, the first task is to decide on the set of attributes that are actually to be communicated to the user: a selection has to be made from the full database entry for the book. We propose four different criteria:

1. attributes that serve to identify the book (author, title)
2. attributes that are – independent of the context – unusual and thus a priori 'important': book is very long or very short; very old or very recent
3. attributes where the book mis-/matches the user model
4. attributes where the book mis-/matches the book presented just before

We call the set of attributes thus determined the 'propositions' that enter the verbalization stages. But first they receive an evaluation: will the user appreciate them or not? The propositions that relate the book to the user model receive a label POS or NEG indicating the dis-/agreement, or NEUT in case the user model is not specified for the attribute. Next, the POS and NEG propositions are counted and the overall *communicative goal* is computed on the basis of the distribution. It is one of *describe* (neutral; first book to be presented), *recommend-mildly* (the book is quite suitable for the user), *recommend-strongly* (the book fits very well), or *describe-and-compare*, *recommend-mildly-and-compare*, *recommend-strongly-and-compare* (another book was presented already). Furthermore, an additional *evaluative* proposition can be computed that summarizes the overall "value" of the book. The text will then contain a sentence like *This book suits your needs very well.*

After this step of content selection and evaluation, we have a communicative goal and a set of propositions, which are assigned one of the types 'identificational' (ID), 'evaluative' (EVAL), or 'argumentative' (ARG). The ARG type is further subclassified into nine subgroups according to their relationship with the user model (UM-match, UM-mismatch, UM-neutral) and the previous book (PB-match, PB-mismatch, PB-neutral).

3.2   Salience Assignment

We now define **local propositional salience** in terms of THEMATICAL RELATIONS that are derived by investigating the contribution a proposition makes to the comunicative goal (as computed in the previous step). We distinguish three relations: propositions can be

unrelated	iff there is no corresponding or deviating information on PB- or UM-matches available at all,
contrastive	iff they deviate in terms of PB- or UM-matching, and
similar	else.

The thematic relation is computed for each pair of propositions in the set. It is furthermore associated with different *strength* scores expressing an assumed ranking of prototypicality.[2] Type and strength of a thematical relation define the local salience of two propositions $p_1 and p_2$ $(0 \leq \sigma_l(p_1, p_2) \leq 1)$, as shown below. Briefly, local propositional salience is higher if the thematical relation indicates similarity in argumentative function, and lower for contrastivity; the lowest value applies to propositions that are unrelated.[3]

Global propositional salience depends on the communicative goal, on its overlap with the argumentative function of the proposition and on the static importance weights assigned to facts in the database. We thus define $\sigma_g(p)$ as the product ($\wedge$) of these factors, i.e. $\sigma_g(p) = i(p) \cdot \delta(p) \cdot \alpha$ with $\delta(p)$ as a measure of compatibility between p and the communicative goal; $i(p)$ representing the

---

[2] For example, we treat a thematical relation as more prototypically contrastive the higher the number of deviating features and the lower the number of similar features of the propositions it connects are.

[3] In a more comprehensive model of local propositional salience, one would also consider event/knowledge structure [1], and cohesion arising from lexical chains.

Table 1. Thematical relations and local propositional salience

relation	unrelated	contrastive			similar	
strength	0	3	2	1	1	2
UM-relation	n.a.	≠	≠ n.a.	≠ =	= n.a.	=
PB-relation	n.a.	≠	n.a. ≠	= ≠	n.a. =	=
$\sigma_l(p_1,p_2)$	0	0.2	0.4	0.6	0.8	1

=: both propositions have UM/PB-mismatch/match
≠: one proposition has UM/PB-mismatch, the other one UM/PB-match
n.a.: one proposition is UM/PB-neutral

conventional importance of the proposition p, and α expressing the influence of the overall communicative goal:

$$\delta(p) = \begin{cases} 0.25 & \text{if UM-neutral} \\ & \text{and PB-mismatch} \\ 0.5 & \text{if UM-match} \\ & \text{and PB-match,} \\ 0.75 & \text{if UM-match} \\ & \text{and PB-neutral,} \\ 1 & \text{if UM-match} \\ & \text{and PB-mismatch,} \\ 0 & \text{else} \end{cases}$$

$i(p) \in [0,1]$ (pre-defined) weights of the facts in p

$$\alpha = \begin{cases} 1 & \text{iff. } recommend\text{-}strongly \\ 0.5 & \text{iff. } recommend\text{-}mildly \\ 0 & \text{iff. } describe \end{cases}$$

The technical definition of global salience as above is problem-specific, of course. Nevertheless it reflects some basic insights in communicative universals making it likely to be adaptable to other domains as well.

First, global salience is not a property of the discourse entity itself, but depends on mental states the speaker has and the hearer is expected to have. In our domain, we only distinguish three degrees of recommendations as possible communicative goals. We introduce $\delta(p)$ to reflect the impact a given piece of information has with respect to these goals, i.e. any information making the current book preferable (UM-match) or interesting (PB-mismatch) will result in a higher global salience.

The main function of global salience in the current framework is to generate nuclearity preferences, cf. the principle of **importance** as stated above. Applying this assumption on two propositions p_1 and p_2 to be conjoined into an elementary tree, we suggest that one of them is preferred to appear as nucleus of an asymmetric rhetorical relation holding between them if it is more globally salient than the other one. Otherwise, if there is no clear preference for a single nucleus, we would prefer a symmetric relation. If global salience is mainly defined in terms of $\delta(p)$ as proposed above, it seems less likely to generate asymmetric relations (emphasizing positive information about the current book) if the communicative goal is to describe rather than to recommend. This is reflected by α.

Finally, $i(p)$ provides a mechanism to include external knowledge on prominent information such as general prominence of a given feature a book has, deviations from the user model, and the like.

We treat all of these components of global salience to be necessary conditions, not sufficient ones. Therefore, a given piece of information will be salient only if all of these factors are fulfilled. This is expressed by the multiplication as the analogon of a logical $\wedge$.

For reasons of space, we can illustrate the salience assignments only with a short example here. Assume that the following three propositions were part of a book recommendation (goal *recommend-strongly-and-compare*): (`in-german BOOK1`) (t_1), (`has-audience BOOK1 NOVICE-AUDIENCE`) (t_2), (`deals-with BOOK1 MODAL-LOGICS`) (t_3). According to their argumentative subtypes, they are assigned local and global salience scores as illustrated in Figure 1. (When the system actually plans a paragraph, there are about 15 propositions forming a network of this kind.)

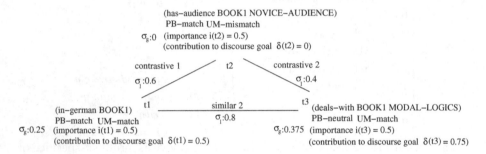

Fig. 1. Sample propositions with type definitions, inferred thematical relations and resulting salience scores

3.3 Text Structuring

The basic idea of our approach is to mix top-down schema application with bottom-up processes that build up small rhetorical trees to fill the slots of the best-suited schema. We first explain the procedure for combining elementary trees (the propositions produced above), then illustrate our notion of schema, and finally show the search procedure combining the two methods.

Combining elementary trees. The main operation in the bottom-up process is combining two elementary trees t_1, t_2 into a more complex one $t_{1 \circ 2}$. This step involves the following sub-tasks:

1. Determine the rhetorical relation holding between t_1 and t_2 in $t_{1 \circ 2}$

$$t_{1 \circ 2} = \begin{cases} (\text{SUBORD } t_1 \ t_2) & \text{iff } t_1 \text{ is significantly more globally salient than } t_2 \\ (\text{SUBORD } t_2 \ t_1) & \text{iff } t_1 \text{ is significantly less globally salient than } t_2 \\ (\text{COORD } t_1 \ t_2) & \text{else} \end{cases}$$

'Significance' depends on a threshold b, for which we experimentally determined the value 0.2. SUBORD and COORD are placeholders for specific subordinating/coordinating rhetorical relations, which depend, inter alia, on the thematical relations holding between t_1 and t_2. In our domain, important relations to be derived include JOINT and BACKGROUND (if `similar` t_1 t_2), and CONTRAST and ANTITHESIS (if `contrastive` t_1 t_2); some further features of the propositions are used to determine the relations.

2. Determine global salience of $t_{1 \circ 2}$

$$\sigma_g(t_{1 \circ 2}) = \begin{cases} 0.5\sigma_g(t_1) + 0.5\sigma_g(t_2) & \text{iff (COORD } t_1 \ t_2) \\ \sigma_g(t_1) & \text{iff (SUBORD } t_1 \ t_2) \end{cases}$$

3. Determine type of $t_{1 \circ 2}$:
   - if (SUBORD t_1 t_2), $t_{1 \circ 2}$ gets the type of its nucleus t_1
   - if (COORD t_1 t_2), $t_{1 \circ 2}$ gets all types that t_1 and t_2 have in common, i.e.
     - if t_1 and t_2 have the same UM-relation, it is propagated to $t_{1 \circ 2}$, but
     - if t_1 and t_2 don't have the same UM-relation, $t_{1 \circ 2}$ will be UM-neutral
     - analoguously for PB-relation
4. Thematical relations and local salience are computed using the type of $t_{1 \circ 2}$

In our small example, we can choose propositions t_1 and t_2 to be conjoined. Given the threshold $b = 0.2$, neither $\sigma_g(t_1)$ nor $\sigma_g(t_2)$ significantly exceeds the other one, so we assert a coordinating relation; since the thematical relation holding between them is contrastive, the relation becomes CONTRAST. With respect to their argumentative types, t_1 and t_2 share a PB-match only, so the type of $t_{1 \circ 2}$ will be PB-match and UM-neutral. Then, thematical relations and local salience scores are computed from this type.

Schema Application. The schemata capture the basic 'rhetorical strategy' used in a paragraph. For each communicative goal, the system has a few schemata at its disposal; which one is the most suitable depends on the configurations of the data and is determined by the search procedure (see below). An example for *recommend-strongly* is (ID Eval UM-match UM-mismatch); one for *recommend-mildly* is (ID UM-match UM-mismatch Eval); one for *describe* is (ID PB-match PB-mismatch). Each slot is labelled with the type that a prospective filler must have.[4]

A schema is applicable to a set of elementary trees, if for each slot there is at least one filler available (i.e., tree with right type), and if for each tree there is exactly one potential slot. Schema filling is trivial if exactly one filler can be assigned to each slot. If there is more than one filler for a slot, they are linked by the JOINT relation. If two slots S1 and S2 are of the same type, we determine nondeterministically a partition of the set of possible fillers.

---

[4] The same type may for rhetorical reasons occur twice in a schema, when for example the 'negative' facts are to be embedded in the 'positive' ones: UM-match UM-mismatch UM-match.

The search procedure. The approach we take toward finding the optimal schema instantiation is a slightly modified beam search. It differs from standard beam search in that we store not just the k best results of the recent generation, but also the i best results of the overall process. This is necessary since scores don't necessarily grow monotonically if we allow changes in type. The rating of a set of elementary trees is defined by local salience and schema match:

1. Apply the preferred schema candidate[5].
2. For each node n with subnodes $n_1, ..., n_k$ in the rhetorical tree built by this schema, calculate the rating.

$$r(n) = \min_{i \in \{1,...,k\}} \min_{j \in \{1,...,k\}} \sigma_l(n_i, n_j)$$

3. The overall rating of a tree $r(t)$ is then defined as the sum of the node ratings, multiplied with the rating of the schema.

To continue our simple example, we abstract from schema application and treat all generated configurations as feasible instances of the same schema; further, we restrict the size of any generation to $k = 1$.

Given the propositions illustrated in Figure 1, we first generate the offspring of the configuration represented by this set. We apply our merging procedure to any possible pairing and rank the results according to the rating function. Therefore, we pick the second configuration as the highest-ranking candidate. See below the resulting tree of the only possible offspring candidate $\{t_{(1 \circ 3) \circ 2}\}$.

configuration	$\{t_{1 \circ 2}, t_3\}$	$\{t_{1 \circ 3}, t_2\}$	$\{t_1, t_{2 \circ 3}\}$
resulting tree	(JOINT t_3 (CONTRAST t_1 t_2))	(JOINT t_2 (BACKGROUND t_1 t_3))	(JOINT t_1 (ANTITHESIS t_2 t_3))
rating r	$\sigma_l(t_3, t_{1 \circ 2}) + \sigma_l(t_1, t_2)$ $= 0 + 0.6$	$\sigma_l(t_2, t_{1 \circ 3}) + \sigma_l(t_1, t_3)$ $= 0.6 + 0.8$	$\sigma_l(t_1, t_{3 \circ 2}) + \sigma_l(t_3, t_2)$ $= 0.6 + 0.4$

```
(ANTITHESIS
    (BACKGROUND                                    ; nuc of ANTITHESIS
        (in-german BOOK1)                          ; t_1
        (deals-with BOOK1 MODAL-LOGICS))           ; t_3
    (has-audience BOOK1 NOVICE-AUDIENCE))          ; sat of ANTITHESIS: t_2
```

The rating of $\{t_{(1 \circ 3) \circ 2}\}$ will be equal to that of $\{t_{1 \circ 3}, t_2\}$, but since it belongs to a later generation, this will be the preferred result of the algorithm.

The eventual output sentence is akin to *Though it is intended for a novice audience, BOOK1 is in German and deals with modal logics, just as requested.*

---

[5] Schemata are organized in a partial order by specificity; the more detailed a schema, the higher its rank.

4   Comparison to Related Work

As indicated, our overall system took inspiration from ILEX [10] and related systems. However, we propose that linearization should strictly *follow* determining hierarchical discourse structure, so that further salience effects can be controlled (e.g., for determining information structure). Also, we do not just generate neutral descriptions of static entities, but also *recommendations*. Therefore, our paragraphs are tailored to the user, as in [2]. Our notion of global propositional salience resembles their measures of evidence strength or "compellingness", but note that neither their proposal nor its adaption by [16] make use of hierarchical discourse structure. Instead, they apply simplified notions of text structuring involving general ordering constraints and goal-dependent representation strategies. Therefore, neither cues indicating different discourse relations nor nuclearity effects on morphosyntax can be generated.

Our bottom-up algorithm is similar to that of Marcu [8]. Unlike his approach, though, we do not assume rhetorical relations between data base entries to be already given. Whereas Marcu applies mean distances as a measure of 'strength' of a relation, our notion of local propositional salience is not a static feature from the data base, but may be determined independently from the rhetorical relation itself.

Text structuring by maximizing local salience is inspired by the use of local coherence metrics holding between adjacent utterances. Whereas existing metrics focus on referential salience or – more technically – centering transitions [6,5], our notion of local propositional salience provides a mechanism to take another structural level into account. Besides this, our notion of global propositional salience corresponds to what has been introduced as "salience of a (data-base) record" or "salience of a feature" in older work on generating descriptions [3] or comparisons [9].

A related concept of salience as a quantity composed of several factors (including extra-linguistic ones) has been studied in the psycholinguistics literature; cf. [11] for a detailed discussion and perspectives on its application in NLG.

Finally, Reed [13] modelled "salience" of a proposition as an additional goal to be fulfilled by a plan operator. This referred to the *effect* an utterance has on the hearer, whereas we define it as a precondition of any proposition to be uttered by the speaker; thus the two proposals cannot be compared directly.

5   Summary

We proposed numerical measures of global and local salience that account both for speaker's intentions and for local coherence effects. This approach seems appropriate for text genres involving both descriptive and argumentative portions, as in our book comparisons and recommendations, but it would also apply for example to commentaries. In our system, the same salience measures are then also used further down the pipeline in sentence planning decisions, which could not be discussed here. The second point we made was building hierarchical discourse structure by combining bottom-up processes and top-down schema application. Again, this is useful for texts that should pay attention to conventionalized orders of presentations, but at the same time have spans where grouping and ordering decisions are to be made on the grounds of local coherence.

Extending the approach to the sentence planning phase is underway. When this is completed, we can address the important issue of evaluating our results, e.g. by adapting and extending the criteria of Eddy [3].

References

1. B.K. Britton, P. Schaefer, M. Bryan, S. Silverman and R. Sorrells (2001). Thinking about bodies of knowledge. In: T. Sanders et al., Text Representation: Linguistic and Psycholinguistic Aspects. John Benjamins, Amsterdam.
2. G. Carenini and J. Moore (2000). A Strategy for Generating Evaluative Arguments. Proc. of INLG-00. itzpe Ramon, Israel, 47-54.
3. B. Eddy (2002). Toward balancing conciseness, readability and salience: an integrated architecture. Proc. of INLG-02. Columbia University/NY, 173-178.
4. T. Givón (2001). Syntax, vol. II. John Benjamins, Amsterdam.
5. N. Karamanis and H.M. Manurung (2002). Stochastic Text Structuring using the Principle of Continuity. Proc. of INLG-02. Columbia University/NY, 81-88.
6. R. Kibble and R. Power (2000). An integrated framework for text planning and pronominalization. Proc. of INLG-00. Mizpe Ramon, Israel, 77-84.
7. W.C. Mann and S.A. Thompson (1988). Rhetorical Structure Theory: Toward a functional theory of text organization. Text 8 (3), 243-281.
8. D. Marcu (1997). From local to global coherence: A bottom-up approach to text planning. Proc. of the 14th National Conference on Artificial Intelligence (AAAI-97), Providence/RI, 629-635.
9. M. Milosavljevic (1997). Content selection in comparison generation. Proc. of the 6th European WS on Natural Language Generation (EWNLG), Duisburg, 72-81.
10. M. O'Donnell, Ch.Mellish, J.Oberlander, and A.Knott (2001). ILEX: An architecture for a dynamic hypertext generation system. Natural Language Engineering 7.
11. Th. Pattabhiraman (1992). Aspects of Salience in Natural Language Generation. PhD Thesis, Simon Fraser University, Vancouver, B.C.
12. E. Prince (1981). Toward a taxonomy of given-new information. In: Cole, P., ed. Radical Pragmatics. New York: Academic Press, 223-256.
13. C.A. Reed (2002). Saliency and the Attentional State in Natural Language Generation. Proc. of the 15th European Conference on AI (ECAI 2002), IOS Press, Lyon.
14. M. Stede (2002). Polibox: Generating desciptions, comparisons, and recommendations from a database. Proc. of the 19th International Conference on Computational Linguistics (Coling), Taipei.
15. D. R. Traum (1994). A Computational Theory of Grounding in Natural Language Conversation, PhD Thesis, Dept. of Computer Science, University of Rochester.
16. A. Stent, M. Walker, S. Whittaker and P. Maloor (2002), User-tailored generation for spoken dialogue: An experiment. Proc.of ICSLP 2002.

Finetuning NLG
Through Experiments with Human Subjects:
The Case of Vague Descriptions

Kees van Deemter

ITRI, University of Brighton, Lewes Road, Brighton BN2 4GJ,
`Kees.van.Deemter@itri.bton.ac.uk`,
http://www.itri.brighton.ac.uk/~Kees.van.Deemter

Abstract. This discussion paper describes a sequence of experiments
with human subjects aimed at finding out how an NLG system should
choose between the different forms of a gradable adjective. This case
study highlights some general questions that one faces when trying to
base NLG systems on empirical evidence: one question is what task to set
a subject so as to obtain the most useful information about that subject,
another question has to do with differences between subjects.

1   Introduction

NLG systems express information in linguistic form. As these systems become
more and more sophisticated, a key problem is choosing between the different
ways in which the same information can be expressed. Although intuition and
general linguistic principles can go a long way, the problem is essentially an
empirical one that can only be resolved by empirical study.

How can we *find out* whether one way of expressing a given input is better than
another? One option is to look at corpora. But large corpora, such as the BNC,
tend not to come with extensive semantic annotation, and even if they do, the
domains with which the texts in the corpus are concerned tend not to have been
formalised. (In NLG *jargon*: We don't know the input from which the corpus was
generated.) In many cases, this is a crucial limitation, necessitating an alternative
method. An alternative is to 'generate' corpora by logging human users' verbal
behaviour during a controlled experiment (e.g., [2], [7]), resulting in corpora
whose domains can be explicitly modelled, and where the truth value of all the
relevant domain facts is known. The present paper focusses mostly on a slightly
simpler method[1], by letting human subjects choose between the different ways in
which the input information may be expressed. Rather than producing a corpus
of extended discourse/dialogue, such experiments can tell us, at least in principle,
which expression is favoured by subjects: the fact that explicit judgements are

---

[1] An partial exception is our third experiment, described in Section 5, which could be
seen as generating a corpus.

A. Belz et al. (Eds.): INLG 2004, LNAI 3123, pp. 31–40, 2004.
© Springer-Verlag Berlin Heidelberg 2004

obtained from subjects might be even thought an advantage. We will focus on issues raised by previous work on referring expressions, focussing on the question how one might inform the generator's choice between the different forms of a gradable adjective in descriptions such as

a. – 'the fat chihuahua' [base form]
b. – 'the fatter chihuahua' [comparative form]
c. – 'the fattest chihuahua' [superlative form]

After discussion of the experiments that we have done to inform this choice, we will discuss two problems: one problem has to do with experimental methodology (e.g., how does one find out what constitutes the optimal use of language), another problem has to do with differences between human subjects' preferences.

2   Generating Vague Descriptions: Research Hypotheses

It was reported in [12] how the module of an NLG system that generates referring expressions can use numerical information in the input to the generator to produce referring expressions like a-c above. Generating such *vague descriptions* is nontrivial partly because properties like 'fat', 'fatter', 'fattest' are not simply true or false of an animal: the fattest chihuahua is not necessarily the fattest dog, for example, or the fattest animal. Unlike the numerical properties that measure the animals' waistelines, properties like these are context dependent, and this has to be taken into account by the generation algorithm. If, for example, the knowledge base were to simply list *all* hippos and *no* chihuahuas as fat, then this would make it impossible to ever refer to a dog as 'the fat chihuahua', and this could even mean that the referent in question cannot be identified uniquely at all (i.e., if there happens to be no combination of other properties that distinguishes it from everything else in the domain). The problems surrounding gradable adjectives have been studied widely (e.g., [3], [10], [4]), but little of this is directly applicable to NLG, let alone to the choice between the different forms of the gradable adjective in descriptions such as a-c above.

In addition to presenting an algorithm for generating vague descriptions, [12] also described an informal experiment that supported the idea that for large classes of adjectives[2], the three forms a,b,c (above) of the vague description are *semantically equivalent* in the sense that, in those cases where they are used referentially, they are often interpreted as having the same reference.[3] The experiment involved numbers; the outcome suggested strongly that, normally, 'the

---

[2] *Evaluative adjectives, such as 'brilliant' or 'stupid' are excluded [1].*

[3] Notable exceptions arise when the description refers anaphorically or in combination with other gradable adjectives. For example, if an entity has been introduced as 'a large dog' then this legitimises later references to it as 'the large dog' even where other, larger dogs are in evidence. The second type of exception arises when, for example, 'the large dog' is juxtaposed with another vague expression such as 'an even larger dog'. For background and elaboration, see [13].

large number' is the same as 'the larger number', which is the same as 'the largest number'. What this experiment did *not* tell us is how to choose between a-c: for all we know, there might be situations in which the use of the superlative, for example, would be highly unnatural (even though it would tend to be interpreted correctly, as the experiment suggested). It is questions of the latter kind that the present paper addresses.

Intuition, supported by pilot experiments and informal study of corpora, suggested to us that there *are* situations where the base form is preferred over the superlative. We will henceforth refer to the difference in the relevant dimension between the intended referent and the nearest relevant object (the nearest 'distractor' removed by the adjective) as the *gap*. This gap itself can have different sizes. Roughly in line with Gricean principles, we hypothesised that when the gap is large, the base form is preferred; in these cases it would be unnecessarily elaborate to say 'the largest number'. Conversely, when the gap is small, we expected the superlative to be preferred. (In such cases, to use the base form sounds like an exaggeration.)

Hypotheses:
1. Small gap ⇒ Superlative > Base
2. Large gap ⇒ Base > Superlative

(*How* large a gap has to be to switch from superlative to base form would have to be assessed separately.) Our first experiment did not take the comparative form into account, but this was added in later experiments. All experiments asked whether subjects considered themselves native speakers of English, fluent, or none of the two; no major differences between the three groups were found.

3   First Experiment: Picking a Numeral

25 academics at the University of Brighton were shown pairs of numerals, one of which appeared in brackets. We chose numerals because numbers come in all possible 'sizes', so when assessing the size or hight of a numeral, the only sensible comparison appears to be with other numerals that the experiment has presented. (Previously seen numerals can be ignored.) The gap between the two numbers was either large (in this case: gap size 7) or small (gap size 1). Eight different patterns involving the numbers $1, 2, 8, 9$ were offered, depending on whether the gap was large or small, in both possible orders, and involving numbers that are somewhat higher (2 and 9 when the gap is large; 8 and 9 when the gap is small) or lower (1 and 8 when the gap is large; 1 and 2 when the gap is small). They were asked

> *Which of the following statements offers the most natural description of this sequence?*
> – *'the large number appears in brackets', or*
> – *'the largest number appears in brackets'?*

Thus, when confronted with the patterns [2 (9)], [(9) 2], [1 (8)], or [(8) 1], we expected to find that more subjects prefer the base form (because the gap is large); when confronted with the patterns [8 (9)], [(9) 8], [2 (1)], or [(1) 2], we expected to find that more subjects prefer the superlative.

Outcomes: The number of choices for each of the different types of adjective can be summarised in a contingency table:

	Base	Superlative
Large Gap	25	75
Small Gap	1	99

The table shows the gap size and adjective type to be non-independent of each other (Chi-square $= 25.464$ with $df = 1$ at $p = 0.001$.) More specifically, the experiment overwhelmingly supported Hypothesis 1. (Only one of the 25 subjects preferred the base form, and only on one occasion.) Equally clearly, however, the experiment failed to confirm Hypothesis 2: in fact, the superlative was chosen in the majority of cases even where the gap was large. *Post hoc*, the experiment suggests that base-form adjectives occur more often when the gap is large than when it is small. (Using the t-test, for example, this is highly significant, with p=.008361 and df=24.) This pattern was confirmed by later experiments.

Note that there was a striking difference between two groups of subjects: all the people in the IT faculty, except one, consistently chose the superlative, while people at the School of Languages showed more variety, including some who chose the base form *if and only if* the gap was large. We will return to the issue of differences between groups of subjects in Section 7.2.

4   Second Experiment: Picking a Number from a Sequence

Confronted with this failure to confirm Hypothesis 2, it is not difficult to find excuses: maybe the gap between the numbers in the experiment had not been large enough, or maybe the question that was asked of the subjects (containing a possibly theory-laden expression like 'natural') was unclear; also, subjects were not offered the possibility of choosing the comparative form ('the larger number'), which is sometimes thought to be preferable when there are only two things to compare. To remove these obstacles, we did the following experiment, which varies on the same numerical theme.

Fourteen subjects (participants at the 2001 EACL conference in Toulouse) were shown sequences of two, three or four numbers, one or two of which appeared in brackets. There were 18 patterns, including, for example, [1 (59)] (large gap), [1 (59) (58)] (large gap), [55 (59) 54] (small gap), [(59) 55 (59) 55] (small gap), and [(59) 1 (59) 0] (large gap). Subjects were asked, in each of these cases, to say *Which description do you consider most likely to have been produced by a native speaker?*, where they could choose between

- *'the large numbers appear in brackets'* or
- *'the larger numbers appear in brackets'* or
- *'the largest numbers appear in brackets'*?

Based on the previous experiment, we refined our hypotheses. Given this subjects were offered a choice between three options, it seemed reasonable to compare the numbers of base forms with each of the two other forms separately:

Hypotheses:
1a. Small gap $\Rightarrow$ Comparative > Base
1b. Small gap $\Rightarrow$ Superlative > Base
2a. Large gap $\Rightarrow$ Base > Comparative
2b. Large gap $\Rightarrow$ Base > Superlative

Outcomes: The data can be summarised as follows:

	Base	Comparative	Superlative
Large Gap	43	37	42
Small Gap	2	65	59

Chi-square suggests a dependency between gap size and adjective type (at $p = 0.001$, $df = 2$, Chi-square $= 47.851$). Using a t-test, we see that, in line with the first experiment, Hypotheses 1a and 1b were confirmed but, crucially, Hypotheses 2a and 2b were not. The following table lists the number of choices for each of the three types of adjectives, for each of those 9 patterns of numbers where the gap was large. (The gap was small in patterns b,c,d,e,h,i,k,m,q.)[4]

[Large Gap]	Base	Comparative	Superlative
Pattern a	3	8	3
Pattern f	4	1	9
Pattern g	3	3	8
Pattern j	6	5	3
Pattern l	4	6	4
Pattern n	5	5	3
Pattern o	4	2	7
Pattern p	7	2	5
Pattern r	7	5	2

Focussing on Hypothesis 2a, we find that the two-tailed P value is not significant at 0.4774 ($t = 0.7276$, $df = 16$). Hypothesis 2b is even further off the mark with $P = 0.9120$ ($t = 0.1123$). As before, there were substantial differences between subjects, including some who used the base form *if and only if* the gap was small. Also as before, the base form was used much more often when the gap was large than when the gap was small.

---

[4] The numbers for patterns n and o do not add up to 14 because one subject had failed to enter a clearly legible choice.

5   Third Experiment: Describing Triangles

Going by the two experiments reported so far, it appears that superlatives are preferred, even in situations where the gap is very large. Again, one can think of excuses. *Asking* subjects about their preferences may not be the best way of assessing them: perhaps speakers cannot always tell how they use language (just like most of us cannot say how they walk). Also, numbers have their peculiarities: contrary to what was assumed in Section 2, one might argue that some numbers (the number 0, for example, given that we only used non-negative numbers) *are* intrinsically small. For these reasons, we shifted the subject matter from numbers to geometrical shapes, and we designed the experiment in such a way that subjects could produce their own referring expressions (instead of being offered a forced choice). 34 Subjects (students of an HCI module at the University of Brighton) were shown a piece of paper showing two isosceles, and approximately equilateral triangles,[5] one of which was circled. To encourage the use of size-related descriptions (like 'the large triangle', 'the biggest of the two figures', but unlike 'the figure on the top left'), the instructions asked subjects to imagine themselves on the phone to someone holding a copy of the same sheet of paper, but not necessarily with the same orientation (e.g., possibly upside down). To discourage lengthy descriptions, the space for text was limited:

```
Q: Which triangle on this sheet
   was circled?
A: The ........... triangle
```

Each of the 34 subjects saw six pairs of triangles, one of which was smaller than the other. Triangles came in three sizes, so the 'gap' between the two triangles could either be large (when the smallest of the three was juxtaposed to the largest of the three) or small (when the mid-size triangle was juxtaposed to either the smallest one or the largest one). The same hypotheses were used as in the previous experiment (see Section 4).

Results: Rather pleasingly, all except one subject used brief, size-related descriptions throughout. There were a few occurrences of descriptions like 'the top triangle', 'the bottom triangle', 'the tiny triangle', yet the data allow a remarkably simple summary:

12 subjects chose **superlatives** throughout (i.e., 6 items)
6 subjects chose **comparatives** throughout
3 subjects chose **Base form** throughout
6 subjects oscillated between Superlative and Comparative
6 subjects oscillated between Base form and some other form

---

[5] Only two triangles were shown at a time, since the use of larger sequences in the second experiment had payed no obvious benefit. The lengths of the bases of the triangles were $5mm, 8mm$, and $16mm$ respectively.

As before, Hypotheses 2a and 2b were not confirmed (while Hypotheses 1a and 1b were confimed). Once again, these findings appear to suggest that superlatives are preferred regardless of circumstance.

6 Fourth Experiment: Recognising Human Behaviour

It seemed plausible that the fact of being under scrutiny (being tested!) might have encouraged 'pedantic' behaviour in our subjects, causing this unexpected run of results. We therefore made one more attempt at getting at subjects' normal behaviour, using a procedure reminiscent of the Turing test, which involves letting subjects judge whether a given pattern of behaviour is likely to have been produced by a real person as opposed to, for example, a computer or a linguist [11]. We showed results (or, in one case, fake results) from the previous experiment to 14 students of the School of Languages, at the University of Brighton. (Each subject in the third experiment gave answers to six answers to questions of the form *Which triangle (...)?*, so each subject produced a sequence of six answers, e.g., smallest large smaller smaller larger larger.) We told our new subjects that each output was produced by one of our subjects (**a,b,c,** and **d**) in an earlier experiment:

> a: smallest largest smallest smallest largest largest
> b: smaller larger smaller smaller larger larger
> c: small large smaller smaller larger larger
> d: smaller larger small small large large

(Subjects were also shown the geometrical patterns on which the four sets of judgments were based.) Subjects **a** and **b** show completely uniform output; **c** mixes base forms and comparatives in a manner consistent with our Hypotheses; **d** (constructed by hand, because no such output had been produced by a real subject) reverses the patterns produced by **c**, using a base form where **c** had produced a comparative and conversely. We asked:

> *Which of the four sequences of responses is most likely to have been produced by a real person, in your opinion? Circle one of the options: Subject* **a, b, c, d.**

In line with our earlier expectations, we hypothesised that **c** would be favoured over all others: that (i) **c** > **a**, that (ii) **c** > **b**, and that (iii) **c** > **d**

Results. The data are as follows:

- 9 subjects thought **b** was most likely
- 4 subjects thought **c** was most likely
- 1 subject thought **a** was most likely
- 0 subjects thought **d** was most likely

On the positive side, this suggests that a generator programmed to behave in accordance with our Hypotheses (leading to output as in **c**) would be judged to be quite natural. But the more striking conclusion is surely that subjects rated completely uniform behaviour even more highly. The number of subjects partaking in this fourth experiment may be too small to warrant firm conclusions but the experiment clearly does little to confirm Hypothesis (ii).

7   Discussion

Two themes emerge: the question how to set up experiments in such a way that their outcomes reflect the linguistic preferences of the subjects; and the question how to cope with differences between subjects.

7.1   Eliciting 'Natural' Use of Language

Our experiments suggest that vague descriptions in the base form are almost always dispreferred in comparison with comparatives and/or superlatives. To us at least, this seems counterintuitive.[6] Otherwise, the experiments diverge. For example, superlatives came out on top of the third experiment, but were trumped by comparatives in the fourth. Note that such surprises are not easily explained along the lines of [5]. There, Oberlander invokes an asymmetry between speakers' inclinations and hearer's expectations, because speakers may be subject to factors that hearers cannot be aware of before the utterance is made (e.g., its propositional content). Our experiments, however, appear to make subjects aware of all the factors that writers/speakers would be aware of. (More specifically, the third and fourth experiments gave their subjects exactly the same information about the triangles and their properties.)

It is, of course, well known that questionnaire-type experiments are sensitive to subtle differences in formulations, and it is possible that our experiments have failed to capture spontaneous language use. One might therefore insist on naturalistic settings where subjects are given immersive real-world tasks to make them less self-conscious, and experiments of this kind (involving the narration of bedtime stories for children) are currently being prepared. The analysis of such experiments (involving unconstrained language use) tends to be difficult and time consuming, however. More importantly, one can always doubt the validity of the experiment by asking whether the task was immersive *enough*.

Perhaps most worryingly, our experiences cast doubt on previous findings: if questions of the form *Which description do you consider most likely to have been produced by a native speaker?* lead to outcomes that misrepresent writers/speakers' inclinations, then how do we know that the answers to other,

---

[6] As was explained in Section 1, it would be no simple matter to test our hypotheses using a corpus like the BNC: even though base-form descriptions *are* much more frequent there than the two other types of descriptions, it would be no trivial matter to filter out attributive, anaphoric, and other uses which, collectively, are much more frequent than the referring expressions on which this paper has focussed.

similar questions that psycholinguists ask (e.g., 'How would you continue this sentence?' [9]; similarly for other types of questions relating to generation of referring expressions, e.g., [6]) are safe?

7.2   Honouring Style Differences

In recent work, Reiter and Sripada have argued that corpora can be a slippery basis on which to base the decisions of a generator [8]. Our own findings suggest a similar conclusion in connection with controlled experiments: one ignores style differences at one's peril. The underlying point is a simple mathematical one: Suppose a given input can be expressed in three ways: A, B, and C, where there are two different sub-styles, say **1** and **2**. Suppose expression A is most frequent in none of the two styles, while occupying a very solid second place in both:

Substyle **1**: $B > A >> C$
Substyle **2**: $C > A >> B$
Overall: $A > B > C$

If the construction of a generator was based on overall frequencies, it would express the input as A, the most frequent expression overall. But this would cause the generator to be a poor imitator of anyone's language use, since no existing substyle would be modelled. It would be better to choose either B or C since, at least, this would capture what is most frequent in one substyle.

8   Conclusion

When gathering data to inform natural language generation, controlled experiments are a natural complement to the study of corpora. This discussion paper has used a sequence of experiments to highlight two types of problems with the experimental approach, one of which (section 7.1) is specific to the experimental approach, while the other echoes similar problems in the study of language corpora (section 7.2).

Acknowledgements

Support for the TUNA project from the EPSRC under grant number GR/S13330 is gratefully acknowledged. Further thanks are due to Paul Piwek and to my TUNA colleagues: Albert Gatt, Emiel Krahmer, Richard Power, and Sebastian Varges, all of whom have contributed to this paper in some way or other.

References

1. Bierwisch, M.: The semantics of gradation. In M.Bierwisch and E.Lang (Eds.) *Dimensional Adjectives*. Berlin, Springer Verlag, (1989) pp.71-261.

2. Jordan, P.W.: Can Nominal Expressions Achieve Multiple Goals?: An Empirical Study. Procs. of ACL-2000, Hong Kong (2000).

3. Kamp, H.: Two theories about adjectives. In "Semantics for natural language", ed. E. Keenan. Cambridge University Press (1975).

4. Klein E.: A semantics for positive and comparative adjectives. *Linguistics and Philosophy* **4** (1980).

5. Oberlander, J.: Do the right thing ... but expect the unexpected. Computational Linguistics, **24** (3), (1998) 501-507.

6. Pechmann, Th.: Incremental Speech Production and Referential Overspecification. *Linguistics* **27** (1989) 98-110.

7. Piwek, P. Cremers, A.: Dutch and English Demonstratives: A Comparison. Language Sciences **18** (3-4), (1996) pp. 835-851.

8. Reiter, E. Sripada, S.: Should Corpora Texts Be Gold Standards for NLG? In Proceedings of INLG-02 (2002) pages 97-104.

9. Stevenson, R.J., Crawley, R.A., and Kleinman, D.: Thematic roles, focus and the representation of events. *Language and Cognitive Processes* **9** (1994) 519-548.

10. Synthese. Special issue of the journal *Synthese* on semantic vagueness. *Synthese* **30** (1975).

11. Turing, A.: Computing Machinery and Intelligence. *Mind* **59**, No. 236 (1950) pp. 433-460.

12. van Deemter, K.: Generating Vague Descriptions. In Procs. of Int. Conf. on Natural Language Generation (INLG-2000) (2000) Mitzpe Ramon.

13. van Deemter, K.: Computational Generation of Vague Descriptions. Manuscript, ITRI, University of Brighton.

Indirect Supervised Learning of Content Selection Logic

Pablo A. Duboue

Columbia University Dept. of Computer Science
New York, NY, 10025, USA
pablo@cs.columbia.edu
http://www.cs.columbia.edu/~pablo/

Abstract. I investigate the automatic acquisition of Content Selection
(CS) rules; a desirable goal, as the CS problem is quite domain dependent. My learning uses a loosely aligned Text-Data corpus, a resource
increasingly popular in learning for NLG because they are readily available and do not require expensive hand labelling. However, they only
provide indirect information about the selected or not selected status of
each semantic datum. Indirect Supervised Learning is my proposed solution to this problem, a solution common to other learning from loosely
aligned Text-Data corpora problems in NLG. It has two steps; in the first
step, the loosely aligned Text-Data corpus is transformed into a data set
with classification labels. In the second step, supervised learning machinery acquires the CS rules from this data set. I evaluate the approach by
comparing the output of my system with the information selected by
human authors in unseen texts.

1 Introduction

CONTENT SELECTION (CS), the problem of choosing the right information to
communicate in the output, is in general a highly domain dependent task; new
CS rules must be developed for each new domain. This is typically a tedious
task, as a realistic knowledge base contains large amounts of data selected.

I am interested in automatically acquiring a set of CS rules in a biographical
description domain. I want to learn these rules from a training data set consisting
of input data and classification labels (selected or not-selected). These rules
decide whether or not to include a piece of information based solely on the
semantics of the data (e.g., the relation of the information to other data in the
input). However, that would require expensive hand-labelling. Instead, I turn to
a loosely aligned Text (Figure 1 (a)) and Data (Figure 1 (b)) corpus. Loosely
aligned Text-Data corpora are increasingly popular in learning for NLG because
they are readily available[1] and do not require expensive hand labelling. However,

---

[1] Examples of domains with available text data corpora include Biology (e.g., the bi-
ological KB and species descriptions); Geography (e.g., CIA fact-book and country
descriptions); Financial Market (e.g., Stock data and market reports); and Enter-
tainment (e.g., Role Playing character sheets and character descriptions).

A. Belz et al. (Eds.): INLG 2004, LNAI 3123, pp. 41–50, 2004.

they only provide indirect information about the selected or not selected status of each semantic datum. Indirect Supervised Learning[2] is my proposed solution to this problem, arguably a solution common to other learning from Text-Data corpora problems in NLG. It has two steps; in the first step, the Text-Data corpus is transformed into a training data set of selected or not-selected classification labels. In the second step, CS rules are learned in a supervised way, from the training data set constructed in the previous step.

Actor, born Thomas Connery on August 25, 1930, in Fountainbridge, Edinburgh, Scotland, the son of a truck driver and charwoman. He has a brother, Neil, born in 1938. Connery dropped out of school at age fifteen to join the British Navy. Connery is best known for his portrayal of the suave, sophisticated British spy, James Bond ...

(a) Text.

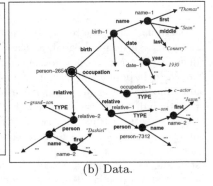

(b) Data.

Fig. 1. Loosely aligned Text-Data corpus.

The output of my machine learning system (Figure 4) will select data that can be further filtered and ordered by later stages in the generation pipeline (e.g., see the spreading activation algorithm used in ILEX [1]). Because my knowledge representation allows for cycles, the actual knowledge representation is as a graph: each frame is a node on it and there are edges labelled with the attribute names joining the different nodes. Atomic values are also represented as special nodes. In this way, my CS rules contain decision logic only for these special atomic nodes. In this paper, expressions such as "a piece of data to be selected" are formalized as one of these atomic nodes in the graph.

In previous work [2], we presented a version of our system for learning CS rules from a Text-Data corpus. The type of rules mined were very general, in the form of SELECT-ALL/SELECT-NONE type of rules (e.g., select all relative first names or do not select any of them). In this work, I defined a rule language and perform a Genetic Search over the possible rules on that language, picking the one that better explains a training data set, built from the Text-Data corpus. This new, improved approach let me augment the quality of the learned rules, making them closer to the type of rules NLG practitioners write to solve CS tasks.

---

[2] Indirect Supervised Learning, where the system learns from indirect, teacher provided examples is not to be confused with Semi-supervised learning. The latter is a bootstrapping method while the former is related to reinforcement learning.

This paper is organized as follows: in the next Section, my domain (together with the loosely aligned Text-Data corpus internals) is introduced. My methods are presented in Section 3 followed by the experimental results. Related work and conclusions are summarized at the end of the paper.

2   Domain: Biographical Descriptions

My technique applies to descriptive texts which realize a single, purely infor- mative, communicative goal, as opposed to cases where more knowledge about speaker intentions are needed. In particular, I focus on biography generation, an exciting field that has attracted practitioners of NLG in the past [3, 4, 5, 6].

I have gathered a loosely aligned Text-Data corpus in this domain. The Data part contains information related to the person the biography talks about (and that the system will use to generate that type of biography). However, not all that information will necessarily appear in the biography. That is, the Data part is not the semantics of the *target text* but the larger set of all things that could possibly be said about the person in question.

To collect the Data, I crawled 1,100 HTML pages containing celebrity fact- sheets from the *E! Online* website.[3] I then proceeded to transform the informa- tion in the pages to a frame-based knowledge representation (the final corpus contains aprox. 50K frames).

The text part was mined from two different web-sites, biography.com, con- taining typical biographies, with an average of 450 words each; and imdb.com, the Internet movie database, 250-word average length biographies.

3   Methods

I present here my two step learning process. In the first step (Section 3.1), I use the Text-Data corpus to infer the classification labels, selected or not-selected, in the data side (that constitutes the training instances for the supervised learning). In the second step (Section 3.2), I train a supervised classifier for the CS task.

3.1   Data Set Construction

The data selected for inclusion in the text can be divided into two classes: data that appears verbatim in the text and data that is somehow verbalized. To deal with the data copied verbatim, I search for it in the text, in a process I call *exact matching*, described next. Finally, the rest of the selected data is verbalized (e.g., c-comedian $\Rightarrow$ *"comedian"*). I introduce a *statistical selection* process to target these harder cases.

---

[3] This process is not required to build a loosely aligned Text-Data corpus, I crawled fact-sheets to provide structured knowledge while I was building the Knowledge Component (that uses information extraction) for the PROGENIE generator [7].

Exact Matching. Exact matching aims to identify pieces from the input that are copied verbatim to the output. When I found a piece of data appearing in the text, I conclude that the data must be selected for inclusion in the text. The output of this process is a set of labels (selected or not-selected) for each datum in the input. This training data set is to be used for supervised learning of CS rules.

The overall matching operation is prone to two type of errors: omission (if the atomic value is symbolic in nature, e.g., `c-comedian` appears in the text as *"he performed comedy for several years"* or a different verbalization, e.g., *"MA"* instead of *"Maryland"*) and over-generation (if there are several values for it, e.g., *"Smith"* appears in the text and it is simultaneously the name of the father and a brother). The latter errors were addressed with a post-processing step based on automatically mined defeasible rules [8], that I cannot detail here by lack of space. More interestingly, the former type of errors are addressed with the statistical selection technique described below.

Statistical Selection. My statistical selection algorithm aims to identify variations on the data that produce variations on the text side. For example, all the comedians (a semantic distinction induced from the data side) may have their biographies with words such as *"comedy,"* *"stand-up"* and the like occurring on them more often than in the rest of the biographies. To this end, I first generate meaningful variations on the data side and then apply statistical filters to the resulting partition of documents on the text side.

In previous work [2], we employed clustering on the atomic values to induce the variations in the data side. I extend that work by replacing the clustering step with an enumeration process. To see the reasons behind this extension, consider the following example: in [2], we clustered all people who were born in November and compared their biographies with the ones of the people born in December. That approach turned up to do well. But now consider that clustering on the atomic values (November, December, etc.) will not necessarily be so informative in cases such as first names. Putting together all the relatives with named *"John"* against the relatives named *"Peter"* is not a semantically meaningful distinction on the data-side. In this extension, therefore, I was interested in enumerating all rules that partition the input semantic data into two sets of a minimum size (or *minimum support*). I employed then *complete level-wise search*[4] [9] to obtain them.

These rules belong to the same language of the final rules mined by the system (Figure 4). They are used to discriminate the full set of knowledge representations. If any node on a knowledge representation is selected when the rule is applied to it (that is, the rule returns **true**), then the whole knowledge

---

[4] Complete level-wise search is employed to search for all instances verifying a certain property. Each instance has an associated complexity (its *level*) and the property must be anti-monotonic: the higher the level, the smaller the number of instances that verify the property. By enumerating the instances in a level-wise manner, all instances that verify the property are guaranteed to be found in an efficient fashion.

representation is selected for the cluster. The rules are enumerated as follows: for each data-path, I record all possible atomic values and measure its support. I then perform a number of passes (normally between 2 or 3), joining atomic values (in the form of IN(...) rules). At all times, I keep only the ones that have enough *support*.

After the atomic rules have been enumerated, I grow paths on the graph, also by doing a number of passes (normally between 3 to 5). In each pass, a working set goes through a number of steps. In the forward step, I take all the nodes reachable from the nodes in the data class through a path in the working set and record which labels **depart** from them. The extension of the paths using these edges form a candidate set that I then filter for paths without enough support. In the backward step, I build now a candidate set by taking the paths in the working set and going back to their parents. Again, I filter the paths by support. The new paths constitute the working set for the next round. Finally, I combine all the paths that had enough support in this enumeration process with the atomic values from the previous step to form TRAVERSE rules. The paths alone are also employed to form TRAVERSE-EQ rules. The resulting rule set is again checked for having enough support and for rules selecting the same set of instances (that are deemed as synonyms and all but one are discarded).

Finally, I create advanced rules with AND and OR. These rules do not follow level-wise behavior, and I thus only select a subset of them, up to some complexity level. I combine rules from a working set a number of times (normally 2 or 3).

With this rule-induced partition of the training data I then look at the text side, looking for difference on the language employed in each partition. In previous work, I employed cross-entropy of the language models induced by the partition. This solution is satisfactory in pin-pointing a global variation on the overall texts, but I wanted to obtain further information about the difference between the partitions.[5] In this work, I investigated statistical tests on the counts for each word on either partition. For example, if the partition is induced by putting aside all comedians and writers in the input data, I then want to conclude that their associated biographies contain the words *"comedian," "wrote,"* and *"producer"* more than expected by chance on this corpus (Figure 2).

Finally, I am left with two training data sets containing classification labels for each piece of input data: one data set produced by the exact matching process and another data set produced by the statistical selection process. I need to combine them into a sole data set for the supervised learning. I investigated two ways to combine the data: full union and selected union. In the full union, I just performed a logical OR of the information contained in both data sets. However, this degraded the results, because the statistical selection data is much noisier than the exact match data. Therefore, I introduced selected union, where the data sets are pre-screened and certain types of input data are marked as

---

[5] Cross-entropy is a feasible solution to this problem, but its results are difficult to interpret. Furthermore, the extracted words of the new statistical tests can be later on used to obtain training material for learning ordering (not only selection).

---

for relative #TYPE rule IN("c-sister-in-law", "c-sister"); words: *sister, often*

for occupation #TYPE –
  – rule EQ("c-occupation-writer"); words: *during, which, own,* **writer,** *from, years, also, success*
  – rule IN("c-occupation-model", "c-occupation-comedian"); words: ***modeling,*** *appearances, turning*
  – rule   TRAVERSE("../#TYPE",f, IN("c-occupation-comedian", "c-occupation-writer")); words: *producer, wrote, comedian, which, own, from, order, success*

Fig. 2. Extracted Words.

always exact matched (if the number of exact matched instances is higher than a percentage threshold on their total number). This ensures a balance between the information coming from the exact match data set and the statistical selection data set, augmenting the signal-to-noise ratio in the final data set.

3.2   Supervised Learning

From the Data Construction step, I have a data set consisting of classification labels (selected, not-selected) for each piece of input data. I want to learn that mapping (from datum to classification label) and capture that knowledge in the form of CS rules. Moreover, a robust machine learning methodology has the chances of improving my results from the noise of the automatically constructed data sets . The information available to the learner is thus the frame knowledge representation (a graph) plus the labels. This implies learning from structural information (as compared to learning from flat feature vectors). To this end, several alternatives are possible, including using memory-based learning, inductive logic programming, combinatorial algorithms and kernel methods [10]. The high dimensionality of the decision space over graphs made me decide for a Genetic Search over the space of all possible rules (Figure 3), with the operators explained below.

As fitness function, I employed the F_α^* measure (weighted f-measure from Information Retrieval) of the classification task of recovering all selected labels on the training data sets. Because I wanted to obtain rules with higher recall that precision, I employed $\alpha = 2.0$ (recall is doubly important than precision). I added a MDL term to the fitness function to avoid over-fitting the data (by memorizing all training instances).

As operators, I have a sexual reproduction operator that takes the two rules and combine them in a new one, by traversing simultaneously both rule trees and randomly deciding whether to combine both rules or stick to one of the parents. I also have several mutation operators that disturb an already existing rule. As initial population, I employ rules enumerated as described in Section 3.1.

> TRUE() Always select.
> IN(list of atomic values) Select if the value is in the list.
> TRAVERSE(path in the graph,rule) Select if the node at the of the path are se-
>   lected by the rule.
> TRAVERSE-EQ(path in the graph) Select if the value of the node at the end of the
>   path is equal to the value of the current node.
> AND(rules) Select if all the rules select the current node.
> OR(rules) Select if any of the rules select the current node.

Fig. 3. Rule Language. All rules are of the form $f :$ node $\rightarrow \{T, F\}$, that is, they take a node in the knowledge representation and return true or false.

4   Experiments

I perform two rounds of training and testing. In the first round, I use 102 biographies from `biography.com` and associated framesets from E! Online. Of these 102, 11 were separated and tagged by hand as test-set.[6] In the second round, I used 205 biographies from ImDB. From these 205, 14 were separated as test-set. Some of the rules I mined are shown in Figure 4.

> **name first TRUE(); name last TRUE()**
>   Always say first and last names.
> **education place country IN("Scotland","England")**
>   As I used U.S. biographies, the country of education is only mentioned when it
> is abroad.
> **significant-other #TYPE IN("c-husband", "c-wife")**
>   Mention husband and wives (but not necessarily boyfriends, girlfriends or lovers).

Fig. 4. Learned rules.

My experimental results are summarized in the following table, where I see the goodness of different approaches in the task of recovering the classification labels. I measure precision, recall and $F_{0.5}$-measure:[7]

---

[6] While my system uses heuristics to approximate the selected data and then learns to select that approximated selected content, the final evaluation is not heuristic: a human judge analyzes each of the kept-aside texts and marks each piece of data as appearing or not in the text.

[7] I used $F_{2.0}$ for the fitness function, but I report the quality of the system with the standard $F_{0.5}$. Results with $F_{2.0}$ will be higher, but difficult to compare.

Experiment	development				imdb.com			
	Selected	Prec.	Rec.	F*	Selected	Prec.	Rec.	F*
random	162	0.29	0.48	0.36	369	0.25	0.50	0.33
select-all	1129	0.26	1.00	0.41	1584	0.23	1.00	0.37
previous work[2]	550	0.41	0.94	0.58	891	0.36	0.88	0.51
only exact match	359	0.64	0.61	0.62	432	0.48	0.65	0.55
combined	292	0.57	0.81	0.67	432	0.49	0.68	0.57
test set	293	-	-	-	369	-	-	-

The table shows that my new system outperforms our previous work and two baselines. As the selected data can be further filtered, recall is more important than precision for my task. My combined exact match and statistically trained supervised learner obtains higher recall than the exact match trained learner, with a small penalty in precision. The `imdb.com` corpus is less homogeneous than `biography.com`, making it a harder test set, although I still observe an improvement over our previous system.

I also performed an evaluation of my data set Construction step: I put together all test and training corpus (102 Text-Data pairs) and obtain labelled data sets as described in Section 3.1. I then separated the 11 data sets corresponding to the test set and evaluated its goodness. I evaluated the exact match obtained data set separated from the statistically obtained one. I also evaluated the two ways to combine them (one of them with three different thresholds).[8]

Exp.	Exact Match	Statistical	Full Union	Sel. 20%	Sel. 30%	Sel. 40%
Prec.	**0.75**	0.36	0.68	0.73	0.70	0.67
Rec.	0.64	0.13	**0.70**	0.69	0.61	0.53
F*	0.69	0.19	0.69	**0.71**	0.65	0.60

The table shows the level of noise of the statistical selection process. When directly joined with the exact match data, the precision drops sharply, but there is new training material available in that data set that cannot be captured by the exact match. The overall effect is that recall grows and there is no impact on F^*-measure. The selected union remedies that, picking the best from both data sets.

Comparing both tables I can also see that my system outperforms in recall its training data. I therefore conclude that my supervised learning is generalizing for my task beyond its initial training material, a very desirable goal.

5   Related Work

The CS literature in NLG is quite vast [11, 12, 13, 14, 1] highlighting the importance of the problem.[9] One of the most felicitous CS algorithms proposed in

---

[8] This is not akin to evaluate on the training corpus, because the labelling task is unsupervised.

[9] For a more thorough discussion of related work see [2, 15].

the literature is the spread activation used in the ILEX project [1], where most salient pieces of data are first chosen (by hard-coding its salience in a field of the knowledge representation) and coherence is used to later select other data. My approach can be thought as empirically grounded mean to obtain the most salient pieces of data. This salience problem is also addressed in a summarization context [16], where human annotation are employed to provide salience scores used later for the evaluation of summaries.

The work of Reiter et al. [13] addresses also Knowledge Acquisition for CS. Different from us, although, they employ non-automatic, traditional Knowledge Engineering (and comment about how laborious is such task).

Text-Data corpora are recently gaining momentum as a resource for Statistical NLG [17, 18, 19, 20]. They have been employed for learning elements at the content planning [17], lexical choice [18, 19] and other levels [20].

Working on the problem of learning similar substructures in graphs, the novel field of Graph Data Mining [10] is related to my supervised learning task. I think the recent invention of graph kernels [21] is of particular importance for the learning of CS logic.

6   Conclusions and Further Work

I have presented an improved method for learning CS rules, a task that is tedious to perform manually and is domain dependent. My new system improves on previously published results on two data sets.

I have mined these CS rules from a Text-Data corpus by means of Indirect Supervised Learning. This two-step learning approach is conceptually easy to grasp and it may apply to other learning from Text-Data corpora problems.

My new statistical test mines words that are related to a particular concept or concepts in the input data. In further work, I would like to relate this to ongoing research on the acquisition of linguistic data from non-linguistic sources [20] and bootstrapping learning of named-entity tags [22].

Finally, I would like to compare my Supervised Learning solution (Stochastic Search) with a kernel method, most specifically graph kernels [21].

Acknowledgements

The author wish to acknowledge the support of ARDA through AQUAINT contract MDA908-02-C-0008. He is also thankful to Kathleen McKeown, Vasileios Hatzivassiloglou, Michel Galley, Noemie Elhadad, and Juan Lipari for thoughtful comments and discussion. He is especially thankful to the three anonymous reviewers of the INLG conference.

References

[1] Cox, R., O'Donnell, M., Oberlander, J.: Dynamic versus static hypermedia in museum education: an evaluation of ILEX, the intelligent labelling explorer. In: Proc. of AI-ED99. (1999)

[2] Duboue, P.A., McKeown, K.R.: Statistical acquisition of content selection rules for natural language generation. In: Proc. EMNLP, Sapporo, Japan (2003)

[3] Kim, S., Alani, H., Hall, W., Lewis, P., Millard, D., Shadbolt, N., Weal, M.: Artequakt: Generating tailored biographies with automatically annotated fragments from the web. In: Proc. of the Semantic Authoring, Annotation and Knowledge Markup Workshop in the 15th European Conf. on Artificial Intelligence. (2002)

[4] Schiffman, B., Mani, I., Conception, K.: Producing biographical summaries: Combining linguistic knowledge with corpus statistics. In: Proc. of ACL-EACL. (2001)

[5] Radev, D., McKeown, K.R.: Building a generation knowledge source using internet-accessible newswire. In: Proc. of the 5th ANLP. (1997)

[6] Teich, E., Bateman, J.A.: Towards an application of text generation in an integrated publication system. In: Proc. of 7th IWNLG. (1994)

[7] Duboue, P.A., McKeown, K.R.: ProGenIE: Biographical descriptions for intelligence analysis. In: Proc. 1st Symp. on Intelligence and Security Informatics, Tucson, AZ, Springer-Verlag (2003)

[8] Knott, A., O'Donnell, M., Oberlander, J., Mellish, C.: Defeasible rules in content selection and text structuring. In: Proc. of EWNLG, Duisburg, Germany (1997)

[9] Agrawal, R., Srikant, R.: Fast algorithms for mining association rules. In: Proc. of VLDB, Morgan Kaufmann (1994) 487–499

[10] Washio, T., Motoda, H.: State of the art of graph-based data mining. SIGKDD Explor. Newsl. **5** (2003) 59–68

[11] Sripada, S.G., Reiter, E., Hunter, J., Yu, J.: A two-stage model for content determination. In: ACL-EWNLG'2001, Toulouse, France (2001) 3–10

[12] Bontcheva, K., Wilks, Y.: Dealing with dependencies between content planning and surface realisation in a pipeline generation architecture. In: Proc. IJCAI. (2001)

[13] Reiter, E., Robertson, R., Osman, L.: Knowledge acquisition for natural language generation. In: Proc. of INLG-2000. (2000)

[14] Lester, J., Porter, B.: Developing and empirically evaluating robust explanation generators: The knight experiments. Comp. Ling. (1997)

[15] Duboue, P.A., McKeown, K.R.: Statistical acquisition of content selection rules for natural language generation. Technical report, Columbia Univ., CS Dept. (2003)

[16] Nenkova, A., Passonneau, R.: Evaluating content selection in summarization: The pyramid method. In: Proc. of HLT-NAACL, Boston, MA (2004)

[17] Duboue, P.A., McKeown, K.R.: Content planner construction via evolutionary algorithms and a corpus-based fitness function. In: Proc. of INLG. (2002)

[18] Barzilay, R., Lee, L.: Bootstrapping lexical choice via multiple-sequence alignment. In: EMNLP-2002, Philadelphia, PA (2002)

[19] Sripada, S., Reiter, E., Hunter, J., Yu, J.: Exploiting a parallel text-data corpus. In: Proceedings of Corpus Linguistics 2003. (2003)

[20] Barzilay, R., Reiter, E., Siskind, J.M., eds.: Workshop on Learning Word Meaning from Non-Linguistic Data. In Barzilay, R., Reiter, E., Siskind, J.M., eds.: HLT-NAACL03, Edmonton, Canada, ACL (2003)

[21] Kashima, H., Inokuchi, A.: Kernels for graph classification. In: Proc. of Int. Workshop on Active Mining. (2002) 31–35

[22] Niu, C., Li, W., Ding, Jihong Srihari, R.K.: Bootstrapping for named entity tagging using concept-based seeds. In: Proc. of HLT-NAACL, Edmonton, Canada (2003)

Generating Referring Expressions
Using Perceptual Groups

Kotaro Funakoshi[1], Satoru Watanabe[1],
Naoko Kuriyama[2], and Takenobu Tokunaga[1]

[1] Department of Computer Science, Tokyo Institute of Technology
Tokyo Meguro Ôookyama 2-12-1, Japan
{koh,satoru_w,take}@cl.cs.titech.ac.jp
[2] Department of Human System Science, Tokyo Institute of Technology
Tokyo Meguro Ôookyama 2-12-1, Japan
kuriyama@hum.titech.ac.jp

Abstract. Past work of generating referring expressions mainly utilized attributes of objects and binary relations between objects to distinguish the referent from other objects. However, such an approach does not work well when there is no distinctive attribute among objects. To overcome this limitation, this paper proposes a method utilizing the perceptual groups of objects and n-ary relations among them. With the proposed method, an expression like "the leftmost ball in the left cluster of three balls" can be generated. The key is to identify groups of objects that are naturally recognized by humans. We conducted psychological experiments with 42 subjects to collect referring expressions in such situations, and built a generation algorithm based on the results. The evaluation using another 23 subjects showed that the proposed method could effectively generate proper referring expressions.

1   Introduction

Generating referring expressions is one of the important research issues of natural language generation, and many researchers have studied it [1, 2, 3, 4, 5, 6, 7, 8, 9].

Most past work [1, 2, 3, 4, 5, 6, 7, 8] makes use of attributes of an intended object (the target) and binary relations between the target and others (distractors) to distinguish the target from distractors. Therefore, these methods cannot generate proper referring expressions in situations where no significant surface difference exists between the target and distractors, and no binary relation is useful to distinguish the target. Here, a *proper* referring expression means a concise and natural linguistic expression enabling hearers to distinguish the target from distractors.

For example, consider indicating object b to person P in the situation shown in Figure 1. Note that person P does not share the label information such as a and b with the speaker. Because object b is not distinguishable from objects a or c by means of their appearance, one would try to use a binary relation between object b and the table, i.e., *"A ball to the right of the table"*. [3] However, *"to the right of"* is not a discriminatory

---

[3] In this paper, we assume that all participants share the appropriate reference frame[10].

A. Belz et al. (Eds.): INLG 2004, LNAI 3123, pp. 51–60, 2004.

relation, for objects a and c are also located to the right of the table. Using a and c as a reference object instead of the table does not make sense, since a and c cannot be uniquely identified because of the same reason that b cannot be identified.

Van der Sluis and Krahmer [9] proposed using gestures such as pointing in situations like those shown Figure 1. However, pointing and gazing are not always available depending on the positional relation between the speaker and the hearer.

In the situation shown in Figure 1, a speaker can indicate object b to person P with a simple expression "the front ball" without using any gesture. In order to generate such an expression, one must be able to recognize the salient perceptual group of the objects and use the n-ary relative relations in the group. [4]

In this paper, we propose a method of generating referring expressions that utilizes n-ary relations among members of a group. Our method recognizes groups by using Thórisson's algorithm [11].

Although there are several types of relations in groups other than positional relation, such as size, e.g., "the *biggest* one", we focus on positional relations in this paper.

Speakers often refer to multiple groups in the course of referring to the target. In these cases, we can observe two types of relations: the *intra-group relation* such as "the front two *among* the five near the desk", and the *inter-group relation* such as "the two *to the right of* the five". We define that a subsumption relation between two groups is an intra-group relation.

In what follows, Section 2 explains the experiments conducted to collect expressions in which perceptual groups are used. The proposed method is described in Section 3, and the evaluation is described in Section 4. Finally, we conclude the paper in Section 5.

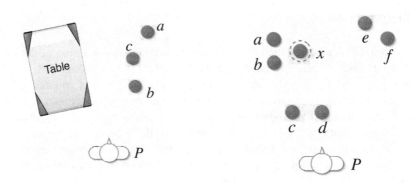

Fig. 1. An example of problematic situations

Fig. 2. A visual stimulus of the experiment

---

[4] Although Krahmer *et al.* claim that their method can handle n-ary relations [8], they provide no specification. We think their method cannot directly handle situations we discuss here.

2 Data Collection

We conducted a psychological experiment with 42 Japanese undergraduate students to collect referring expressions in which perceptual groups are used. In order to evaluate the collected expressions, we conducted another experiment with a different group of 44 Japanese undergraduate students. There is no overlap between the subjects of those two experiments. Details of this experiment are described in the following subsections.

2.1 Collecting Referring Expressions

Method Subjects were presented 2-dimensional bird's-eye images in which several objects of the same color and the same size were arranged and the subjects were requested to convey a target object to the third person drawn in the same image. We used 12 images of arrangements. An example of images presented to subjects is shown in Figure 2. Labels $a, \ldots, f, x$ in the image are assigned for purposes of illustration and are not assigned in the actual images presented to the subjects. Each subject was asked to describe a command so that the person in the image picks a target object that is enclosed with dotted lines. When a subject could not think of a proper expression, she/he was allowed to abandon that arrangement and proceed to the next one. Referring expressions designating the target object were collected from these subjects' commands.

Analysis We presented 12 arrangements to 42 subjects and obtained 476 referring expressions. Twenty eight cases were abandoned in the experiment. Observing the collected expressions, we found that starting from a group with all of the objects, subjects generally narrow down the group to a singleton group that has the target object. Therefore, a referring expression can be formalized as a sequence of groups (SOG) reflecting the subject's narrowing down process.

The following example shows an observed expression describing the target x in Figure 2 with the corresponding SOG representation below it.

"hidari oku ni aru mittu no tama no uti no iti-ban migi no tama."
(the rightmost ball among the three balls in the back-left side)

SOG: $[\{a, b, c, d, e, f, x\}, \{a, b, x\}, \{x\}]$ [5]
where
   $\{a, b, c, d, e, f, x\}$ denotes all objects in the image (total set),
   $\{a, b, x\}$ denotes the three objects in the back-left side, and
   $\{x\}$ denotes the target.

Since narrowing down starts from the total set, the SOG representation starts with a set of all objects and ends with a singleton group with the target. Translating the collected referring expressions into the SOG representation enables us to abstract and classify the expressions. On average, we obtained about 40 expressions for each arrangement, and classified them into 8.4 different SOG representations. The summary of collected data is shown in Table 1.

Although there are two types of relations between groups as we mentioned in Section 1, the expressions using only intra-group relations made up about 80% of the total.

---

[5] We denote a SOG representation by enclosing groups with square brackets.

Table 1. Summary of the collected data

Arrangement ID	1	2	3	4	5	6	7	8	9	10	11	12	Average
Number of expressions obtained	41	40	41	41	42	37	42	32	42	41	41	36	39.7
Number of different SOGs	5	6	8	8	6	12	4	15	4	11	5	17	8.4

2.2 Evaluating the Collected Expressions

Method Subjects were presented expressions collected in the experiment described in Section 2.1 together with the corresponding images, and were requested to indicate objects referred to by the expressions. The presented images are the same as those used in the previous experiment except that there are no marks on the targets. At the same time, subjects were requested to express their confidence in selecting the target, and evaluate the conciseness, and the naturalness of the given expressions on a scale of 1 to 8.

Because the number of expressions that we could evaluate with subjects was limited, we chose a maximum of 10 frequent expressions for each arrangement. The expressions were chosen so that as many different SOG representations were included as possible. If an arrangement had SOGs less than 10, several expressions that had the same SOG but different surface realizations were chosen. The resultant 117 expressions were evaluated by 44 subjects. Each subject evaluated about 32 expressions.

Analysis Discarding incomplete answers, we obtained 1,429 evaluations in total. 12.2 evaluations were obtained for each expression on average.

We measured the quality of each expression in terms of an *evaluation value* that is defined in (1). This measure is used to analyze what kind of expressions are preferred and to set up a scoring function (5) for machine-generated expressions as described in Section 3.

$$(evaluation\ value) = (confidence) \times \frac{(naturalness) + (conciseness)}{2} \tag{1}$$

According to our analysis, the expressions with only intra-group relations obtained high evaluation values, while the expressions with inter-group relations obtained lower evaluation values. We provide a couple of example expressions indicating object x in Figure 2 to contrast those two types of expressions below.

- without inter-group relations (i.e., with intra-group relations only)
  - "the rightmost ball among the three balls in the back-left side"
- with inter-group relations
  - "the ball behind the two front balls"

In addition, expressions explicitly mentioning all the objects obtained lower evaluation values. Considering these observations, we built a generation algorithm using only intra-group relations and did not mention all the objects explicitly.

The summary of the analysis is shown in Table 2. The first column "w/o inter-group" shows the data concerning the expressions with intra-group relations only. The second

Table 2. Statistics of the human evaluation

		w/o inter-group	w/ inter-group	total
Number of expressions		86	31	117
Accuracy	: Range (%)	9 - 100	0 - 100	0 - 100
	: Average (%)	93.51	70.02	87.29
	: Std. Dev.	16.28	35.04	23.61
Evaluation Value	: Range	11.66 - 55.54	10.49 - 49.54	10.49 - 55.54
	: Average	34.40	25.16	31.95
	: Std. Dev.	10.14	11.42	10.89
Confidence	: Range	3.93 - 7.75	3.36 - 7.36	3.36 - 7.75
	: Average	6.36	5.59	6.15
	: Std. Dev.	0.91	1.17	1.01
Briefness	: Range	2.85 - 7.36	2.25 - 7.00	2.25 - 7.36
	: Average	5.53	4.59	5.28
	: Std. Dev.	1.00	1.26	1.09
Naturalness	: Range	2.75 - 7.18	2.33 - 6.18	2.33 - 7.18
	: Average	5.09	4.09	4.83
	: Std. Dev.	1.07	1.28	1.17

column "w/ inter-group" shows the data concerning the expressions with inter-group relations.

Among these expressions, we selected those with which the subjects successfully identified the target with more than 70% accuracy. The selected expressions are used to build a generation algorithm. One might think this threshold is too low. However, since the average number of evaluations for each expression is not so large, deleting incomplete evaluations further reduces the number of evaluations, and thus decreases the reliability. 70% is a compromised threshold value. These expressions are used to extract parameters of our generation algorithm in the next section.

3   Generating Referring Expressions

Given an arrangement of objects and a target, our algorithm generates referring expressions by the following four steps:

Step 1: enumerate perceptual groups based on the proximity between objects
Step 2: generate the SOG representations by combining the groups
Step 3: calculate the scores of each SOG representation
Step 4: translate the SOG representations into linguistic expressions

In the rest of this section, we illustrate how these four steps generate referring expressions in the situation shown in Figure 2.

Step 1: Generating Perceptual Groups. To generate perceptual groups from an arrangement, Thórisson's algorithm [11] is adopted.

Given a list of objects in an arrangement, the algorithm generates groups based on the proximity of the objects and returns a list of groups. Only groups containing the target, that is x, are chosen because we handle intra-group relations only as mentioned before, and that implies that all groups mentioned in an expression must include the target. Then, the groups are sorted in descending order of the group size. Finally a singleton group consisting of the target is added to the end of the list if such a group is missing in the list. The resultant group list, GL, is the output of Step 1.

For example, the algorithm recognizes the following groups given the arrangement shown in Figure 2:

$$\{\{a, b, c, d, e, f, x\}, \{a, b, c, d, x\}, \{a, b, x\}, \{c, d\}, \{e, f\}\}.$$

After filtering out the groups without the target and adding a singleton group with the target, we obtain the following list:

$$GL = \{\{a, b, c, d, e, f, x\}, \{a, b, c, d, x\}, \{a, b, x\}, \{x\}\}. \tag{2}$$

Step 2: Generating the SOG Representations. In this step, the SOG representations introduced in Section 2 are generated from the GL of Step 1, which generally has a form like (3), where G_i denotes a group, and G_0 is a group of all the objects. Here, we narrow down the objects starting from the total set (G_0) to the target ($\{x\}$).

$$GL = \{G_0, G_1, \ldots, G_{m-2}, \{x\}\} \tag{3}$$

First, given a group list GL, all possible SOGs are generated. From a group list of size m, 2^{m-2} SOG representations can be generated since G_0 and $\{x\}$ should be included in the SOG representation. For example, from a group list of $\{G_0, G_1, G_2, \{x\}\}$, we obtain four SOGs: $[G_0, \{x\}]$, $[G_0, G_1, \{x\}]$, $[G_0, G_2, \{x\}]$, and $[G_0, G_1, G_2, \{x\}]$.

Second, among these generated SOG representations, those that contain more than four groups are discarded at this stage for the sake of conciseness. This filtering was introduced considering the observation of the collected data.

For example, one of the SOG representations generated from list (2) is

$$[\{a, b, c, d, e, f, x\}, \{a, b, x\}, \{x\}]. \tag{4}$$

Step 3: Calculating Scores. This step calculates the score of SOG representations. Currently, the score is calculated only based on the SOG representation, that is, features of linguistic expressions such as phrase length, are not considered.

The total score of an SOG representation is calculated by averaging the scores given by functions f_1 and f_2 whose parameters are dimension ratios between two consecutive groups as given in (5), where n is the number of groups in the SOG representation.

$$score(SOG) = \frac{1}{n-1} \left\{ \sum_{i=0}^{n-3} f_1 \left(\frac{dim(G_{i+1})}{dim(G_i)} \right) + f_2 \left(\frac{dim(\{x\})}{dim(G_{n-2})} \right) \right\} \tag{5}$$

The dimension of a group dim is defined as the average distance between the centroid of the group and that of each object. The dimension of the singleton group $\{x\}$ is defined as a constant value. Because of this idiosyncrasy of the singleton group $\{x\}$ compared to other groups, function f_2 was introduced separately from function f_1 even though both functions represent the same concept as described below.

We assume that, when a speaker tries to narrow down an object group from G_i to G_{i+1}, there is an optimal ratio between the dimensions of G_i and G_{i+1}. In other words, narrowing down a group from a very big one to a very small one might cause hearers to become confused. For example, consider the following two expressions that both indicate object x in Figure 2. Hearers would prefer (A) to (B) though (B) is simpler than (A).

(A) "the rightmost ball among the three balls in the back-left side"
(B) "the fourth ball from the left"

The optimal ratio between two groups, and that from a group to the target were found through the quadratic regression analysis of data collected in the experiment described in Section 2.2. Functions f_1 and f_2 are the two regression curves found through the analysis representing correlations between dimension ratios and values calculated based on human evaluation as in (1).

Step 4: Generating Linguistic Expressions. In the last step, the SOG representations are translated into linguistic expressions. Since Japanese is a head-final language, the order of linguistic expressions for groups are retained in the final linguistic expression for the SOG representation. That is, an SOG representation $\{G_0, G_1, \ldots, G_{n-2}, \{x\}\}$ can be achieved as shown in (6), where $E(X)$ denotes a linguistic expression for X, $R(X, Y)$ denotes a relation between X and Y, and '+' is a string concatenation operator.

$$E(G_0) + E(R(G_0, G_1)) + E(G_1) + \ldots + E(R(G_{n-2}, \{x\})) + E(\{x\}) \quad (6)$$

As described in Section 2.2, expressions that explicitly mention all the objects obtain lower evaluation values, and expressions using intra-group relations obtain high evaluation values. Considering these observations, our algorithm does not use the linguistic expression corresponding to all the objects, that is $E(G_0)$, and only uses intra-group relations for $R(X, Y)$.

Possible expressions of X are collected from the experimental data in Section 2.1, and the first applicable expression is selected when realizing a linguistic expression for X, i.e., $E(X)$.

For example, the SOG representation (4) is realized as follows.

$$[\{a, b, c, d, e, f, x\}, \{a, b, x\}, \{x\}]$$

$$\rightarrow E(R(\{a, b, c, d, e, f, x\}, \{a, b, x\})) + E(\{a, b, x\})$$
$$+ E(R(\{a, b, x\}, \{x\})) + E(\{x\})$$

$$\rightarrow \quad \text{"}hidari\ oku\ no\text{"} + \text{"}mittu\ no\ tama\text{"} + \text{"}no\ uti\ no\ migihasi\ no\text{"} + \text{"}tama\text{"}$$
$$\quad\ \ \text{(in the back-left) (three balls)} \quad\ \ \text{(rightmost \ldots among) \quad (ball)}$$

Note that there is no mention of all the objects, $\{a, b, c, d, e, f, x\}$, in the linguistic expression.

Table 3. Summary of evaluation

	Accuracy (%)	Naturalness	Conciseness	Confidence	Eval. val.	Agreement (%)
Human-1	87.3	4.82	5.27	6.14	32.0	N/A
Human-2	97.0	5.05	5.49	6.38	34.2	N/A
System-A	91.0	5.60	6.25	6.32	40.1	53.3
System-B	88.4	5.09	5.65	6.25	35.2	45.0
System-Average	89.2	5.24	5.82	6.27	36.6	46.7

4   Evaluation

We implemented the algorithm described in Section 3, and evaluated the output with 23 undergraduate students. The subjects were different from those of the previous experiments but were of the same age group, and the experimental environment was the same. The evaluation of the output was performed in the same manner as that of Section 2.2.

The results are shown in Table 3. "Human-1" shows the average values of all expressions collected from humans as described in Section 2.2. "Human-2" shows the average values of expressions by humans that gained more than 70% in accuracy in the same evaluation experiment. Our algorithm tries to emulate the expression of "Human-2", thus this would be the baseline of the algorithm.

"System-A" shows the average values of expressions generated by the algorithm for the 12 arrangements used in the data collection experiment described in Section 2.1. The algorithm generated 18 expressions for the 12 arrangements, which were presented to each subject in random order for evaluation.

"System-B" shows the average values of expressions generated by the algorithm for 20 randomly generated arrangements that generate at least two linguistic expressions. The algorithm generated 48 expressions for these 20 arrangements, which were evaluated in the same manner as that of "System-A".

"System-Average" shows the micro average of expressions of both "System-A" and "System-B".

"Accuracy" shows the rates at which the subjects could identify the correct target objects from the given expressions. Comparing the accuracies of "Human-2" and "System-A", we find that the algorithm generates very good expressions. Moreover, the algorithm is superior to human in terms of "Naturalness" and "Conciseness". However, this result should be interpreted carefully. Further investigation of the expressions revealed that humans often sacrificed naturalness and conciseness in order to describe the target as precisely as possible for complex arrangements.

The last column, "Agreement", shows to what extent the scores of expressions given by the algorithm conform with the human evaluation. The agreement is calculated as follows. First, the generated expressions are ordered according to the algorithm's score given by (5) in Section 3 and the human evaluation given by (1) in Section 2.2. All binary order relations between two expressions are extracted from these two ordered lists of expressions respectively. The agreement is defined as the ratio of the same binary order relations among the number of all binary orders. We find that the current scoring function does not conform with the human evaluation very well.

5 Concluding Remarks and Future Work

This paper proposed an algorithm that generates referring expressions using perceptual groups and n-ary relations among them. The algorithm was built on the basis of the analysis of expressions that were collected through linguistic experiments. The performance of the algorithm was evaluated by 23 subjects and it generated promising results.

In the following, we look at future work to be done.

Recognizing Lines: Thórisson's algorithm [11] cannot recognize objects in linear arrangement as a group, although such an object arrangement is quite salient for humans. This is one of the reasons for the disconformity of the evaluations between those of the algorithm and those of the human subjects.

For example, in the arrangement shown in Figure 3, Thórisson's algorithm will recognize groups $G1$, $G2$, and $G4$ but not group $G3$ because the distance between objects x and c is a little bit longer than other distances between objects. However, a line formed by group $G3$ is salient for humans, and it would be preferred to use $G3$ to generate expressions such as "the second one from the left among the four balls in back".

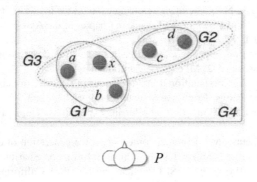

Fig. 3. An example arrangement forming a line

Using Relations Other Than Positional Relations: In this paper, we focused on positional relations of perceptual groups. Other relations such as degrees of colors and sizes should be treated in the same manner.

Designing a Better Scoring Method: As shown by the evaluation in Section 4, our scoring method described in Section 3 does not conform with the human evaluation. The method uses only the dimension ratio of groups in the course of the narrowing down process. This would be an effective factor for generating appropriate referring expressions but not necessarily the primary one. Further research is required to explore other factors to be incorporated into the scoring method.

Integrating with the Conventional Methods: In this paper, we focused on the limited situation where inherent attributes of objects are useless, but this is not the case in general. The algorithm integrating the conventional attribute-based methods and the proposed method should be investigated to achieve the end goal.

A possible direction would be enhancing the algorithm proposed by Krahmer et al. [8]. They formalize an object arrangement (*scene*) as a labeled directed graph in which vertices model objects and edges model attributes and binary relations, and regard content selection as a subgraph construction problem. Their algorithm performs searches directed by a cost function on a graph to find a subgraph that has no isomorphic subgraphs on the same graph.

By considering a perceptual group as an ordinary object, their algorithm is applicable. However, introducing perceptual groups as vertices makes it difficult to design the cost function. A well-designed cost function is indispensable for generating concise and comprehensible expressions. Otherwise, an expression like "a ball in front of a ball in front of a ball" for the situation shown in Figure 1 would be generated.

References

[1] Appelt, D.E.: Planning english referring expressions. Artificial Intelligence **26** (1985) 1–33
[2] Dale, R., Haddock, N.: Generating referring expressions involving relations. In: Proceedings of the Fifth Conference of the European Chapter of the Association for Computational Linguistics(EACL'91). (1991) 161–166
[3] Dale, R.: Generating referring expressions: Constructing descriptions in a domain of objects and processes (1992) MIT Press, Cambridge.
[4] Dale, R., Reiter, E.: Computational interpretations of the gricean maxims in the generation of referring expressions. Cognitive Science **19** (1995) 233–263
[5] Heeman, P., Hirst, G.: Collaborating referring expressions. Computational Linguistics **21** (1995) 351–382
[6] Krahmer, E., Theune, M.: Efficient context-sensitive generation of descriptions (2002) In Kees van Deemter and Rodger Kibble, editors, Information Sharing: Givenness and Newness in Language Processing. CSLI Publications, Stanford, California.
[7] van Deemter, K.: Generating referring expressions: Boolean extensions of the incremental algorithm. Computational Linguistics **28** (2002) 37–52
[8] Krahmer, E., van Erk, S., Verleg, A.: Graph-based generation of referring expressions. Computational Linguistics **29** (2003) 53–72
[9] van der Sluis, I., Krahmer, E.: Generating referring expressions in a multimodal context: An empirically oriented approach (2000) Presented at the CLIN meeting 2000, Tilburg.
[10] Levinson, S.C., ed.: Space in Language and Cognition. Cambridge University Press (2003)
[11] Thórisson, K.R.: Simulated perceptual grouping: An application to human-computer interaction. In: Proceedings of the Sixteenth Annual Conference of the Cognitive Science Society. (1994) 876–881

The Use of a Structural N-gram Language Model in Generation-Heavy Hybrid Machine Translation

Nizar Habash

University of Maryland University Institute for Advanced Computer Studies
University of Maryland College Park
habash@umiacs.umd.edu

Abstract. This paper describes the use of a statistical structural N-gram model in the natural language generation component of a Spanish-English generation-heavy hybrid machine translation system. A structural N-gram model captures the relationship between words in a dependency representation without taking into account the overall structure at the phrase level. The model is used together with other components in the system for lexical and structural selection. An evaluation of the machine translation system shows that the use of structural N-grams decreases runtime by 60% with no loss in translation quality.

1 Introduction

Statistical N-gram models capturing patterns of local co-occurrence of contiguous words in sentences have been used in various hybrid implementations of Natural Language Generation (NLG) and Machine Translation (MT) systems [1,2,3,4,5]. Other types of language models that capture long-distance relationships, such as probabilistic context-free grammars (PCFG) or lexicalized syntax models, have been used in the parsing community with impressive improvements in parsing correctness [6,7,8,9]. In comparison, only one large-scale system built with NLG in mind uses a structural language model [4]. Additionally, the IBM Air Travel Reports system, which implements a dependency n-gram model, uses templates and focuses on travel reports only [10]. A recent study using the Charniak parser [11] as a lexicalized syntax model for generation purposes demonstrated the usefulness of these models in a variety of NLG tasks [12].

The focus of this paper is on the contributions of a specific type of a structural language model, Structural N-grams (SN-gram model)[1], for NLG in the MT context. Whereas syntax models address both parent-child relationships and sisterhood relationships, the SN-gram model characterizes the relationship between words in a dependency representation of a sentence without taking into account the overall structure at the phrase level. In other words, an independence in the behavior of the children relative to each other (their sisterhood relationships) is assumed in SN-grams.

Figure 1 exemplifies the differences between SN-grams (dashed arrows) and N-grams (solid arrows). In addition to capturing long-distance relationships between words (e.g., *have/has* and *lining*), SN-grams are based on uninflected lexemes not on inflected

---

[1] To distinguish between *Surface* N-gram models and *Structural* N-gram models, I will refer to them as N-gram and SN-gram models, respectively.

A. Belz et al. (Eds.): INLG 2004, LNAI 3123, pp. 61–69, 2004.

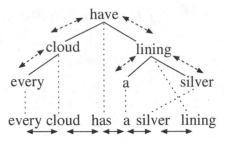

Fig. 1. SN-grams vs N-grams

surface forms. Therefore SN-grams can model more general relationships between lexical items. Moreover, the effect of SN-grams is only seen on lexical selection whereas the N-gram statistical ranking determines both lexical selection and linearization. Therefore, the two models are complementary in many ways.

Two particular hybrid NLG systems are relevant to the work presented here: Nitrogen/Halogen and FERGUS. Nitrogen is a hybrid NLG system that uses N-grams models to rank through symbolically overgenerated lattices of possible output. A later version of Nitrogen, Halogen, improves on time-space efficiency by compressing the search space into *forests*, compact non-redundant syntactically-derived representations of lattices [13]. Although structural syntactic information is used in constructing forests, the only SLM used in Halogen is a surface N-gram model. FERGUS (Flexible Empiricist/Rationalist Generation Using Syntax) extends the use of N-gram models with a tree-based statistical model, SN-gram model and a lexicalized tree-based syntactic grammar [4]. The use of SN-grams for lexical selection was tested through an artificial expansion of words using WordNet supersynsets [14]. The experiment showed that lexical choice was improved using structural language models.

This paper describes the use of a statistical structural N-gram (SN-gram) model in EXERGE (Expansive Rich Generation for English), the natural language generation (NLG) component of the Spanish-English generation-heavy hybrid machine translation (GHMT) system Matador [15]. The next section is an overview of Matador and EXERGE. Section 3 describes the different uses of SN-grams in EXERGE. Finally, Section 4 presents an empirical evaluation of the contribution of SN-grams in EXERGE.

2   Overview of Matador and EXERGE

Matador is a Spanish-English MT system implemented in the Generation-heavy Hybrid MT (GHMT) approach [16,15]. The focus of GHMT is addressing resource poverty in MT by exploiting symbolic and statistical target language resources in source-poor/ target-rich language pairs. Expected source language resources include a syntactic parser and a word-based translation dictionary. No transfer rules, complex interlingual representations or parallel corpora are used. Rich target language symbolic resources such as word lexical semantics, categorial variations and subcategorization frames are used to overgenerate multiple structural variations from a target-glossed syntactic dependency representation of source language sentences. This symbolic overgeneration is constrained by multiple statistical target language models including N-grams and SN-grams. Some of the advantages of systems developed in this approach include: ease of retargetability to new source languages due to source-target asymmetry, performance stability across different genres due to lack of need to train on parallel text, and improved grammaticality as compared to systems that do not use deep linguistic resources (for an evaluation comparing Matador to a statistical MT system, see [15]).

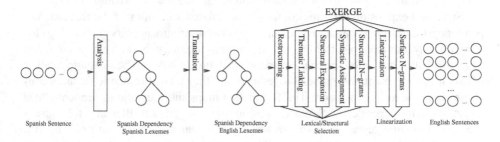

Fig. 2. Matador: Spanish-English Generation-Heavy Hybrid Machine Translation

Figure 2 describes the different components of Matador. There are three phases: Analysis, Translation and Generation. The last phase is marked as EXERGE — EXpansivE Rich Generation for English — a source-language-independent generation module for English. These three phases are very similar to other paradigms of MT: Analysis-Transfer-Generation or Analysis-Interlingua-Generation. However, these phases are not symmetric. The output of Analysis is a deep syntactic dependency that normalizes over syntactic phenomena such as passivization and morphological expressions of tense, number, etc. Translation converts the Spanish lexemes into ambiguous sets of English lexemes. The dependency structure of the Spanish is maintained. The last phase, Generation, is where most of the work is done to manipulate the input lexically and structurally and produce English sequences. The rest of this section discusses EXERGE's resources and major components.

EXERGE utilizes three symbolic and two statistical English resources. The first of the symbolic resources is the word-class lexicon, which defines verbs and prepositions in terms of their subcategorization frames and lexical conceptual primitives. A single verb or preposition can have multiple entries for each of its senses. For example, among other entries, run_1 as in ($John_{agent}$ $ran_{cause-go_{identificational}}$ $store_{theme}$) is distinguished from run_2 as in ($John_{theme}$ $ran_{go_{locational}}$). Second, the categorial-variation lexicon relates words to their categorial variants. For example, $hunger_V$, $hunger_N$ and $hungry_{AJ}$ are clustered together. So are $cross_V$ and $across_P$; and $stab_V$ and $stab_N$. The third symbolic resource is the syntactic-thematic linking map, which relates syntactic relations (such as subject and object) and prepositions to the thematic roles they can assign. For example, while a subject can take on just about any thematic role, an indirect object is typically a *goal, source* or *benefactor*. Prepositions can be more specific. For example, *toward* typically marks a *location* or a *goal*, but never a *source*.

EXERGE consists of seven steps (Figure 2). The first five are responsible for lexical and structural selection and the last two are responsible for linearization. Initially, the source language syntactic dependency, now with target lexemes, is normalized and restructured into a syntactico-thematic dependency format. The thematic roles are then determined in the thematic linking step. The syntax-thematic linking is achieved through the use of thematic grids associated with English (verbal) head nodes together with the syntactic-thematic linking map. This step is a *loose* linking step that does not enforce the subcategorization-frame ordering or preposition specification. This looseness is important for linking from unknown non-English subcategorization frames.

Structural expansion explores conflated and inflated variations of the thematic dependency. Conflation is handled by examining all verb-argument pairs (V_{head}, Arg) for *conflatability*. For example, in *John put salt on the butter, to put salt on* can be conflated as *to salt* but *to put on butter* cannot be conflated into *to butter*. The thematic relation between the argument and its head together with other lexical semantic features constrain this structural expansion. The fourth step maps the thematic dependency to a target syntactic dependency. Syntactic positions are assigned to thematic roles using the verb class subcategorization frames and argument category specifications. The fifth step prunes ambiguous nodes using a SN-gram model. The purpose of this step is to constrain the overgeneration of the previous steps in preparation for further expansion by the linearization step.

Next is the linearization step, where a rule-based grammar implemented using the linearization engine oxyGen [17] is used to create a word lattice that encodes the different possible realizations of the sentence. Finally, the word lattice is converted into a Halogen-compatible forest to be ranked with Halogen's statistical forest ranker [13].

In terms of input complexity and the balance of symbolic and statistical components, EXERGE is in between the hybrid NLG systems Nitrogen and FERGUS. FERGUS requires the shallowest input (closest to the target-language surface form) and employs the most in statistical and symbolic power. Nitrogen's input is the deepest (semantic representation) and its resources the simplest (an overgenerating grammar and n-gram model).

3   SN-grams in EXERGE

SN-grams are used in EXERGE for (1) lexical selection and (2) structural selection. First, SN-grams are used to prune the ambiguous nodes in the forest of syntactic dependencies produced after the structural expansion and syntactic assignment steps. This pruning is motivated by the need to control the size of the word lattices passed on to the n-gram language model, which tends to be the most expensive step in the whole system. For each tree, T in the forest, a bottom-up dynamic programming algorithm is used to calculate the maximum (joint) frequency of $(word, parent_{word})$ over all $words$ in the $nodes$ of T.[2] Once the scoring is completed, selecting the best unambiguous tree using the dynamic programming tables is straightforward.

---

[2] In a different version of the system, the conditional probability, $P(word|parent_{word})$, is used with no significant effect. This is consistent with findings in the parsing community [18].

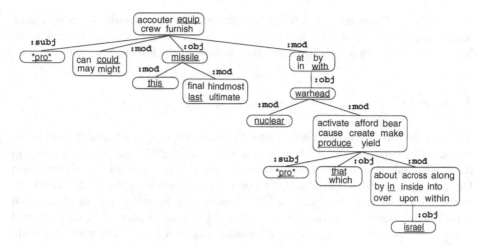

Fig. 3. SN-gram-based Lexical Selection

As an example, Figure 3 displays the input to EXERGE resulting from the parsing and word-based translation for the Spanish sentence *Este último misil puede equiparse con ojivas nucleares que se están produciendo en Israel.* "This last missile can be equipped with nuclear warheads which are currently produced in Israel." The under-lined lexical items in Figure 3 are what the SN-gram model selected for this example. These lexemes are later linearized into a lattice of possible sequences. The top ranked sequence based on a surface bigram model is *This last missile could be equipped with nuclear warheads that are being produced in Israel.*

Secondly, since the symbolic resources used in the structural expansion phase fo-cus on verbs only, a SN-gram-driven approach is used to expand the structure of *noun phrases*. This addresses cases where the direct modification relationship between two English nouns is expressed in Spanish using a preposition.[3] This process is done as fol-lows. For every *parent-child* pair of nominal nodes separated by a *preposition*, the pair is determined to prefer a direct modification relation over *preposition* if the SN-gram frequency of (*child, parent*) is higher than the frequency of (*child, preposition*) or the frequency of (*preposition, parent*). For example, the preposition in the Span-ish *el mundo en desarrollo (the world in development/developing)* is replaced by a direct modification relationship since the SN-gram (*developing world*) is more com-mon than (*world in*) and (*in development/developing*) in English.[4] Structural variations in noun-noun modification are common in translation between English and other lan-guages (e.g., Japanese [20]).

---

[3] The technique presented here for structural selection using SN-grams can be used in reverse to allow translation of direct noun modification in the source language to prepositional modi-fication in English.

[4] A relevant discussion of the translation of noun-noun compounds from Spanish to English is available in [19].

The use of SN-grams in EXERGE for both lexical and structural choice in a large scale trans-lingual setting is a major difference from FERGUS's use of SN-grams for lexical choice only in a monolingual setting. Nitrogen does not use SN-grams.

4   Evaluation

The contribution of SN-grams is evaluated by comparing translation quality and system efficiency of two versions of Matador, one implementing SN-grams and one without them. The evaluation metric used for translation quality is Bleu (BiLingual Evaluation Understudy) [21]. Bleu is a method of automatic translation evaluation that is quick, inexpensive and language independent.[5] The Bleu score is basically an N-gram precision variation calculated as the ratio of the number of N-gram sequences in the generated string that appear in the reference (gold standard) string to the total number of N-gram sequences in the generated string. Bleu is used with 1 to 4-grams and without case sensitivity.[6] System efficiency is measured in terms of CPU time (in seconds). [7]

The blind test set evaluated contained 2,000 Spanish sentences[8] from the UN Spanish-English corpus [24]. The gold standard translations used as references for the Bleu evaluation are the English side of the 2,000 sentences. There was one reference per sentence.

The SN-gram (structural bigram) model was created using 127,000 parsed sentences from the English UN corpus covering over 3 million words. The parsing was done using Connexor's English parser [25]. The resulting noisy treebank was traversed and parent-child instance (lexeme) pairs were counted to create the model. The language model totals 504,039 structural bigrams for 40,879 lexemes. A human checked Treebank was not used to collect SN-gram statistics because none that exist cover the domain of the test set.

The N-gram model was built using 500 thousand sentences from the UN corpus (50,000 from the UN Spanish-English corpus [24] and 450 thousand sentences from the English side of the Arabic-English UN corpus [26]). The Halogen ranking scheme used is bigrams with length normalization. One issue relevant to the N-gram model is the use of bigrams instead of trigrams, which are known to perform better. This decision is purely based on technical issues, namely that Halogen's runtime performance with trigrams is prohibitively long [12].

The runtime and resulting Bleu scores are presented in Table 1. A breakdown of the time over the different Matador modules is presented in Figure 4. The Expansion module refers to the first five steps in EXERGE (see Figure 2). The use of SN-grams decreases runtime by 59.45% with no negative effect on text quality. Running the SN-gram pruning doubles the runtime of the expansion module. However the payoff is a

---

[5] Other metrics for evaluating natural language generation include tree-based metrics and combined (string-based and tree-based) metrics [22]. For excellent surveys of machine translation evaluation metrics and techniques, see [23].

[6] Throughout this paper, Bleu scores are presented multiplied by 100.

[7] The system ran on a SparcIII, with 750Mhz and 1GB of memory.

[8] Average sentence length in test set is 15.39 words/sentence.

Table 1. Structural N-gram Evaluation

	Bleu Score	Overall Runtime	Runtime (sec/sentence)
with Structural N-grams	18.01 +/- 1.00	14,155 sec ≈ 3.9 hours	7.08
without Structural N-grams	17.94 +/- 1.04	34,908 sec ≈ 9.7 hours	17.45

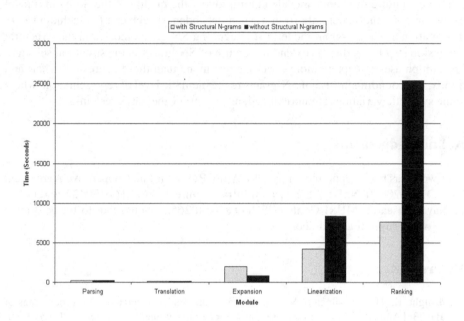

Fig. 4. Overall Runtime per Matador Module: with/without SN-grams

50% decrease in runtime of linearization and ranking, both of which are significantly costlier time-wise than expansion.

An investigation of the type of errors resulting from the use of SN-grams reveal the following two issues. First, the lack of syntactic knowledge such as part-of-speech information in the current implementation of SN-grams often leads to confusing relationships and erroneous selections, especially in a language like English where Verb/Noun homographs are common. [4] reported a slight increase in text accuracy when POS information was used as part of a structural language model. And secondly, the current implementation of SN-grams is only aware of bigram relations. This, together with the lack of part-of-speech information can lead to erroneous selections such as *they continued to their efforts to do X* instead of *they continued in their efforts to do X*. The facts that a noisy treebank was used to collect the statistics and that the coverage was limited to 3 million words are possible explanations for some of the errors resulting from using the SN-gram model.

5   Conclusions and Future Work

This paper described the use of a SN-gram model in EXERGE for lexical and structural selection. The use of SN-grams in a Spanish-English GHMT system decreases runtime by 59.45% with no loss in translation quality. The general lesson of this work is that the use of SN-grams as a pruning tool is desirable especially when there is a concern for efficiency. Future directions include (1) improving the quality of the SN-gram model by using more and better data from a clean dependency treebank; (2) including POS information in the SN-gram model; (3) integrating SN-grams models in the structural expansion step for verbs; (4) extending the use of SN-grams in the structural selection of noun phrases to capture more general phenomena than those addressed so far; and finally, (5) extending the use of SN-grams to the thematic level of representation, where some syntactic variations are normalized, using a noisy thematic treebank.

Acknowledgements

This work has been supported, in part, by Army Research Lab Cooperative Agreement DAAD190320020, NSF CISE Research Infrastructure Award EIA0130422, and Office of Naval Research MURI Contract FCPO.810548265. I would like to thank Bonnie Dorr for her support and advice.

References

1. Knight, K., Hatzivassiloglou, V.: Two-Level, Many-Paths Generation. In: Proceedings of the 33rd Annual Meeting of the Association for Computational Linguistics (ACL-95), Cambridge, MA (1995) 252–260
2. Brown, R., Frederking, R.: Applying Statistical English Language Modeling to Symbolic Machine Translation. In: Proceedings of the Sixth International Conference on Theoretical and Methodological Issues in Machine Translation, Leuven, Belgium (1995) 221–239
3. Langkilde, I., Knight, K.: Generating Word Lattices from Abstract Meaning Representation. Technical report, Information Science Institute, University of Southern California (1998)
4. Bangalore, S., Rambow, O.: Corpus-Based Lexical Choice in Natural Language Generation. In: Proceedings of the 38th Annual Meeting of the Association for Computational Linguistics (ACL 2000), Hongkong, China (2000)
5. Habash, N., Dorr, B., Traum, D.: Hybrid Natural Language Generation from Lexical Conceptual Structures. Machine Translation **17** (2003)
6. Collins, M.: Three Generative, Lexicalised Models for Statistical Parsing. In: Proceedings of the 35th Annual Meeting of the ACL (jointly with the 8th Conference of the EACL), Madrid, Spain (1997)
7. Charniak, E.: Statistical parsing with a context-free grammar and word statistics. In: Proceedings of the AAAI, Providence, RI, AAAI Press/MIT Press (1997) 598–603
8. Charniak, E.: Immediate-head parsing for language models. In: Proceedings of the 39th Annual Meeting of the Association for Computational Linguistics. (2001)
9. Sima'an, K.: Tree-gram parsing: Lexical dependencies and structural relations. In: Proceedings of 38th Annual Meeting of the Association for Computational Linguistics (ACL'00), Hong Kong, China (2000)

10. Ratnaparkhi, A.: Trainable Methods for Surface Natural Language Generation. In: Proceedings of the 1st Annual North American Association of Computational Linguistics, NAACL-2000, Seattle, WA (2000) 194–201

11. Charniak, E.: A maximum-entropy-inspired parser. In: Proceedings of the First Meeting of the North American Chapter of the Association for Computational Linguistics NAACL-2000, Seattle, Washington (2000)

12. Daumé, H., Knight, K., Langkilde-Geary, I., Marku, D., Yamada, K.: The importance of lexicalized syntax models for natural language generation tasks. In: Proceedings of the International Natural Language Generation Conference (INLG-02), new York, New York (2002)

13. Langkilde, I.: Forest-based statistical sentence generation. In: Association for Computational Linguistics conference, North American chapter (NAACL'00). (2000)

14. Fellbaum, C.: WordNet: An Electronic Lexical Database. MIT Press (1998)

15. Habash, N.: Matador: A Large-Scale Spanish-English GHMT System. In: Proceedings of the Ninth Machine Translation Summit (MT SUMMIT IX), New Orleans, USA (2003)

16. Habash, N.: Generation-Heavy Machine Translation. In: Proceedings of the International Natural Language Generation Conference (INLG'02) Student Session, New York (2002)

17. Habash, N.: oxyGen: A Language Independent Linearization Engine. In: Fourth Conference of the Association for Machine Translation in the Americas, AMTA-2000, Cuernavaca, Mexico (2000)

18. Johnson, M.: Joint and Conditional Estimation of Tagging and Parsing Models. In: Proceedings of the 39th Annual Meeting of the Association for Computational Linguistics (ACL-2001), Toulouse, France (2001)

19. Aymerich, J.: Generation of Noun-Noun Compounds in the Spanish-English Machine Translation System SPANAM. In: Proceedings of the Eighth Machine Translation Summit (MT SUMMIT VIII), Santiago de Compostela, Spain (2001)

20. Tanaka, T., Baldwin, T.: Translation Selection for Japanese-English Noun-Noun Compounds. In: Proceedings of the Ninth Machine Translation Summit (MT SUMMIT IX), New Orleans, USA (2003)

21. Papineni, K., Roukos, S., Ward, T., Zhu, W.: Bleu: a Method for Automatic Evaluation of Machine Translation. Technical Report RC22176(W0109-022), IBM Research Division, Yorktown Heights, NY (2001)

22. Bangalore, S., Rambow, O., Whittaker, S.: Evaluation Metrics for Generation. In: Proceedings of the 1st International Conference on Natural Language Generation (INLG 2000), Mitzpe Ramon, Israel (2000)

23. Hovy, E.: MT Evaluation Bibliography. In: The ISLE Classification of Machine Translation Evaluations International Standards for Language Engineering (ISLE), Information Sciences Institute, Los Angeles, CA (2000) http://www.isi.edu/natural-language/mteval/2e-MT-bibliography.htm.

24. Graff, D.: UN Parallel Text (Spanish-English), LDC Catalog No.: LDC94T4A (1994) Linguistic Data Consortium, University of Pennsylvania.

25. Tapanainen, P., Jarvinen, T.: A non-projective dependency parser. In: 5th Conference on Applied Natural Language Processing / Association for Computational Linguistics, Washington, D.C. (1997)

26. Jinxi, X.: UN Parallel Text (Arabic-English), LDC Catalog No.: LDC2002E15 (2002) Linguistic Data Consortium, University of Pennsylvania.

On Referring to Sets of Objects Naturally

Helmut Horacek

Saarland University, Department of Computer Science
P.O.Box 151150, D-66041 Saarbrücken, Germany

Abstract. Several algorithms have been proposed for the generation of
referring expressions to identify sets of objects, including incremental,
best-first, and exhaustive searches. However, most of these algorithms
produce uniform combinations of descriptors, some even including disjunctions and negations, which may not always be adequately expressible
by natural language surface forms. In order to better support the production of descriptions considered natural, we apply and enhance a best-
first searching procedure, which enables us to produce a larger variety
of expressions of limited complexity. We incorporate restrictions which
express constraints on preferred surface forms, and we enhance the repertoire of descriptions by compositions of partially identifying expressions
and by descriptions of objects to be excluded. The results show that
our algorithm produces reasonable specifications for surface expressions,
with a significantly increased repertoire compared to its predecessors.

1   Introduction

Generating referring expressions is a central task in natural language generation.
Recently, its scope has been expanded from identifying single objects to sets of
objects. Several algorithms have been proposed for this purpose, including incremental, best-first, and exhaustive searches. The most ambitious among these
algorithms produce combinations of descriptors including disjunctions and negations. In more complex cases, however, expressing these specifications adequately
by natural language surface forms may turn out to be extremely hard.

In order to better support the production of descriptions considered natural,
we apply and enhance our best-first search procedure [10], which enables us
to produce a larger variety of expressions of limited complexity. We incorporate
restrictions which express constraints on preferred surface forms, and we enhance
the repertoire of descriptions by compositions of partially identifying expressions
and by descriptions of objects to be excluded.

This paper is organized as follows. First, we provide some background and
review previous work. Then we motivate our goals, based on deficits of other
methods, and we sketch measures addressing them. We follow by illustrating the
functionality of our algorithm. Finally, we discuss a working example, we give
some implementation details, and we illustrate some expressions the algorithm
can generate and performs better than previous approaches.

A. Belz et al. (Eds.): INLG 2004, LNAI 3123, pp. 70–79, 2004.

2   Background and Previous Approaches

In the scope of this paper, we adopt the terminology originally formulated by Dale [4] and later used by others. A *referential description* [6] serves the purpose of letting the hearer or reader identify a particular object or set of objects in a given situation. The referring expression to be generated is required to be a *distinguishing description*, that is a description of the *intended referent(s)*, the *target set*, but not to any other object in the *context set*. A context set is defined as the set of the entities the addressee is currently assumed to be attending to – this is similar to the set of entities in the focus spaces of the discourse focus stack in Grosz' and Sidner's [8] theory of discourse structure. Moreover, the *contrast set* (or the set of *potential distractors* [15]) is defined to entail all elements of the context set except the intended referents.

Generating referring expressions is pursued since the eighties [1,2,13]. Subsequent years were characterized by a debate about computational efficiency versus minimality of the elements appearing in the resulting referring expression [4,17,18], with divergent interpretations of minimality. In the mid-nineties, this debate seemed to be settled in favor of the incremental approach [5] – motivated by results of psychological experiments [14,16], certain non-minimal expressions are tolerated in favor of adopting the fast strategy of incrementally selecting ambiguity-reducing attributes from a domain-dependent preference list.

With the extension of the algorithm's scope to the identification of sets of objects rather than individuals [3,20,12], the incremental strategy was in some sense overstressed. Since only few attributes typically apply to all intended referents, van Deemter [20] has extended the set of descriptors to boolean combinations of attributes, including disjunctions and negations, for obtaining a distinguishing description. For such a repertoire of descriptors, he has proved that there always exists a joint distinguishing description for a set of intended referents, provided each of them can be identified individually. However, the incremental strategy may lead to the inclusion of too many redundant descriptors in the final specification, even in simple situations. This deficit disappeared through the use of exhaustive [7] and best-first searching procedures [10].

3   Motivation

Throughout this paper, we refer to the scenario consisting of a set of 12 vehicles as defined in Figure 1, comprising their subcategories, color, location, size, and age. All vehicles are identifiable individually, which we always assume for the identification task to be meaningful. Some of these vehicles are distinguished by minor differences only. This makes the identification task challenging, since accomplishing it requires the production of expressions with several disjunctions.

Despite the improvement obtained by exhaustive and best-first searches, the goal of producing a single, uniform expression that identifies a set of referents may turn out to be overambitious in increasingly complex situations. Satisfying this goal may require the verbalization of comparably complex specifications built out of descriptors, which we feel to be unsuitable in several aspects:

Descriptor	x_0	x_1	x_2	x_3	x_4	x_5	x_6	x_7	x_8	x_9	x_{10}	x_{11}	x_{12}
						Objects							
vehicle	•	•	•	•	•	•	•	•	•	•	•	•	•
car			•	•	•	•	•			•	•	•	•
sportscar						•	•					•	•
truck	•	•						•	•				
blue		•								•			•
red						•		•	•		•	•	
white	•		•		•								
center						•	•			•		•	
left		•							•				•
right		•		•			•	•					
big		•	•	•						•		•	•
small						•	•	•	•	•	•		
new		•			•	•			•		•		•
old			•	•			•	•		•		•	

Fig. 1. Example scenario with 12 vehicles and one dummy object

- *Length of expressions*
  For identifying subsets of the vehicles in the situation defined in Figure 1, we have obtained non-redundant specifications with up to 8 descriptors. The mere length of the expressions makes identification too difficult for humans.
- *Operators in expressions*
  Expressions identifying intended referents may contain several disjunctions, which may result in structurally ambiguous expressions [7]. It is well-known from other areas, such as deductive inferences [11], that humans have difficulties with boolean expressions, especially those with disjunctions. Johnson-Laird argues that understanding disjunctions is difficult for humans because it requires building several mental models. For instance, the expression "trucks and sportscars which are white or in the center" refers to x_1, x_5, x_{11} (Figure 1) by a single expression. It entails four alternatives, combining categories with properties, even though only "the sportcars in the center and the white truck" are the intended referents (one of the sportcars is also white).
- *Form of expressions*
  Ambitious algorithms build specifications that describe the entire set of intended referents by expressions of the form $\wedge_{i=1,n} (\vee_{j=1,m} P_{ij})$, where each P_{ij} is a positive or a negative property applying to at least one of the intended referents. This technique only exploits a limited repertoire of boolean combinations. In addition, the top level operators may be disjunctions instead of conjunctions, yielding an enumeration or a composition of descriptions of subsets of the intended referents. Moreover, nested expressions may be in the scope of a negation, which yields a complementing description of objects not intended as referents, that is, a description of some distractors.

4 Extending the Repertoire of Descriptions

In order to address these deficits, we extend the repertoire of descriptions:

- *Identifying referents through exclusion, by describing their distractors*
  Describing some of the distractors still to be excluded may occasionally lead
  to shorter expressions than further expanding the partial description of the
  intended referents generated so far. In simple cases, this exclusion measure
  is even possible within the expression $\wedge_{i=1,n} (\vee_{j=1,mi} P_{ij})$. When $mi = 1$
  holds for some i, and P_{i1} is a negative property that is expressible as a
  category, i. e., as a head noun, this portion of the identifying description can
  be expressed as "..., but not the $< P_{i1} >$". In general, such a description
  yields a conjoined expression, which we address by building full descriptions
  of distractors as alternatives to enhancing those of the intended referents.
  Consider, for example, "the vehicles on the right, but not the red truck",
  identifying x_1, x_3, and x_6 by excluding x_7 in the locally restricted context.
- *Resolving multiple disjunctions – no reference to non-existing compositions*
  Even in moderately complex instances of the expression $\wedge_{i=1,n} (\vee_{j=1,mi} P_{ij})$,
  several elements in this conjoined expression may consist of disjunctions of
  more than one descriptor. This may introduce ambiguities and unnecessary
  complications, which make the identification task for the reader more difficult than it need to be. In such a constellation, we pick up one of these
  disjunctions, for example $\vee_{j=1,mk} P_{kj}$ for some k, and transform the entire
  expression by applying distributivity. This amounts to partitioning the set
  of intended referents into subsets, where each of the components of the new
  top level disjunction describes one of these subsets. Moreover, simplifications
  may be possible in these expressions. Consider, for example, "the sportscars
  that are not red and the small trucks" identifying x_5, x_7, x_8, and x_{12} in two
  components rather than by the involved one-shot "the vehicles that are a
  sportscar or small, and either a truck or not red".
- *Partitioning the identification into subtasks – to avoid complex descriptions*
  We incorporate specifications that define length limitations on the surface
  form of descriptions, including places for the head noun, pre- and postnominal modifiers, and relative clauses, for the description applying to the
  intended referents, as well as for the description applying to potential distractors. Maximum numbers for each of these positions can be given, also
  specifying places as alternative ones, to limit the number of components in
  conjoined expressions. These specifications allow one to control the surface
  structure of the resulting descriptions. In accordance with these specifications, a description is generated that excludes as many distractors as possible. If insufficient, further descriptions are generated, within the restricted
  context of the descriptions generated so far, producing a sequence of descriptions rather than a single one. Consider, for example, "one of the trucks and
  the sportscars, all not white. The truck stands on the right", identifying x_6,
  x_7, x_{11}, and x_{12} out of all 12 vehicles (in Figure 1) in two passes.

	Descriptors				
Surface position	vehicle type	color	location	size	age
head noun	•				
prenominal modifier		•	•	•	•
postnominal modifier			•		
relative clause	•	•	•	•	•

Fig. 2. Possible surface positions of the descriptors of the scenario defined in Figure 1

5   Details of the Algorithm

In order to implement the tasks discussed in the previous section through dedicated methods, we build on our best-first searching algorithm [10]. The basic mechanism of this algorithm is a generalization of the incremental version: instead of successively adding attributes to the full expression generated so far, all intermediate results are accessible for this operation. To make this process efficient, expansion is guided by linguistically motivated preferences, similar to the incremental version of the algorithm. The best-first searching algorithm does not generate redundant descriptions, as the incremental algorithm is likely to do in more complex situations. Moreover, a number of efficiency-enhancing search techniques make it competitive with the exhaustive search. Its main advantage over the exhaustive search, which is realized as a constraint solver [7], is the increased process transparency through its explicit control and data structures. This gives us some flexibility of use, which is the main motivation for choosing this algorithm. In particular, it enables us to incorporate enhancements to the algorithm, and to exploit intermediate results as partial descriptions.

The first enhancement addresses restrictions concerning the surface form of the expression that is ultimately generated. In order to control these restrictions during the descriptor selection process, we associate each descriptor with surface positions it can take (see Figure 2, for the descriptors given in Figure 1). Some descriptors can be realized in limited ways only, according to the categories of the words by which they can be expressed. However, it is important that there is at least one form by which all descriptors can be expressed, which is a relative clause in English. Otherwise, some boolean combinations would not be expressible at all, which is in contrast to the assumption of the descriptor selection algorithm.

Next, recasting a description through applying distributivity is illustrated in Figure 3. Any of the subformulas in the conjoined expression may be used for partitioning according to the descriptors contained in it (2 alternatives in Figure 3). Moreover, there may be alternatives of partitioning the objects if several of the descriptors in the subexpression chosen apply to one of the objects (x_5 for partitioning into subsets for 'sportscar' and 'small' in Figure 3). Finally, simplifications are carried out in case some of the descriptors in the subexpressions not partitioned do not apply to any of the referents in corresponding subset, and the

$\{x_5, x_7, x_8, x_{12}\}$ identified by (sportscar $\vee$ small) $\wedge$ (truck $\vee\neg$ red)
3 possible partitionings, according to the subexpression chosen and objects it covers:

1. (sportscar $\wedge$ (truck $\vee\neg$ red)) $\vee$ (small $\wedge$ (truck $\vee\neg$ red)) for $\{x_{12}\}$, $\{x_5, x_7, x_8\}$
2. (sportscar $\wedge$ (truck $\vee\neg$ red)) $\vee$ (small $\wedge$ (truck $\vee\neg$ red)) for $\{x_5, x_{12}\}$, $\{x_7, x_8\}$
3. (truck $\wedge$ (sportscar $\vee$ small))$\vee$ ($\neg$ red $\wedge$ (sportscar $\vee$ small)) for $\{x_7, x_8\}$, $\{x_5, x_{12}\}$
2. and 3. (1. not) can be both simplified to (truck $\wedge$ small) $\vee$ ($\neg$ red $\wedge$ sportscar)

Fig. 3. An example of the result of performing the partitioning procedure

simplest variant is chosen. This applies to both partial expressions in variants 2 and 3 in Figure 3, which yield identical expressions. Unlike the other extensions proposed, this partitioning method can be combined with all algorithms that generate a distinguishing description including disjunctions and negations for sets of intended referents. In some sense, the method is dual to the aggregation techniques applied by Bateman [3], but we can also handle negation.

All extensions except to the composition of identification subtasks manifest themselves in the procedure for selecting a boolean descriptor combination (see Figure 4). This combination is to expand a partial description considered best by the embedding best-first searching algorithm. In accordance with best-first and incremental approaches, descriptor combinations are generated with increasing complexity, and they are then tested whether they subsume all intended referents and exclude at least one potential distractor. We assume the function Next-descriptor to perform this standard task, while the embedding procedure Select takes care of additional tests and modifications with descriptor combinations.

If the description generated so far refers to the original intended referents (*Swap* is false), Next-descriptor is also called for the "dual" case, with distractors and intended referents exchanged (1). If the "dual" descriptor is simpler, it becomes the next candidate (2). If the chosen combination is more complex than the maximum number of positions would allow, which is computed a priori on the basis of combining all restrictions, no descriptor combination is generated (3). Otherwise the possible places associated with each element in the chosen combination are considered, and their intersection is built (4). The resulting combinations are then incorporated into the set of possible combinations of the descriptors generated so far (5), and a test is made whether any of the augmented combinations are still in accordance with the specified limitations (6). If this test is successful, the descriptor combination generated is returned. If it fails, the descriptor combination is reorganized through applying distributivity, simulating the separation of the intended referents into subsets (7), and the above test is repeated. If it is successful this time, the descriptor combination generated is returned. Otherwise, the whole procedure is repeated with the next descriptor combination (8). If the procedure Select fails to deliver a descriptor combination for the node considered within the specified complexity limits, the embedding best-first search chooses another node as the next candidate for expansion. If none of them can be expanded due to the limitations specified, the search stops with a partial solution.

Procedure Select (*Referents, Distractors, Swap*)

1 *Descriptors* ← Next-descriptor(*Referents, Distractors*)
  Loc-swap ← false
  if not *Swap*
      then *Dual-descriptors* ← Next-descriptor(*Distractors, Referents*)   (1)
      if <*Dual-descriptors* simpler than *Descriptors*>
          then *Descriptors* ← *Dual-descriptors*
                Loc-swap ← true   (2)
      endif
  endif
  if <the complexity of *Descriptors* is larger than maximum number of positions>
      then return nil   (3)
  endif
  Pos ← <Intersection of positions of each descriptor in the combination used>   (4)
  Pos ← <Integrate *Pos* in combinations of the partial description built so far> (5)
  if not <Any of the combinations in *Pos* is compatible with restrictions>   (6)
      then <Build partitions of *Referents* resp. *Distractors*>   (7)
      if <Any of the combinations for this is compatible with the restrictions>
          then return <*Descriptors, Loc-swap*>
          else goto 1   (8)
      endif
  endif
  return <*Descriptors, Loc-swap*>

Fig. 4. Schema of the procedure for selecting descriptor combinations

The top-level generation algorithm, as given in Figure 5, consists of possibly multiple call to the (best-first) search procedure for building referential descriptions, according to a maximum specified complexity. These calls are activated by recursive calls to the procedure Generate. The results of these calls, which may be a description identifying the intended referents or a partial solution excluding as many distractors as possible, are collected in a list named *Description*. First, a simple call to the procedure Search is performed (9). The result is returned as the global result (11), if the identification goal is fully accomplished (10). Otherwise, the search is repeated with the distractors not excluded by the best partial description found (12). This is done for each partition separately, if the resulting description has been transformed into several descriptions, each identifying a subset of the intended referents (14). In some of these partitions, the subset of intended referents may already be identified, so that a recursive call is not required for this partition (13).

6   Examples

We illustrate the behavior of the algorithm by a small example. Let $\{x_1, x_3, x_6\}$ in Figure 1 be the set of intended referents. Specifications for maximum complex-

Procedure Generate (*Referents*, *Distractors*)

Description ← Search (*Referents*, *Distractors*)   (9)
if <Intended referents are all identified>   (10)
   then return *Description*   (11)
   else *Distractors* ← <*Distractors* not excluded by the best partial solution> (12)
   for <All partitions built by *Description*> **do**
      if not <Intended referents in this partition are all identified> (13)
         then *Local-referents* ← <Referents in this partition>
         Description ←
         Append (*Description*, Generate (*Local-referents*, *Distractors*)) (14)
      endif
   return *Description*
   next
endif

Fig. 5. Schema of the top level generation procedure

ity of surface forms allow head nouns, pre- and postnominal modifiers, at most one of them as a conjoined expression, and a relative clause or a "but"-modifier expressing an exception. Only two descriptors apply to all intended referents, 'vehicle' and 'right'. Even if 'vehicle' is chosen first, subsequent searching only expands on the partial description with 'right', since it excludes a superset of the distractors 'vehicle' does: only x_7 is remaining. The next simplest descriptor combination is (car ∨ white), which allows full identification of the intended referents. Since it can only be expressed by a relative clause, for which conjoined expressions are not allowed, partitioning is attempted. This yields (car ∧ right) ∨ (white ∧ right) as a possible solution. Since a head noun is required for the second part, adding a further descriptor, an attempt is made to improve the solution, through finding an alternative to (car ∨ white). Describing the complement constitutes such an alternative, since identification is required for x_7 only. This is done by selecting 'truck' and any of the descriptors 'red', 'small', and 'old' (let us say, we pick 'red'). This yields (right ∧¬ (truck ∧ red)) as an alternative solution, 'vehicle' being added to obtain a head noun.

Altogether, a surface generator could then generate "the vehicles on the right, but not the red truck", resp. "the cars and the white vehicle, both on the right" – the latter with a clever aggregation module. Through choosing 'truck' instead of 'vehicle' for the head noun, "right" could be omitted for "white truck", but we did not investigate this optimization. It is hard to judge which of these expressions is better; more elaborate preference criteria about competitive NP structures are required, on a general empirical basis or on application-specific grounds. Both expressions, which we consider reasonable, cannot be generated by other approaches. However, we have to note that the generation of surface expressions, which we did not address, is far from trivial for these specifications.

Among others, it requires clever ordering of descriptors and partial descriptions, introduction of quantifiers and disambiguation markers.

We have implemented the algorithm in CommonLisp, on an Intel Pentium processor with 2600 MHz, and we have tested it with all subsets of intended referents of the scenario in Figure 1, ranging from 2 to 6 elements. We have restricted the surface form specifications to keep the number of descriptors below 6, to avoid too complex descriptions, which also would run very long due to combinatorics. These specifications may lead to sequences of descriptions in some cases. Running times are 30 seconds for the most complex cases, and significantly lower for simpler ones. Since producing an identifying description is also challenging for humans in more complex situations, it is hardly surprising that running times may become considerable in some situations.

Finally, we illustrate the quality improvements obtained by our algorithm by contrasting some expressions it can generate with the kind of expressions previous approaches can produce. When identifying x_1, x_3, and x_6, describing a distractor to exclude it in the local context of a partial description ("the vehicles on the right, but not the red truck") sounds more natural than a mere description of the intended referents, as in "the vehicles on the right, which are white or sportscars". Moreover, identifying x_3, x_4, and x_6 by partitioning the set of intended referents ("the cars on the right and the small red car") is better structured than the somehow clumsy "the cars which are white or small, stand on the right or are red". Similarly, the reorganized expression for identifying x_5, x_7, x_8, and x_{12} ("the sportscars which are not red and the small trucks", see Figure 3) is preferable to the original "the vehicles which are sportscars or small and trucks or not red", which mixes categories and attributes in an odd way. If the joint identification requires a longish expression, partitioning the set of intended referents and the associated descriptions may yield considerable reductions. Consider "one of the trucks and the sportscars, all not white. The truck stands on the right", identifying x_6, x_7, x_{11}, and x_{12}, which is a great improvement over "some of the sportcars and trucks, all of which are not white, big or old, and new or stand on the left".

7   Conclusion

We have presented extensions to a best-first search algorithm that can produce referring expressions for uniquely identifying sets of objects. These extensions give our algorithm a number of advantages over its predecessors:

- The repertoire of expressions it is able to produce is larger, due to the incorporation of exclusion descriptions, and partitioning of the identification task through (1) descriptions identifying disjoint and covering subsets of intended referents, and (2) combining partially identifying descriptions.
- The algorithm has some sort of a limited view of the capabilities of realization facilities, through the categorization of descriptors and the associated composition restrictions, so that major impacts on realization can be taken into account during searching (similar to the approach in [9]).

– The algorithm is to able accommodate empirical findings, to produce preferred expressions, and it can be adapted to specifics of an application.

References

1. Appelt, D.: Planning English Referring Expressions. Artificial Intelligence 26 (1985) 1–33
2. Appelt, D., Kronfeld, A.: A Computational Model of Referring. In Proc. of the 10th International Joint Conference on Artificial Intelligence (IJCAI-87) (1987) 640–647
3. Bateman, J.: Using Aggregation for Selecting Content when Generating Referring Expressions. In Proc. of the 37th Annual Meeting of the Association for Computational Linguistics (ACL-99) (1999) 127–134
4. Dale, R.: Generating Referring Expressions in a Domain of Objects and Processes. PhD Thesis, Centre for Cognitive Science, Univ. of Edinburgh (1988)
5. Dale, R., Reiter, E.: Computational Interpretations of the Gricean Maxims in the Generation of Referring Expressions. Cognitive Science 18 (1995) 233–263
6. Donellan, K.: Reference and Definite Description. Philosophical Review 75 (1966) 281–304
7. Gardent, C.: Generating Minimal Definite Descriptions. In Proc. of the 41st Annual Meeting of the Association for Computational Linguistics (ACL-02) (2002) 96–103
8. Grosz, B., Sidner, C.: Attention, Intention, and the Structure of Discourse. Computational Linguistics 12 (1986) 175–206
9. Horacek, H.: An Algorithm for Generating Referential Descriptions with Flexible Interfaces. In Proc. of the 35th Annual Meeting of the Association for Computational Linguistics and 8th European Chapter of the Association for Computational Linguistics (ACL-EACL'97) (1997) 206–213
10. Horacek, H.: A Best-First Search Algorithm for Generating Referring Expressions. In Proc. of the 10th European Chapter of the Association for Computational Linguistics (EACL'03) (short paper) (2003) 103–106
11. Johnson-Laird, P., Byrne, R.: Deduction. Ablex Publishing (1990)
12. Krahmer, E., v. Erk, S., Verleg, A.: A Meta-Algorithm for the Generation of Referring Expressions. In Proc. of 8th European Workshop on Natural Language Generation (EWNLG-01) (2001)
13. Kronfeld, A.: Donellan's Distinction and a Computational Model of Reference. In Proc. of the 24th Annual Meeting of the Association for Computational Linguistics (ACL-86) (1986) 186–191
14. Levelt, W.: Speaking: From Intention to Articulation. MIT Press (1989)
15. McDonald, D.: Natural Language Generation as a Process of Decision Making under Constraints. PhD thesis, MIT (1981)
16. Pechmann, T.: Incremental Speech Production and Referential Overspecification. Linguistics 27 (1989) 89-110
17. Reiter, E.: The Computational Complexity of Avoiding Conversational Implicatures. In Proc. of 28th Meeting of the Association of Computational Linguistics (ACL-90) (1990) 97–104
18. Reiter, E., Dale, R.: Generating Definite NP Referring Expressions. In Proc. of the 14th International Conference on Computational Linguistics (COLING-92) (1992)
19. Stone, M.: On Identifying Sets. In Proc. of the First International Natural Language Generation Conference (2000)
20. van Deemter, K.: Generating Referring Expressions: Boolean Extensions of the Incremental Algorithm. Computational Linguistics, 28(1) (2002) 37–52

An ATMS Approach to Systemic Sentence Generation

Hasan Kamal[1] and Chris Mellish[2]

[1] Department of Computer Science, University of Bahrain, Bahrain
hasank@itc.uob.bh
[2] Department of Computing Science, University of Aberdeen King's College,
Aberdeen AB24 3UE, United Kingdom
cmellish@csd.abdn.ac.uk

Abstract. This paper introduces a new NLG architecture that can be sensitive to surface stylistic requirements. It brings together a well-founded linguistic theory that has been used in many successful NLG systems (Systemic Functional Linguistics, SFL) and an existing AI search mechanism (the Assumption-based Truth Maintenance System, ATMS) which caches important search information and avoids work duplication. It describes a technique for converting systemic grammar networks to dependency networks that an ATMS can reason with. The generator then uses the translated networks to generate natural language texts. The paper also describes how surface constraints can be incorporated within the new architecture. We then evaluate the efficiency of our system.

1 Introduction

Given the wide range of applications NLG systems might be part of, it is very important that they master their job in an aesthetic and sophisticated manner. Some applications may require that the generation component produces text with certain rhyme, alliteration or even poetic aspects [6]. Such tasks may require redoing syntactic and lexical choices under constraints from different levels.

In this work, surface stylistic constraints (SSC) are those stylistic requirements that are known beforehand but cannot be tested until after the utterance or (in some lucky cases) a proper linearised part of it has been generated. For example, the French pronouns *le, la* cannot precede words starting with *e*. When that happens, both are abbreviated to *l'*. Now, if we want to generate (in French) an unambiguous utterance, the choice between the feminine pronoun *la* and *Sarah* depends on the next word [11]. Although simple, this example shows that there are cases where generators cannot make a final decision on lexical choice until after the surface form has been linearised and its words inflected.

Another example is text size limits. Some lexical choices result in longer utterances because of the way in which each word packages information. The cumulative effect of such verbose choices can be longer texts. However, the exact length of text is not known until after the text is generated and only then can it be compared to the size limit it is allowed to occupy. In the STOP project,

A. Belz et al. (Eds.): INLG 2004, LNAI 3123, pp. 80–89, 2004.
© Springer-Verlag Berlin Heidelberg 2004

Reiter discusses how even things like punctuation, inflection, and font type can play a role in keeping the text within the allowed limit [10].

Current systemic generation algorithms are prone to surface stylistic problems because they need to make decisions at different choice points before the surface form or part of it has been built. When there is not enough information to make a decision, current generators resort to one of two strategies: selection of a default or selection of a random alternative. [5] show that neither strategy guarantees problem-free surface forms, as "the default choices frequently are not the optimal ones" and the alternative of randomized decisions entails "the risk of producing some non-fluent expressions".

This paper approaches the crucial notion of choice differently to previous systems using SFL. It relaxes the choice process in that choosers are not obliged to deterministically choose a single alternative allowing SSC to influence the final lexical and syntactic decisions. On the other hand, instead of introducing into the system the well-known problems of backtracking [4], we use a Truth Maintenance System (TMS) to efficiently manage the choices and their dependencies.

2   The ATMS Framework

A Truth Maintenance System (TMS) is attached to a problem solver so that it can focus on the particulars of the given task and the TMS on the bookkeeping of beliefs and assumptions [4]. The problem solver passes the TMS "reasoning information". In the case of the Assumption-based Truth Maintenance System (ATMS), this reasoning information comes in three kinds: nodes, justifications and no-goods. A *node* is associated with an instance of a data structure which is being manipulated by the problem solver: a problem-solver datum. The actual content of this problem-solver datum is of no interest to the ATMS. It is the problem solver which requests the ATMS to create an autonomous node, thus informing the ATMS it is reasoning with the associated data.

A *justification* is a statement indicating that the truth of a conjunction of nodes is sufficient to conclude the truth of a node. Or, a justification can be defined as an implication equivalent to: $\langle n_1 \wedge ... \wedge n_k \rightarrow n_x \rangle$, where each n_i is a node. Some nodes, as decided by the problem solver, are called assumptions. The *assumptions* are the nodes on which any datum ultimately depends. They are considered true until proven false.

Evidence against the presumed truth of assumptions comes in the form of no-goods. A *no-good* is a set of nodes which cannot all be true at the same time. More precisely, it is a conjunction of nodes which is impossible: $\langle n_1 \wedge ... \wedge n_k \rightarrow \bot \rangle$, where each n_i is a node. Often, falsity is represented by a specially constructed node $\bot$.

As nodes, justifications and no-goods are added, the ATMS maintains a label for each node. A *label* is the set of environments, representing the disjunction of those environments, which supports the associated node. An *environment* is a set of assumptions representing the conjunction of these assumptions. If an environment $E = \{a_1, ..., a_m\}$ is in the label of a node n, the ATMS has deduced that $\langle a_1 \wedge ... \wedge a_m \rightarrow n \rangle$, or $E \Rightarrow n$. Each label of a node n of an ATMS is guaranteed to be consistent, sound, minimal, and complete. The job of the ATMS is to determine under what conditions any conclusion holds. Introducing a new justification (e.g. $\langle antecedents \rangle \rightarrow C$) may cause any belief to change. Therefore, it updates the label of C and *propagates* the changes to all the consequences of C and from there on. However, if C is found to be contradictory then all the labels are *pruned* accordingly. In this sense, backtracking becomes unnecessary as the ATMS labels are always up-to-date.

The ATMS spends precious time performing set unions and subset tests. Fortunately, efficient implementations do exist in which sets, for example, are represented using bit-vectors to speed things up [3]. Examples of ATMS applications include planning, diagnosis and constraint satisfaction problems [7].

3   ATMS-based NLG

Our architecture has two main stages: translation and generation. First, systemic grammar networks are transformed into dependency networks, a representation that the ATMS can reason with. We established the logical connection between both representations based on the logical interpretation of system networks given in [8], [1] and [2]. The translation algorithm also accounts for the effect of the realization statements as well. Functions are inserted at different points in a system network. Different network paths (or selection expressions) conflate functions into various function bundles. Moreover, the preselection operations on a given function bundle determine the rank of that bundle and hence the system network that should be traversed as a realization for it. Certain paths require that the function bundles be linearized in a particular order. All of this is compiled by the translation algorithm and stored in what we call a network snapshot, since the re-translation of a system network yields exactly the same ATMS representation.

Our generation strategy is similar, in spirit, to that of other systemic generators in that it starts with the clause rank and uses a stack to hold the unexpanded constituents [9]. However, the constituents pushed onto the stack at each step are not those of a single path through the system network but of multiple paths.

The generation algorithm starts with a snapshot of the clause network. Based on the conceptual input and the choosers' response, it cuts out irrelevant parts of the complete network snapshot (note that our choosers are not obliged to choose between system features if they cannot make informed decisions). Then each function bundle of the tailored network is pushed on the stack to be realized later on.

In order to produce a complete sentence, the immediate constituents of the top-most unit need to be expanded. That is, a pass through the network whose rank is implied by the constituent's preselection operations is necessary. It is only when the current constituent is of word rank that we consider it complete and no further expansion is necessary.

4   Example

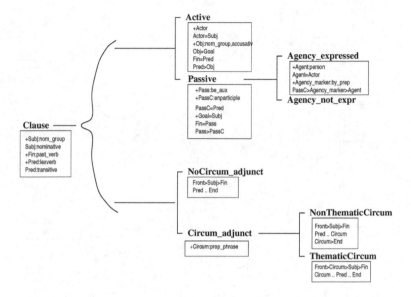

Fig. 1. Clause network fragment

We give an example that shows the kind of representation various stages deal with. To keep the example within limits, we will consider only a fragment of the WAG clause network (see Figure1). SNAC, the translation component of our system, translates this system network into an ATMS dependency network as shown in Figure2 (circles and boxes represent nodes and lines indicate justifi- cations). The dependency network states that the goal node $s(1)$ is true if the assumption *clause* and its associated system $s(2)$ are true. $s(2)$ is true if both $s(3)$ and $s(4)$ are true (i.e. they are simultaneous). In turn, $s(3)$ is true if the assumption *active* is true along with its associated nodes. Note that selecting the feature *active* brings with it three function bundles (represented by SANC as $f(1)$, $f(3)$ and $f(6)$). These are function bundles which might stand for *subj*, *pred*, and *obj*. Note also that each assumption implies some ordering rules. This is indicated by a justification such as $active \rightarrow order(subj, pred)$ which says that selecting *active* implies that *subj* precedes *pred* in order. We call such a config- uration (Figure2) a realization triangle. Therefore, a realization triangle in its abstract form has a goal node as its head and a set of assumptions and derived nodes on the base side. The assumptions represent the features of the systemic network; and the derived nodes represent the compiled function bundles. Each of these bundles will need to be realized in the same manner. If a function is of word rank, it is realized simply by attaching to it applicable lexemes. This process of triangle interfacing is depicted in Figure3. Finally, STAGE, the gen-

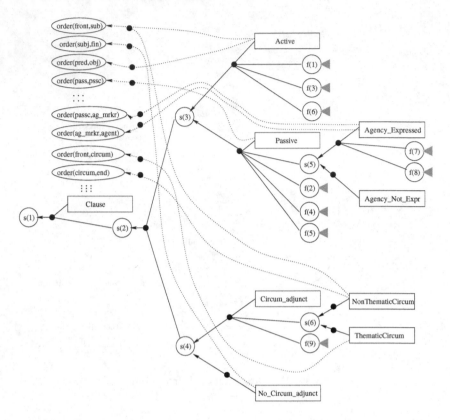

Fig. 2. The dependency network constructed from the clause snapshot

eration component of our architecture, reads off the label of the goal node that represents the topmost clause unit and passes it to a post-processor which prints out the actual sentences. For the input we provided and the lexicon we used, and without any surface constraints, the system generated around 9450 sentences with different syntactic and lexical choices. Some of the generated sentences are shown below:

```
Dartmaul annihilated the Jedis.
The last ruthless warrior exterminated the Jedis on Friday.
On Friday, the last ruthless warrior exterminated the Jedis.
...
...
The black bearded Jedis were massacred.
The black bearded Jedis were massacred by Dartmaul.
The black bearded Jedis were massacred on Friday.
On Friday, the Jedis were annihilated.
The Jedis were annihilated by the warrior on Friday.
On Friday, the Jedis were annihilated by the last ruthless warrior.
...
...
```

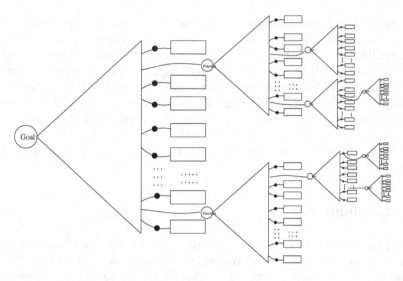

Fig. 3. Interfacing of realization triangles

5 Incorporating Stylistic Constraints

Figure4 shows how surface stylistic constraints (SSC) can be used, in conjunction with the usual realization triangles, to filter out any source of surface stylistic faults. The lower dependency network is a realization triangle as introduced in

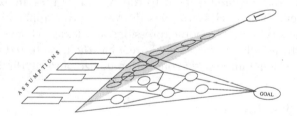

Fig. 4. The stylistic dimension of the generation process

the above discussion. We call the upper dependency network a stylistic triangle. The similarity between the two triangles is simply that they are both ATMS networks with distinctive head nodes forming a triangular configuration. The realization triangle preserves the dependency relations between its nodes (e.g. systems, features) as specified by the underlying systemic grammar networks; whereas the stylistic triangle maintains dependency between a different set of derived nodes (e.g. realization nodes and their implications) as specified by the given surface stylistic requirements. Both triangles in the figure are supported by the same set of assumptions. This way, both the pure syntactic realization triangle and the stylistic triangle together determine the surviving sets of assumptions and hence the final problem-free utterances. Both triangles work hand in hand to generate the final utterances. If a node in the stylistic triangle is found to be contradictory — according to the given stylistic requirements — then the ATMS notes that all the sets of assumptions labelling it lead to a contradiction (or surface stylistic problem in our case). The ATMS then removes these contradictory sets, which form the seeds for possible surface problems, and all their supersets from the labels of the remaining nodes, including the nodes of the lower (syntactic) triangle. This restricts the number of generated sentences — which can be read off the GOAL node label — to only those free of surface problems.

6   Implementation

The implementation of an automatic procedure for the translation of general systemic grammars into the ATMS representation has been carried out. The translator, called System Network to ATMS Converter (SNAC), is implemented in SICStus Prolog. SNAC was tested on an existing systemic grammar (WAG's complete grammatical resources, called the Dialogue grammar) that was written without any ATMS dependency networks in mind. The Dialog grammar has 158 systems and 340 features.

The generation component STAGE (STylistics-Aware GEnerator) takes as an input a micro-semantic representation and generates surface forms that follow the stylistic constraints specified. STAGE depends heavily on the ATMS component in generating the required utterances. It only decides what bits of the problem are to be communicated to the ATMS. It uses an existing neutral ATMS implementation which is not biased towards NLG applications. The computation of the surviving selection expressions and lexical choices are delegated for the ATMS to handle. As far as SSC are concerned, we tested our system on three different style requirements: collocational, size, and rhythmic constraints.

7   System Evaluation

The idea of using the ATMS for processing systemic grammars is new and we need to know what factors affect the performance of the system. At first, we can think of many factors that may influence generation time, these might be:

- the degree of under-specificity of the input
- the number of open paths incurred by the relaxed choosers
- the generosity of the lexicalization process, or the number of available/allowed synonyms for a give concept
- the size of the underlying networks
- the size and complexity of the string to be generated

Of course some of these factors might be related to others in some way. For example, an under-specified semantic input might decrease the choosers' appetite to select particular features resulting in many open paths to be explored; hence expanding the search space. Next, we analyze the plain mode of the generation process and then we turn our attention to the other mode.

7.1 Plane-Mode Generation

Although the ATMS-based generation system can deterministically generate a single sentence for a given semantic input just like classical systemic generators, the way it usually works is to have its choosers keep many alternative paths active for further discovery, resulting in many paraphrases for the same input. Table 1 shows the cpu time needed by the ATMS-based generator to deterministically generate one sentence on the one hand and nondeterministically many sentences (9450 sentences for the particular example we tried) on the other hand.

Table 1. Deterministic and nondeterministic runs of the the ATMS-based system

	Deterministic	Nondeterministic
No. of Sentences	1	9450
Generation Time	0.770 secs	125.16 mins
Time per Sent.	0.770 secs	0.794 secs

A relevant question at this point is: how does the deterministic behaviour of the ATMS-based generator compare to traditional systemic generators? A rough answer comes from the comparison of our system (operating deterministically) with a similar system stripped of the ATMS machinery, which shows that the ATMS is putting around 45% overhead on the system. Figure5 shows how the total generation time increases as larger and larger search spaces need to be explored. In this figure, the number of lexemes per function is fixed (3 lexemes per function in this particular experiment). The increase in search space is due to increasing network sizes.

7.2 Stylistics-Aware Mode

For a given semantic input, many selection expressions might arise due to the relaxed nature of choosers. To cope with this complexity, the system uses the surface stylistic specifications to prefer (partial) realizations over others. We analyzed the system performance with respect to the three different sets of stylistic requirements.

Table 2 shows the system's performance in the stylistics-aware mode under the three sets of surface stylistic requirements. It reveals more details in addition to the increase in the generation time shown in the plot of Figure5. It gives an

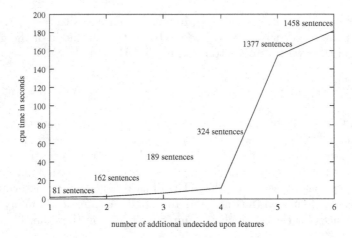

Fig. 5. Effect of nondeterminism on generation time

Table 2. Improvement in generation time for different sets of SSC

	None	Adjacency Constraints	Metre Constraints	Size Constraints
No. of Sentences	9450	16	1	10
Time (minutes)	125.16	1.222	0.621	13.294
Union operations	27209	7565	4602	24572
Derived Nodes	324	423	387	391
Assumption Nodes	242	242	242	242
Label sizes Sum	10638	1014	1012	4652
Improvement in gen. Time	—	99.02%	99.50%	89.38%

idea of the size of the network in terms of the number of derived and assumption nodes. It also counts the number of the primitive union operation. We count this operation because it reflects the amount of work done by the ATMS. Any activity which requires that a node label is updated triggers a series of union operations. The union operation is at the heart of ATMS label update algorithms. The table shows a significant improvement over the generate and test approach, had we chosen to generate the solutions in the plain mode and then check which sentences conform to the surface stylistic requirements. This supports our initial expectation that the ATMS-based generator is best appreciated when used in the stylistics-aware mode.

8   Discussion

Since the stylistics-aware mode is the normal way we intend to use the system, what matters is the performance of the system under this mode and we should not be put off by the generation time taken in the plain mode. The latter mode represents the generate and test possibility which was considerably outperformed by the stylistics-aware mode.

The results show that for generation without stylistics, our system can be competitive to deterministic systemic generators when the process is less likely to succeed the first time. The ATMS overhead will start to pay off after the first failure. Incorporating SSC greatly improved the non-deterministic generation time per sentence. For poetry, word adjacency, and size constraints, the times are 0.004, 0.008, and 0.003 seconds per sentence respectively.

We emphasize here that the ATMS we are currently using is written in an interpreted high-level language. Only a few attempts were made to optimise efficiency (e.g. bit vector representation of sets). The number of candidate solutions increases exponentially as both the number of functions in a sentence and the number of lexemes per function increase.

9 Conclusion

The paper presented an ATMS-based architecture that can be sensitive to surface stylistic requirements. The new approach promises to allow for the efficient generation of sentences that have required surface stylistic features. The generation architecture is modular in that it keeps the grammar, lexicon and stylistic knowledge separate. This way, the stylistic restrictions can parameterize the generation process. Despite the limited stylistic constraints implemented so far, the approach is promising and extensible.

References

[1] Chris Brew. Systemic classification and its efficiency. *Computational Linguistics*, 17(4):375–408, December 1991.

[2] Jo Calder. The horn subset of systemic networks. In *Proceedings of the 6th Meeting on Mathematics of Language, MOL6*, University of Central Florida, Orlando, Florida, USA, July 23-25, 1999.

[3] Johan de Kleer. An assumption-based TMS. *Artificial Intelligence*, 28:127–162, 1986.

[4] Kenneth D. Forbus and Johan de Kleer. *Building Problem Solvers*. MIT Press, Cambridge, Massachusetts, 1993.

[5] K. Knight and V. Hatzivassiloglou. Two-level, many-paths generation. pages 252–260.

[6] H. Manurung, G. Ritchie, and H. Thompson. A flexible integrated architecture for generating poetic texts. In *Proceedings of the Fourth Symposium on Natural Language Processing (SNLP 2000)*, pages 123–132, Chiang Mai, Thailand, 10-12 May 2000.

[7] David McAllester. Truth maintenance. In *Proceedings AAAI90*, pages 1109–1116. Morgan Kaufmann Publishers, 1990.

[8] Chris Mellish. Implementing systemic classification by unification. *Computational Linguistics*, 14(1):40–51, Winter 1988.

[9] Michael O'Donnell. *Sentence Analysis and Generation – a Systemic Perspective*. PhD thesis, Department of Linguistics, University of Sydney, 1994.

[10] Ehud Reiter. Pipelines and size constraints. *Computational Linguistics*, 26(2):251–259, 2000.

[11] Ehud Reiter and Robert Dale. *Building Natural Language Generation Systems*. Cambridge University Press, Cambridge, UK, 2000.

A Corpus-Based Methodology for Evaluating Metrics of Coherence for Text Structuring

Nikiforos Karamanis[1], Chris Mellish[2], Jon Oberlander[1], and Massimo Poesio[3]

[1] University of Edinburgh, School of Informatics, 2 Buccleuch Place,
Edinburgh EH8 9LW, UK,
{nikiforo,jon}@cogsci.ed.ac.uk,
http://www.iccs.informatics.ed.ac.uk/~nikiforo/, http://www.cogsci.ed.ac.uk/~jon/
[2] University of Aberdeen, Department of Computing Science, King's College,
Aberdeen AB24 3UE, UK,
cmellish@csd.abdn.ac.uk, http://www.csd.abdn.ac.uk/~cmellish/
[3] University of Essex, Department of Computer Science, Wivenhoe Park,
Colchester, CO4 3SQ, UK
poesio@essex.ac.uk,
http://cswww.essex.ac.uk/staff/poesio/

Abstract. This paper presents a novel corpus-based methodology for comparing metrics of coherence with respect to their potential usefulness for text structuring. Different definitions of such metrics, all using notions from Centering Theory, are discussed, and the methodology is applied to existing data derived from the MPIRO generation system.

1   Introduction

NLG systems such as ILEX [13] and MPIRO [4] need to structure short descriptions of objects, typically museum artefacts, depicted in a picture. These systems represent the information to be communicated to the user in the form of database facts, each of which corresponds to a sentence, for instance:

Database fact	Sentence
subclass(ex1, amph)	→ This exhibit is an amphora.
painter-story(p-Kleo, en4049)	→ The Painter of Kleofrades used to decorate big vases.
current-location(ex1, wag-mus)	→ This exhibit is currently displayed in the Martin von Wagner Museum.
exhibit-depicts(ex1, en914)	→ This exhibit depicts a warrior performing splachnoscopy before leaving for the battle.
painted-by(ex1, p-Kleo)	→ This exhibit was decorated by the Painter of Kleofrades.
museum-country(wag-mus, ger)	→ The Martin von Wagner Museum is in Germany.

We assume a *search-based* approach to text structuring in which many candidate solutions are evaluated according to scores assigned by a *metric* of coherence

A. Belz et al. (Eds.): INLG 2004, LNAI 3123, pp. 90–99, 2004.

[11,7,5]. Furthermore, our hypothetical text structuring component simply orders the facts by applying a bias in favour of the best scoring ordering among the candidate solutions for the preferred output. Hence, the output of text structuring, as in similar work [2,10], is simply an *ordering* of the selected facts.

For this work, we view text structuring independently from its possible interactions with other generation tasks. We assume that no information is added or deleted once content selection has been performed, and that the preferred ordering is passed to the other generation modules which account for the selection of appropriate referring expressions, pronominalisation, lexicalisation, etc.

Most research on search-based text structuring focuses on employing a metric during the generation process and evaluating its output. Because this metric is usually defined intuitively, it represents only one of the different, perhaps equally plausible, options which in most cases remain unexplored. Our earlier work presents an example of this problem by showing how Centering Theory [17] gives rise to a number of metrics all of which could be used for the type of text structuring assumed in this paper [6]. Hence, a general methodology for identifying which of the many possible metrics represent the most promising candidates for text structuring is required. These candidates can then be tested more extensively using human subjects.

In this paper, we outline a novel methodology for selecting the metrics which are most suitable for text structuring **prior** to the actual generation process. Our methods are automatic and corpus-based instead of relying on generally more expensive psycholinguistic techniques.

We experiment with a subset of the metrics from [6], although these metrics might not represent the best way of doing text structuring when compared with other more informed methods. However, because these metrics exemplify the problem of having to choose between various alternatives in a simple way, they serve as a very appropriate application area for our experiments. Crucially, our methodology can be extended to choose between more complicated metrics for less simplified text structuring approaches as well.

In the following section, we discuss briefly how Centering Theory (henceforth CT) is applied in our domain giving rise to many different metrics of coherence.[4] Then, we outline the novel corpus-based methodology for selecting the metrics which are most suitable for text structuring. We conclude with the results of our experiments which make use of existing data from the MPIRO system.

2 Applying CT in the MPIRO Domain

As already mentioned in the previous section, we assume each database fact to correspond to a sentence. Example (1) shows an ordering, defined by a domain expert, using the sentences in our example to represent the corresponding facts. Example (2) shows an alternative ordering:

(1) (a) This exhibit is an amphora. (b) This exhibit was decorated by the Painter of Kleofrades. (c) The Painter of Kleofrades used to decorate big vases. (d) This

---

[4] This discussion assumes that the reader is familiar with the basic aspects of CT.

exhibit depicts a warrior performing splachnoscopy before leaving for the battle.
(e) This exhibit is currently displayed in the Martin von Wagner Museum. (f)
The Martin von Wagner Museum is in Germany.

(2) (a) This exhibit is an amphora. (b) This exhibit was decorated by the Painter
of Kleofrades. (d) This exhibit depicts a warrior performing splachnoscopy before
leaving for the battle. (e) This exhibit is currently displayed in the Martin von
Wagner Museum. (f) The Martin von Wagner Museum is in Germany. (c) The
Painter of Kleofrades used to decorate big vases.

According to CT, an important factor for the felicity of each example is
the coherence which arises from certain patterns for introducing and discussing
centers, such as the referents of the NPs "this exhibit" and "the Painter of
Kleofrades". Similarly to e.g. [7], we take the arguments of the underlying facts,
i.e. domain objects such as ex1 and p-Kleo to represent these centers.

As discussed by Walker et al. [17], we compute a list of forward looking centers
(CF list) for each fact, the first element of which is identified as the preferred
center CP. The members of the CF list are ranked according to their argument
positions within the fact.[5] For two subsequent facts F_{n-1} and F_n, giving rise to
CF_{n-1} and CF_n respectively, we define the unique backward looking center of
F_n, CB_n, as the highest ranked element of CF_{n-1} which also appears in CF_n
(CT's Constraint 3). For instance, the CB of (b) for both examples is ex1.

The second and third columns of the following table show the structure of
the CF list and the CB for each fact in the orderings (1) and (2):[6]

Fact	CF list: {CP, other CF}	CB	Transition	CHEAPNESS $CB_n = CP_{n-1}$
Ex. (1): (a)	{ex1, amph}	n.a.	n.a.	n.a.
(b)	{ex1, p-Kleo}	ex1	CONTINUE	+
(c)	{p-Kleo, en4049}	p-Kleo	SMOOTH-SHIFT	*
(d)	{ex1, en914}	-	NOCB/PF-NOCB	+
(e)	{ex1, wag-mus}	ex1	CONTINUE	+
(f)	{wag-mus, ger}	wag-mus	SMOOTH-SHIFT	*
Ex. (2): (a)	{ex1, amph}	n.a.	n.a.	n.a.
(b)	{ex1, p-Kleo}	ex1	CONTINUE	+
(d)	{ex1, en914}	ex1	CONTINUE	+
(e)	{ex1, wag-mus}	ex1	CONTINUE	+
(f)	{wag-mus, ger}	wag-mus	SMOOTH-SHIFT	*
(c)	{p-Kleo, en4049}	-	NOCB/PF*-NOCB	+

Following Kibble and Power [7], we call the requirement that CB_n be the same
as CB_{n-1} the principle of COHERENCE and the requirement that CB_n be the same

---

[5] We assume here that the argument positions reflect a rough order of importance.
This is the main difference between our approach and that of Kibble and Power [7],
who also compute the CF list for a fact on the basis of its argument structure, but
allow for more than one potential CP.

[6] We use the indexes of sentences (a)-(f) in the examples to refer to each corresponding
fact. Note that in accordance with CT, we do not compute a CB for (a), but allow
for more than one potential CP.

as CP_n the principle of SALIENCE. Each of these principles can be satisfied or violated, while their various combinations give rise to the standard transitions of CT [1], which are shown in the fourth column of the table, with one difference. When CF_n and CF_{n-1} do not have any centers in common, we compute the NOCB transition for F_n [7]. Moreover we follow Karamanis [6] in setting the artefact-to-be-described (in our examples this corresponds to the center ex1) as the focal entity of the whole description (PageFocus). Karamanis distinguishes between two types of NOCB: PF-NOCB where CF_{n-1} and CF_n do not have centers in common, but the CP_n is the same as the PageFocus (fact (d) of example (1)) and PF*-NOCB where CF_{n-1} and CF_n do not have centers in common and the CP_n is **not** the same as the PageFocus (fact (c) of example (2)).[7] Finally, one can make use of the requirement that CB_n be the same as CP_{n-1}, known as the principle of CHEAPNESS [16]. The last column of the table shows the violations of CHEAPNESS (denoted with an asterisk).[8]

3 Defining CT-based Metrics of Coherence

Following Karamanis [6], the CT concepts previously presented can be used to define many different metrics of coherence which might be useful for text structuring, including:

M.NOCB - picks the ordering with the fewest NOCBs (of both kinds) as the preferred output [5]. Because of its simplicity, M.NOCB serves as our baseline metric.

M.CHEAP - picks the ordering with the fewest violations of CHEAPNESS.

M.KP - sums up the NOCBs (of both kinds) and the violations of CHEAPNESS, COHERENCE and SALIENCE, preferring the ordering with the lowest total cost, as in [7].

M.MIL - picks the ordering with the fewest NOCBs (of both kinds) and ROUGH-SHIFTs. This is inspired by [12].

M.BFP - employs the preferences between standard transitions as expressed by Rule 2 of CT [1]: CONTINUE is preferred to RETAIN, which is preferred to SMOOTH-SHIFT, which is preferred to ROUGH-SHIFT. M.BFP selects the ordering with the highest number of CONTINUEs. If there is a tie, the one which has the most RETAINs is favoured. If there is still a tie, the number of SMOOTH-SHIFTs is used, etc.

The metrics presented so far do not distinguish between PF-NOCBs and PF*-NOCBs. Following [6], for each metric we define a PF-modification of the metric. This first of all computes the orderings that have the fewest PF*-NOCBs. Of

---

[7] If the second fact in a sequence F_2 has a CB, then it is taken to be either a CONTINUE or a RETAIN, even if F_1 is classified as a NOCB (as in (e) of example (1)). The same happens for the second fact in the overall sequence (the first fact overall is not assigned a transition).

[8] As for the other two principles, no violation of CHEAPNESS is computed for (a) or when F_n is marked as a NOCB.

these, it then chooses the one which scores best for the other notions of CT taken into account by its unmodified version (e.g. fewest violations of CHEAPNESS for PF.CHEAP, etc).

In the next section, we present a general corpus-based methodology for choosing the most promising candidates for text structuring between these and other similar metrics.

4   Exploring the Search Space of Possible Orderings

In section 2, we discussed how an ordering of facts defined by a domain expert, such as (1), can be translated into a sequence of CF lists, which is the representation that the CT-based metrics operate on. We use the term *Basis for Comparison* (BfC) to indicate this sequence of CF lists. We now discuss how the BfC is used in a search-oriented evaluation methodology which calculates a performance measure for each metric and compares them with each other.

4.1   Computing the Classification Rate

The performance measure we employ is called the *classification rate* of a metric M on a BfC B produced by a domain expert. It estimates the ability of M to produce B as the output of text structuring according to a specific generation scenario. First, we search through the space of possible orderings defined by the permutations of the CF lists that B consists of and divide the explored search space into sets of orderings that score better, equal, or worse than B according to M.

The classification rate is defined according to the following generation scenario: We assume that the better an ordering scores for M, the higher its chance of being selected as the output of text structuring. This is turn means that **the fewer** the members of the set of better scoring orderings, the better the chances of B to be the chosen output.

Moreover, we assume that additional biases are applied for the selection of the output between the orderings that score the same for M. These will be unpredictable, as they depend on the detail of the search mechanism implemented for generation. On average, B is expected to sit in the middle of the set of equally scoring orderings with respect to these biases. Hence, **half** of the equally scoring orderings will have a better chance than B to be selected by M.

The classification rate v of a metric M on B expresses the expected percentage of orderings with a higher probability of being generated than B using M:

$$v(M, B) = Better(M) + \frac{Equal(M)}{2}$$

Better(M) stands for the percentage of orderings that score better than B according to M, whilst *Equal*(M) is the percentage of orderings that score equal to B according to M. If $v(M_x, B)$ is the classification rate of M_x on B, and $v(M_y, B)$ is the classification rate of M_y on B, M_y is a more suitable candidate than M_x for generating B if $v(M_y, B)$ is smaller than $v(M_x, B)$. That is, smaller classification rates are better.

4.2 Approximating the Classification Rate for Longer Texts

If there are n facts to be ordered then the search space to be explored to calculate the classification rate of a metric M on a BfC B contains $n!$ orderings. This can be enumerated exhaustively for small values of n. However, when B consists of many more CF lists, this is impractical. In this section, we summarise an argument that the result returned from a random sample of 1,000,000 permutations is representative of the result from the entire population of valid permutations.[9]

Assume that in the whole population of N valid permutations, there are b permutations that are classified as Better than or Equal to B according to M. Let the variable X be 1 when a randomly selected permutation is classified as Better than or Equal to B, and 0 otherwise. Then the mean value for X is $\mu = b/N$. The variance for X is $\sigma^2 = b/N * (N - b)/N$. Note that the largest value for σ occurs when $\mu = \frac{1}{2}$, in which case σ is also equal to 0.5.

If we take a random sample of k variables like X, the average of the random sample m is equal to: $m = \frac{X_1 + ... + X_k}{k}$. By the Central Limit Theorem when the size of the sample is large enough (i.e. perhaps $k > 30$) m behaves like a normally distributed variable with a mean equal to the population mean μ and standard error $\sigma_m = \frac{\sigma}{\sqrt{k}}$.

Since m is normally distributed, 95% of such sample means are expected to appear within 1.96 standard errors from the population mean. The standard error is $\sigma_m = \sigma/\sqrt{1000000} = \sigma/1000$. Since σ cannot be greater than 0.5, σ_m cannot be greater than 0.0005. This means that we expect the true value of μ to be at most 0.0005*1.96=0.00098 away from m in 95% of our random samples. Due to the very small value of σ_m we are justified to believe that random sampling is unlikely to return significantly different results from exhaustive enumeration for arbitrarily large search spaces. Indeed a simple empirical study has confirmed this claim.

For $n > 12$, the chance of a random sample of 1,000,000 permutations containing many duplicates is very small. Hence the sampling can also be done without replacement, and this can be done very efficiently.

4.3 Generalising Across Many BfCs

In order for the experimental results to be reliable and generalisable, two metrics M_x and M_y should be compared on more than one BfC from a corpus C. In our standard analysis, the BfCs $B_1, ..., B_m$ from C are treated as the random factor in a repeated measures design since each BfC contributes a score for each metric. Then, the classification rates for M_x and M_y on the BfCs are compared with

---

[9] The argument concerns the estimation of the set of Better or Equal permutations. Similar arguments apply to Better, Equal, etc. separately.

each other and significance is tested using the Sign Test.[10] After calculating the number of BfCs that return a lower classification rate for M_x than for M_y and vice versa, the Sign Test reports whether the difference in the number of BfCs is significant, that is, whether there are significantly more BfCs with a lower classification rate for M_x than the BfCs with a lower classification rate for M_y (or vice versa).

5 Experiments in the MPIRO Domain

Our corpus is a subset of the orderings employed in [2]. It contains 122 ordered sets of facts, each set consisting of 6 facts which were derived from the database of MPIRO and treated as a hypothetical input to text structuring. The facts in each set were manually assigned an order to reflect what one domain expert (not from one of the authors' research groups) considered to be the most natural ordering of the corresponding sentences.

5.1 Permutation and Search Strategy

The fact with the "subclass" predicate, which corresponds to sentence (a) in example (1), is always the first fact in the ordering defined by the expert [2]. We assume that a generator for this domain will always use this domain-specific communication knowledge [8] and so we only consider permutations that start with the "subclass" fact. The search space to be explored for each BfC from MPIRO is very small – $(6 - 1)! = 120$ – and so it is enumerated exhaustively in the computation of classification rates.

5.2 Results

The average classification rates of the metrics vary from 12.66% (for PF.KP) to 81.04% (for M.CHEAP). The data for pairwise Sign Tests are shown in Tables 1 to 4. The fact that classification rates are so high indicates clearly that none of these metrics is suitable *on its own* as a basis for text structuring in this domain. Comparing the metrics pairwise, we have the following results:

1. The baseline M.NOCB does better than M.CHEAP and M.KP, but is over-taken by M.MIL. There is no clear winner when M.NOCB and M.BFP are compared (Table 1).[11]

---

[10] The Sign Test was chosen over its parametric alternatives to test significance because it does not carry specific assumptions about population distributions and variance.

[11] No winner is reported for a comparison when the p value returned by the Sign Test is greater than 0.05. Note that despite conducting more than one pairwise comparison simultaneously we refrain from further adjusting the overall threshold of significance (e.g. according to the Bonferroni method, typically used for multiple planned comparisons that employ parametric statistics), since it is assumed that choosing a conservative statistic such as the Sign Test already provides substantial protection against the possibility of a type I error.

Table 1. Comparing M.NOCB with M.CHEAP, M.KP, M.BFP and M.MIL in MPIRO

Pair	M.NOCB			p	Winner
	lower	greater	ties		
M.NOCB vs M.CHEAP	110	12	0	0.000	M.NOCB
M.NOCB vs M.KP	103	16	3	0.000	M.NOCB
M.NOCB vs M.BFP	41	31	49	0.121	ns
M.NOCB vs M.MIL	0	6	116	0.016	M.MIL
N	122				

Table 2. Comparing each unmodified metric (e.g. M.NOCB) with its PF-modified version (e.g. PF.NOCB) in MPIRO

Pair	unmodified metric			p	Winner
	lower	greater	ties		
M.NOCB vs PF.NOCB	3	55	64	0.000	PF.NOCB
M.CHEAP vs PF.CHEAP	15	105	2	0.000	PF.CHEAP
M.KP vs PF.KP	15	105	2	0.000	PF.KP
M.BFP vs PF.BFP	2	53	67	0.000	PF.BFP
M.MIL vs PF.MIL	3	55	64	0.000	PF.MIL
N	122				

Table 3. Comparing PF.NOCB with PF.CHEAP, PF.KP, PF.BFP and PF.MIL in MPIRO

Pair	PF.NOCB			p	Winner
	lower	greater	ties		
PF.NOCB vs PF.CHEAP	67	52	3	0.100	ns
PF.NOCB vs PF.KP	12	27	83	0.013	PF.KP
PF.NOCB vs PF.BFP	9	23	90	0.011	PF.BFP
PF.NOCB vs PF.MIL	0	6	116	0.016	PF.MIL
N	122				

Table 4. Comparing the PF-modified metrics which overtake the baseline with each other in MPIRO

Pair	PF.MIL			p	Winner
	lower	greater	ties		
PF.MIL vs PF.KP	13	21	88	0.115	ns
PF.MIL vs PF.BFP	10	17	95	0.124	ns

Pair	PF.KP			p	Winner
	lower	greater	ties		
PF.KP vs PF.BFP	18	11	93	0.133	ns
N	122				

2. Each PF-modified metric outperforms the corresponding unmodified metric (Table 2).
3. The enhanced baseline PF.NOCB is outperformed by PF.BFP, PF.KP and PF.MIL (Table 3). So the additional CT concepts seem to make a difference when PageFocus is used.
4. The differences between PF.BFP, PF.KP and PF.MIL are not statistically significant (Table 4).

PF.BFP, PF.KP and PF.MIL are identified at this point as the most promising candidates for text structuring in MPIRO from the ten investigated metrics.

6 Related Work

As Reiter and Sripada [15] suggest, results like the ones presented here should be treated as hypotheses which need to be supplemented with additional evidence. For this reason, we applied the novel methodology on a smaller set of data derived by the GNOME corpus [14], verifying the superiority of M.NOCB over M.CHEAP and M.KP. Note, however, that the analysis from GNOME shows that the PF-modification often increases, instead of reduces, the classification rate of the metrics in the new domain.

Lapata [10] recently presented a methodology for automatically evaluating orderings generated by different features of a probabilistic text structuring model on the basis of their *distance* from the observed orderings in a corpus. She takes into account **more than one** optimal solution by compiling a corpus of parallel orderings defined by many judges. The distance between the orderings of the judges serves as the upper bound in her evaluation which promotes those features of her model which minimise the distance between the generated outputs and the upper bound. In contrast, our method shows preference for the metric which favours fewest orderings other than the **unique** optimal solution in our corpus. Because our corpus does not consist of multiple orderings, which might be difficult to compile on a large scale, our approach remains agnostic about the actual felicity of any solution other than the observed one. The other main difference is that whereas Lapata measures *how close* the predictions of a metric are to gold standard texts, in contrast we measure the extent to which a metric makes it likely to generate a gold standard *itself*.

Finally, it should be emphasised that the methodology in section 4 is not specific to the CT-based metrics or the text structuring approach exemplified in this paper. Rather, it can be adjusted for choosing between any number and type of metrics each of which assigns a score to a text structure in a corpus. This text structure does not have to be a simple ordering as assumed in this paper, since exploring the search space is feasible for other types of structure like the one used e.g. by [7] as well.

Acknowledgements

Special thanks to Aggeliki Dimitromanolaki for entrusting us with her data and for helpful clarifications on their use and to David Schlangen for writing the script which translates the acquired data into a format appropriate for our program. The first author was able to engage in this research thanks to a scholarship from the Greek State Scholarships Foundation (IKY).

References

1. Brennan, S., Friedman [Walker], M., Pollard, C.: A centering approach to pronouns. Proceedings of ACL 1987 (1987), 155–162.
2. Dimitromanolaki, A., Androutsopoulos, I.: Learning to order facts for discourse planning in natural language generation. Proceedings of the 9th European Workshop on Natural Language Generation (2003).
3. Grosz, B., Joshi, A., Weinstein, S.: Centering: A framework for modeling the local coherence of discourse. Computational Linguistics 21(2) (1995) 203–225.
4. Isard, A., Oberlander, J., Androutsopoulos, I., Matheson, C.: Speaking the users' languages. IEEE Intelligent Systems Magazine (2003) 18(1) 40–45.
5. Karamanis, N., Manurung, H.: Stochastic text structuring using the principle of continuity. Proceedings of INLG 2002 (2002) 81–88.
6. Karamanis, N.: Entity Coherence for Descriptive Text Structuring. Ph.D. thesis, Division of Informatics, University of Edinburgh (2003).
7. Kibble, R., Power, R.: An integrated framework for text planning and pronominalisation. Proceedings of INLG 2000 (2000) 77–84.
8. Kittredge, R., Korelsky, T., Rambow, O.: On the need for domain communication knowledge. Computational Intelligence 7 (1991) 305–314.
9. Knott, A., Oberlander, J., O'Donnell, M., Mellish, C.: Beyond elaboration: The interaction of relations and focus in coherent text. In T. Sanders, J. Schilperoord, and W. Spooren, editors, Text Representation: Linguistic and Psycholinguistic Aspects, chapter 7, pages 181–196. John Benjamins, Amsterdam (2001).
10. Lapata, M.: Probabilistic text structuring: Experiments with sentence ordering. Proceedings of ACL 2003 (2003).
11. Mellish, C., Knott, A., Oberlander, J., O'Donnell, M.: Experiments using stochastic search for text planning. Proceedings of the 9th International Workshop on NLG (1998) 98–107.
12. Miltsakaki, M., Kukich, K.: The role of centering theory's rough-shift in the teaching and evaluation of writing skills. In Proceedings of ACL 2000 (2000).
13. O'Donnell, M., Mellish, C., Oberlander, J., Knott, A.: ILEX: An architecture for a dynamic hypertext generation system. Natural Language Engineering 7(3) (2001) 225–250.
14. Poesio, M., Stevenson, R., Di Eugenio, B., Hitzeman, J.: Centering: a parametric theory and its instantiations. Computational Linguistics (2004) In press.
15. Reiter E., Sripada, S.: Should corpora texts be gold standards for NLG? Proceedings of INLG 2002 (2002) 97–104.
16. Strube M., Hahn, U.: 1999. Functional centering: Grounding referential coherence in information structure. Computational Linguistics 25(3) (1999) 309–344.
17. Walker, M., Joshi, A., Prince, E.: Centering in naturally occuring discourse: An overview. In Walker, M., Joshi, A., and Prince, E., editors, Centering Theory in Discourse, pages 1–30. Clarendon Press (1998).

Classification-Based Generation Using TAG

Tomasz Marciniak and Michael Strube

EML Research gGmbH
Villa Bosch Schloss-Wolfsbrunnenweg 33
69118 Heidelberg, Germany
http://www.eml-research.de/nlp

Abstract. In this paper we present an application of machine learning to generating natural language route directions. We use the TAG formalism to represent the structure of the generated texts and split the generation process into a number of individual tasks which can be modeled as classification problems. To solve each of these tasks we apply corpus-trained classifiers relying on semantic and contextual features, determined for each task in a feature selection procedure.

1   Introduction

Traditionally, different NLG tasks such as *text structuring*, *lexicalization* or *syntactic realization* have been considered to belong to different problem categories, requiring their own processing methods and representations. In this paper we present a classification-based approach to language generation which affords a uniform treatment of different NLG stages. We decompose the generation process into a sequence of tasks which realize *minimal* elements of the surface grammatical form of an expression, given the meaning to be coded and the realization context. Each task is handled by a separate corpus-trained classifier using semantic and contextual features chosen in a feature selection procedure. To represent the grammatical structure of the generated texts we use the Tree Adjoining Grammar (TAG) formalism which provides an elegant way to account for the syntactic structure of individual sentences as well as the structure of the discourse. We apply our method to generating route directions, focusing on several elements of the grammatical form both at the clause and discourse levels.

The paper is structured as follows: in Section 2 we characterize the semantic and grammatical structure of route directions. In Section 3 we present the classification-based model of generation and in Section 4 we describe our data. The experiments and evaluation are discussed in Section 5 and related work is summarized in Section 6.

2   Route Directions Overview

Route directions are instructional texts providing a detailed specification of the actions that the instructions' recipient should perform in order to reach his/her goal (see Example 1 below). Descriptions of actions (1b, e) are typically accompanied by specifications of *states* (1a) and *events* (1c, d) that may result from the actions or initiate them. As the cover term for actions, states and events we use a single concept of *situation*.

A. Belz et al. (Eds.): INLG 2004, LNAI 3123, pp. 100–109, 2004.

Example 1. (a) Standing in front of the hotel (b) follow Meridian street south for about 100 meters, (c) passing the First Union Bank entrance on your right, (d) until you see the river side in front of you. (e) Then make a left onto North Hills Street.

In our work we focus on the whole process of mapping between the semantic content of route directions and their grammatical form. Hence in this section we discuss meaning elements of the generated texts and present an account of their grammatical structure, which both provide a basis for the generation method described in Section 3.

Table 1. Binary attributes used to specify the aspectual type of a situation

	Binary Representation		
Vendlerian Classes	Stative	Durative	Culminated
States	yes	yes/no	no
Activities	no	yes/no	no
Achievements	no	no	yes
Accomplishments	no	yes	yes

2.1 Semantic Analysis

We analyze the semantic content of instructional texts as comprising three major elements. At the level of individual discourse units it includes the *semantic frame* of the portrayed situation and its *aspectual type*. Furthermore, we associate the discourse-level meaning of such texts with the *temporal structure* of the discourse, based on temporal relations holding between individual situations. The semantic frame provides a schematic representation of a situation, based on its ontological class (e.g. *self-motion*, *visual perception*) which can be further associated with a set of specific semantic roles (e.g. *self mover*, *path* or *goal*) (cf. [1]). The aspectual type of a situation denotes its qualitative temporal structure. To characterize it, we follow the analysis by [2] and associate each situation with three binary attributes (see Table 1). The representation thus obtained allows to discriminate between *Vendlerian* classes of situations [3]. Clause (1b) from the above example tagged with the semantic information is presented below:

$$\left[\text{ follow }\underset{\text{PATH}}{\left[\text{Meridian Street}\right]}\underset{\text{DIRECTION}}{\left[\text{south}\right]}\underset{\text{DISTANCE}}{\left[\text{ for about 100 meters}\right]}\right]\quad\text{SELF\_MOTION, –STATIVE, +DURATIVE, –CULMINATED}$$

The temporal structure of route directions can be modeled as a tree (see Figure 1), with nodes corresponding to discourse units and edges signalling temporal relations. We interpret these relations as holding between the actual situations referred to by each pair of connected nodes. Relation labels that we use include: *initial*, *ongoing* and *subsequent*, which denote the particular time interval of the situation referred to by the parent node during which the situation specified by the child node occurs.

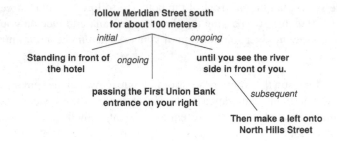

Fig. 1. Temporal Structure

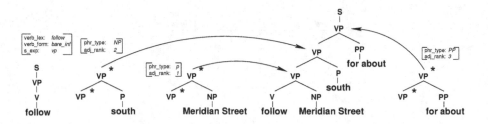

Fig. 2. Elementary trees are represented as feature vectors. Tree selection occurs in a series of classifications which specify individual feature values. Phrasal structures are then adjoined to the tree anchored by the verb in the order determined by one of the features.

2.2   Grammatical Form

To represent the grammatical structure of route directions we use the TAG formalism [4]. A TAG can be defined as a tree rewriting system composed of a set of *elementary* trees which are combined by means of *adjunction* operations to form a derived structure. A selection of elementary trees and the derivation process for clause (1b) are presented in Figure 2.

Note that we do not specify explicitly the subcategorization frame of the verb. All the syntactic patterns necessary to correctly realize a clause are learned directly from the data, so that an explicit model is not necessary. We also abandon the traditional way of augmenting a TAG with semantic information by embedding individual nodes with feature structures (cf. [5], [6]). Instead we acknowledge the fact that virtually *all* elements of the semantic content of an expression may influence realization of *any* element of its grammatical form. We believe that the decision which semantic elements should be considered for each realization step, should be based on empirical grounds.

We base our account of the discourse structure of route directions on DLTAG, a discourse extension to the lexicalized TAG, proposed by [7]. In DLTAG, discourse units function as arguments of *discourse connectives* which anchor elementary trees, labeled as *discourse clauses* (D_c). The derivation process starts with a single initial tree associated with the discourse unit which occupies the root position in the temporal discourse model (cf. Figure 1). All other discourse units are associated with auxiliary trees, which are successively combined to form a derived structure (see Figure 3).

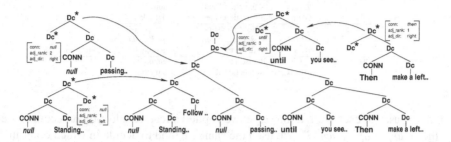

Fig. 3. Selection of elementary trees is based on feature values by means of which individual trees are represented. If two trees are to be adjoined at the same root node, their order is specified by their adjunction rank.

3 Classification-Based Generation

Linguistic realization of an expression is a process involving several steps, in which *minimal* elements of the grammatical structure are assigned specific forms given the meaning to be coded and the context. We define these *minimal* elements as distinctive components of the structure which, depending on the particular form they take, may change the meaning of an expression or render it ill-formed. In the TAG-based representation that we adopted, minimal elements correspond to those elements of a tree which allow to differentiate between two elementary structures. They may include structural elements, such as the adjunction direction, or lexical ones, e.g. the tree anchor. Each such element is modeled as a distinctive feature in the vector representation of elementary trees (see Table 2).

In the approach to generation presented here we formulate realizations of individual features as single classification problems. The entire generation process is then modeled as a cascade of classifiers. As its input, each classifier takes a selection of semantic and contextual features. The first group of features is directly based on the analysis of route directions presented in Section 2. Contextual features specify how the same task has been solved in the preceding discourse, and what forms have been assigned to other elements within the same discourse unit. We narrowed this type of context to the two immediately preceding discourse units. Corresponding feature names have been prefixed with $n\_$ and $nn\_$ respectively. We also used the numerical features *null_prec* and *related_count*, which specify respectively how many discourse units with a *null* connective precede, and how many discourse units are related to the current one.

The architecture of our system consists of a cascade of eight classifiers which incrementally build up a vector representation of the expression's form. As their input the classifiers take a semantic specification of an expression arranged in a feature vector. In addition, those classifiers which occur later in the pipeline may take the output of previous modules as part of their own input. To determine which semantic features

Table 2. Vector representation of elementary trees

Tree Anchor	Feature	Description	Possible Values
discourse connective	*conn*	Connective Lexical Form	*and, until, null,* ...
	adj_rank_dsc	Adjunction Rank	numeric
	adj_dir	Adjunction Direction	right, left
main verb	*s_exp*	S Node Constituents	np_vp, vp
	verb_lex	Verb Lexical Form	*walk, follow, turn,* ...
	verb_form	Verb Form	gerund, bare_inf, finite_pres, ...
verb argument	*phr_type*	Phrase Type	np, pp, p
	adj_rank_phr	Adjunction Rank	numeric

should be used at each realization stage, we applied a feature selection procedure based on the *wrapper approach* [8]. We used the same method to decide in which order individual classifiers should be placed, as this determines the availability of the contextual information at each realization stage. The ordering of tasks and the selected subsets of features are presented in Table 3.

Table 3. Feature subsets used by individual classifiers. Tasks *adj_rank_dsc* and *adj_rank_phr* are further split into a series of binary classifications considering each possible pair of constituents which are to be ordered. Hence two subsets of these features are considered for each binary task.

Task	Semantic Features	Contextual Features
adj_rank_dsc	relation, frame, action, stative, durative	related_count
adj_dir	relation ,n_relation, frame, action, durative, culminated	adj_rank_dsc, related_count
connective	relation, n_relation, action, stative, durative, culminated, n_durative	adj_rank_dsc, adj_dir, n_connective, nn_connective, related_count, null_prec
s_exp	frame, relation, action, stative, durative, culminated	adj_rank_dsc, adj_dir, connective
verb_form	relation, action, stative, durative, culminated	adj_rank_dsc, adj_dir, connective, s_exp, n_verb_form, nn_verb_form, related_count
verb_lex	relation, frame, action, stative, durative, culminated, source_rel, path_rel, goal_rel, dir_rel	connective, verb_form, n_verb_lex, related_count
phr_type	sem_role, arg_rel	verb_lex, s_exp, verb_form,
adj_rank_phr	sem_role, arg_rel	phr_type, verb_lex, s_exp, verb_form, connective

4   Data

Our corpus consists of 70 manually annotated texts, obtained from printed tourist guide books or found on the Internet. Individual texts have a similar structure and their length ranges from 8 to 17 discourse units realized as clauses, yielding a total of 916 clauses in the entire corpus. The annotations comprise markables, i.e. marked text spans falling in four different groups. *Discourse-unit* markables relate to individual situation descriptions and were tagged with attributes specifying the semantic frame of a situation and its aspectual structure. To indicate temporal relations holding between discourse units, markables at this level were combined with directed links labeled with specific relation names. If a pair of related discourse units was connected by means of a conjunction or an adverbial, they were tagged as *Discourse-connective* markables. If no explicit discourse connective was found, a *null* connective was assumed. Main verbs within each

Table 4. Results

Task	Classes	Majority Baseline	Rule-based baseline Accuracy	F-M.	KStar Accuracy	F-M.	Count
1. *adj_rank_dsc*	numeric	-	65.38%	-	87.96%	-	916
1a *precedence*	yes	50%	71.03%	0.76	93.35%	0.93	466
	no			0.64		0.93	466
2. *adj_dir*	right	90.61%	98.25%	0.99	97.82%	0.99	830
	left			0.89		0.89	86
3. *connective*	null	64.52%	63.86%	0.76	79.91%	0.87	591
	and			0.21		0.61	160
	until			0.61		0.86	57
	after			0.54		0.76	31
	as			0.56		0.62	32
	...			...		...	...
4. *s_exp*	vp	78.38%	92.85%	0.94	94.76%	0.97	718
	np_vp			0.82		0.88	198
5. *verb_form*	bare_inf	59.39%	76.31%	0.87	91.05%	0.97	544
	gerund			0.56		0.86	128
	fin_pres			0.78		0.87	169
	will_inf			0.58		0.63	68
	to_inf			0		0.6	7
6. *verb_lex*	walk	13.10%	32.17%	0.26	71.83%	0.65	120
	turn			0.42		0.89	104
	pass			0.45		0.88	66
	follow			0.34		0.64	53
	continue			0.17		0.54	53
	...			...		...	...
7. *phr_type*	pp	40.10%	83.28%	0.84	92.16%	0.94	573
	np			0.83		0.92	667
	p			0.80		0.87	189
8. *adj_rank_phr*	numeric	-	66.15%	-	83.96%	-	1429
8a *precedence*	yes	50%	72.26%	0.73	91.06%	0.91	682
	no			0.72		0.91	682

clause were tagged as *Situation-predicate* markables. Arguments of verbs were tagged as *Situation-argument* markables and were associated with specific semantic roles. All grammatical types of information, such as *verb form* or *constituent type* of verb arguments, were determined automatically during a post-processing stage.

To obtain training and test data from the annotated corpus we used the following procedure. First, we represented each text in the form of a tree (as in Figure 1) . Each node was then described by a vector of feature values, specifying its semantic content and the grammatical structure of the respective discourse unit. We used such constructed discourse representations to generate instances for each classification task, using each time the relevant subset of the semantic features and obtaining the contextual features from the information available at the neighboring nodes.

5   Experiments and Results

To evaluate our system we performed a series of experiments, using an instance-based classifier KStar [9], implemented in Weka [10]. We chose this learning scheme as it performed better on our data than the rule induction algorithm Ripper [11] and the decision-tree learner C4.5 [12].

The results reported in Table 4 were obtained using 10-fold cross-validation for each task. For comparison we also provide the scores of two baseline schemes. They include a *majority* baseline which always selects a class label with the highest frequency in the training data, and a manually-constructed rule-based system which considers up to four semantic and contextual features for each task (see Figure 4). A brief summary of each task and the results are presented below:

Adjunction Rank / Discourse (1, 1a). This numeric task is split into a series of binary *precedence* classifications which consider each pair of elementary trees and decide on their relative order. Results of these sub-tasks are used to sort the relevant trees and assign them a unique rank. The rule-based system reaches 71.03% accuracy at the binary *precedence* task and 65.38% at the main numeric task. The accuracy of KStar at the binary classification lies at 93.35% which yields 87.96% accuracy at the overall adjunction rank task.

Adjunction Direction (2). The majority baseline for this binary task is 90.61%. It is the only task where the rule-based system outperforms the learning algorithm. It assigns *"right"* as a default to all instances with *local rank* higher than *1* or *relation* other than *initial*. Note that the instance-based learner considers more features, which were chosen in the feature selection procedure.

Discourse Connective (3). For this multi-class task the majority baseline lies relatively hight at 64.52% (associated with the *null* connective). The accuracy of the rule-based system is lower here, 63.86%, but it reaches higher F-Measure for other connective classes. KStar proves much better here than the baseline schemes, reaching the accuracy of 79.91%. Table 5 (left) presents a fragment of the confusion matrix with the five most frequent classes. Most misclassifcations occur within narrow groups of classes which in some context may signal similar relations, e.g. *null* vs. *and*, or *as* vs. *after*.

Table 5. Fragments of confusion matrices for *connective*, *verb_form* and *verb_lex* classes

null	and	until	after	as	classified ← as
523	94	11	4	4	null
60	94	2	0	1	and
4	0	53	0	0	until
2	0	0	26	3	after
7	0	0	7	18	as

bare_inf	ger	fin_pres	will_inf	classified ← as
536	6	1	1	bare_inf
21	103	4	0	gerund
3	5	146	12	fin_pres
6	1	21	38	will_inf

walk	turn	pass	continue	classified ← as
86	2	2	3	walk
0	98	0	2	turn
1	0	61	0	pass
14	0	0	28	continue

S Expansion (4). This binary task specifies the main constituent structure of a clause: *NP +VP* vs. *VP* (i.e. if it has no subject). In our domain the majority of clauses is subjectless (78.38%). This task is solved comparatively well by both the rule-based scheme and our system, which reach 92.85% and 94.76% accuracy, respectively.

Verb Form (5). The majority baseline for this task lies at 59.39% (*bare_inf*) and the accuracy of the rule-based system is 76.31%. KStar reaches a much higher score, 91.05%, and improves on the F-Measure for individual classes. Two classes which got lower F-Measure are *to_inf* which has a very low frequency and *will_inf*. The relevant confusion matrix is shown in Table 5 (middle).

Verb Lex (6). This task is concerned with choosing the lexical form of the main verb. It is a multi-class problem, with majority baseline relatively low at 13.10% (*walk*). The overall accuracy of the rule based system reaches 32.17%. The instance-based classifier performs much better here, scoring 71.83% accuracy. A fragment of the confusion matrix for this task is presented in Table 5 (right).

Phrase Type (7). At this task, the phrase type of the verb argument is determined. The majority baseline lies at 40.10% (*PP*). The rule based system performs reasonably well on this task, scoring 83.28%. Our system reaches 92.16% accuracy here.

Adjunction Rank / Phrase (8, 8a). Similarly to (1), this task is split into a series of binary classifications. The rule based system reaches 72.26% at the binary and 66.15% at the main task. Results of our system are much better here: 91.06% and 83.96%.

```
if (relation == subsequent)          if (action == yes)
    if (null_prec == 2)                  verb_form = bare_inf;
        conn = and;                  else if (relation == subsequent)
    else                                 verb_form = fin_pres;
        conn = null;                 else if (relation == ongoing)
else if (relation == ongoing)            if (connective == until)
    if (action == yes)                       verb_form = fin_pres;
        conn = null;                     else
    else                                     verb_form = gerund;
        conn = until;                else if (relation == initial)
else if (relation == subsequent)         ...
    ...
```

Fig. 4. Baseline hand-crafted rules for *connective* (left) and *verb_form* (right) tasks

6   Related Work

Empirical methods were introduced to NLG in the context of syntactic realization [13]. Most current works in this area follow the *ranking* approach which involves overgeneration and then selection of the best candidate, e.g. [14], [15]. Different corpus-based techniques were applied at the discourse planning stage to fact ordering, e.g. [16], [17]. While each of the aforementioned works focused on individual tasks, [18] presented an attempt to merge two trainable modules for different processing stages, which we also do in our work. In contrast to the above works we apply a single trainable method to different NLG tasks, trying to span several stages of the generation process. Our classification model also performs candidate ranking but it considers elements of the grammatical structure and not whole sentences, hence overgeneration is avoided.

The idea that different processing stages in an NLP system can be represented as classification tasks and solved using supervised machine learning methods was stated in [19]. So far this approach was used in NLG for solving individual tasks only [20, 16].

7   Conclusions

In this paper we presented our work on generating route directions, which is a part of a larger project concerned with producing natural language output from a *tourist information system.* We modeled several NLG stages in terms of classification problems which can be solved using machine learning methods. The advantage of this approach is the uniform treatment of different NLG tasks which facilitates adding new modules to the system and re-training it for novel domains.

We found that for almost all tasks machine learning techniques proved much better than hand-crafted rules. This can be explained by the fact that the simple heuristics that we applied considered no more than four information sources (i.e. *features*) at a time, whereas the machine-learning classifiers took advantage of a much more fine-grained instance representation. Arguably, hand-crafting classification rules which take a larger feature space into consideration would require an extensive problem expertise so that the procedure could not be easily replicated for new tasks or domains.

One issue which still requires considerable thought is the evaluation method. Information-retrieval scores such as F-Measure are too strict for many NLG tasks, especially those involving lexical choice. Such tasks can be characterized as *multi-label* problems, in which identical patterns in the data may be associated with different class labels. This is exactly the case in natural language, where more than one lexical or grammatical construction may be appropriate in a given context. Also, in the current work we limited the evaluation to individual tasks only, skipping the overall assessment of the generated discourse. We believe that discourse-level evaluation should be based on human judgements of text coherence and quality. We also want to follow [21] and look for correlations between human qualitative judgements and quantitative measures.

Finally, we plan to extend the scope of our work to cover the remaining NLG tasks (esp. content selection and referring expression generation), and focus on other text sorts in the domain of *tourist information.*

Acknowledgements: The work presented here has been funded by the Klaus Tschira Foundation, Heidelberg, Germany.

References

[1] Baker, C.F., Fillmore, C.J., Lowe, J.B.: The Berkeley FrameNet project. In: Proceedings of the 17th International Conference on Computational Linguistics and the 36th Annual Meeting of the Association for Computational Linguistics, *Montréal, Québec, Canada, 10–14 August 1998.* (1998) 86–90

[2] Moens, M., Steedman, M.: Temporal ontology and temporal reference. Computational Linguistics **14** (1988) 15–28

[3] Vendler, Z.: Verbs and times. In: Linguistics in Philosophy, *Cornell University Press, Ithaca, NY.* (1967) 97–121

[4] Joshi, A.K., Schabes, Y.: Tree-adjoining grammars and lexicalized grammars. In: Maurice Nivat and Andreas Podelski, editors, *Definability and Recognizability of Sets of Trees.* Elsevier. (1991)

[5] Stone, M., Doran, C.: Sentence planning as description using tree adjoining grammar. In: Proceedings of the Thirty-Fifth Annual Meeting of the Association for Computational Linguistics and Eighth Conference of the European Chapter of the Association for Computational Linguistics, *Madrid, Spain, 7 – 12 July 1997.* (1997) 198–205

[6] Bleam, T., Palmer, M., Shanker, V.: Motion verbs and semantic features in TAG. In: Proceedings of the 4th International Workshop on Tree-adjoining Grammars and Related Frameworks (TAG+), *Philadelphia, PA., 1 – 3 August, 1998.* (1998)

[7] Webber, B.L., Joshi, A.: Anchoring a lexicalized tree-adjoining grammar for discourse. In: Proceedings of the COLING/ACL '98 Workshop on Discourse Relations and Discourse Markers, *Montréal, Québec, Canada, 15 August 1998.* (1998) 86–92

[8] Kohavi, R., John, G.H.: Wrappers for feature subset selection. Artificial Intelligence Journal **97** (1997) 273–324

[9] Cleary, J.G., Trigg, L.E.: K*: An instance-based learner using an entropic distance measure. In: Proceedings of the 12th International Conference on Machine Learning, *Tahoe City, Ca., 9–12 July, 1995.* (1995) 108–114

[10] Witten, I.H., Frank, E.: Data Mining - Practical Machine Learning Tools and Techniques with Java Implementations. Morgan Kaufmann, San Francisco, CA (2000)

[11] Cohen, W.W.: Fast effective rule induction. In: Proceedings of the 12th International Conference on Machine Learning, *Tahoe City, Ca., 9–12 July, 1995.* (1995) 115–123

[12] Quinlan, J.R.: C4.5: Programs for Machine Learning. Morgan Kaufmann, San Francisco, CA (1993)

[13] Langkilde, I., Knight, K.: Generation that exploits corpus-based statistical knowledge. In: Proceedings of the 17th International Conference on Computational Linguistics and the 36th Annual Meeting of the Association for Computational Linguistics, *Montréal, Québec, Canada, 10–14 August 1998.* (1998) 704–710

[14] Bangalore, S., Rambow, O.: Exploiting a probabilistic hierarchical model for generation. In: Proceedings of the 18th International Conference on Computational Linguistics, *Saarbrücken, Germany, 31 July – 4 August 2000.* (2000) 42–48

[15] Varges, S., Mellish, C.: Instance-based natural language generation. In: Proceedings of the 2nd Meeting of the North American Chapter of the Association for Computational Linguistics, *Pittsburgh, PA, 2 – 7 June, 2001.* (2001) 1–8

[16] Duboue, P.K., McKeown, K.R.: Empirically estimating order constraints for content planning in generation. In: Proceedings of the 39th Annual Meeting of the Association for Computational Linguistics, *Toulouse, France, 9–11 July 2001.* (2001) 172–179

[17] Dimitromanolaki, A., Androutsopoulos, I.: Learning to order facts for discourse planning in natural language generation. In: Proceedings of the 9th European Workshop on Natural Language Generation, *Budapest, Hungary, 13 – 14 April 2003.* (2003) 23–30

[18] Chen, J., Bangalore, S., Rambow, O., Walker, M.: Towards automatic generation of natural language generation systems. In: Proceedings of the 19th International Conference on Computational Linguistics, *Taipei, Taiwan, 24 August – 1 September, 2002.* (2002)

[19] Daelemans, W., van den Bosch, A.: Rapid development of NLP modules with memory-based learning. In: Proceedings of ELSNET in Wonderland, pp. 105-113. Utrecht: ELSNET, 1998. (1998) 105–113

[20] Hardt, D., Rambow, O.: Generation of VP ellipsis: A corpus-based approach. In: Proceedings of the 39th Annual Meeting of the Association for Computational Linguistics, *Toulouse, France, 9–11 July 2001.* (2001) 282–289

[21] Bangalore, S., Rambow, O., Whittaker, S.: Evaluation metrics for generation. In: Proceedings of the 1st International Natural Language Generation Conference, *Mitzpe Ramon, Israel, 12 – 16 June 2000.* (2000) 1–8

Resolving Structural Ambiguity in Generated Speech

Chris Mellish

Department of Computing Science
University of Aberdeen
King's College
ABERDEEN AB24 3UE, UK
cmellish@csd.abdn.ac.uk,
http://www.csd.abdn.ac.uk/~cmellish/

Abstract. Ambiguity in the output is a concern for NLG in general. This paper considers the case of structural ambiguity in spoken language generation. We present an algorithm which inserts pauses in spoken text in order to attempt to resolve potential structural ambiguities. This is based on a simple model of the human parser and a characterisation of a subset of places where local ambiguity can arise. A preliminary evaluation contrasts the success of this method with that of some already proposed algorithms for inserting pauses for this purpose.

1 Avoiding Structural Ambiguity in NLG

When a Natural Language Generation system has precise communicative goals, it is essential that there is as little ambiguity as possible in its output. However, it is rare for an NLG system actually to check that its output is unambiguous, except in restricted places such as referring expression generation. This paper considers *structural ambiguity*, where a generated sentence can have other syntactic analyses than the one which motivated it.[1] When a sentence is structurally ambiguous, it can be misinterpreted by the reader/hearer. For instance, the sentence *He arrived early in May* could be bracketed in at least the two following ways:

He (arrived early) (in May)
He arrived (early in May)

with corresponding different interpretations. Usually structural ambiguity is avoided (if at all) in NLG by hand crafting (limiting) the grammar, but it is hard to do this reliably. To detect any structural ambiguity, it is probably necessary to perform a full syntactic reanalysis of the output, though we are not aware of any system which has actually done this.

---

[1] By "syntactic analysis" here, we refer to the overall shape of a sentence's phrase structure tree, not, for instance, aspects of scope or labelling which are not apparent from that shape.

A. Belz et al. (Eds.): INLG 2004, LNAI 3123, pp. 110–119, 2004.
© Springer-Verlag Berlin Heidelberg 2004

The long-term goal of the current work is to develop complex speech output interfaces for computer users who are unable to use a conventional computer screen. These will be concept-to-speech (CTS) systems expressing information in both natural and artificial languages (e.g. algebra, programming languages). We thus consider both kinds of languages in this work. For such interfaces, communicative effectiveness is much more important than naturalness. Ambiguity is one of the key problems that must be addressed.

In spoken material, some of the ambiguities might be eliminated by clever addition of special lexical items (corresponding perhaps to written punctuation), but using these exhaustively would yield a much more complex string and there is evidence that this would interfere with memorability [15]. *Intonation* must be exploited, not only because it is the key to reducing the working memory burden in general in interfaces for demanding tasks [9], but also because it has the potential to convey the appropriate structure effectively [12].

Unfortunately, work on the relationship between intonation and human syntactic processing has been criticised for not having led to clear theoretical advances [2]. This is largely because, although human speakers do use various cues to indicate intonational structure [12] and such cues can be perceived by human speakers [14], nevertheless speakers do not use the cues reliably [4]. This seems to be at least because:

- Intonation serves many purposes in natural language: resolving structural ambiguity is just one of them.
- Through laziness, ignorance, lack of time etc., a human speaker is not always ideally sensitive to the exact potential problems of the current hearer.

It seems likely that a CTS system could be designed to use certain intonational effects primarily for resolving potential structural ambiguity. Such a system might be able to use a relatively simple intonational model and yet (though perhaps lacking in some naturalness) be effective as a communication interface where it matters. Also such a system could clearly expend a considerable amount of effort in catering for the needs of the hearer. It follows that the confusing story about human intonation should not necessarily deter attempts to use intonation in interfaces specifically to resolve potential structural ambiguities.

That appropriate intonation in synthesised speech is relevant to resolving ambiguity in practical interfaces is demonstrated clearly by Stevens' important work on the reading of algebra expressions to the blind [16], which was based on experimental work of his own and also on [17]. He demonstrated the effectiveness of using pauses, pitch and amplitude in the speech signal to convey structure in arithmetic expressions which (in spoken form) had many possible structural interpretations.

2   Principles for Using Pauses

This paper considers the particular mechanism of inserting pauses in synthesised speech.[2] Standard models of intonation assume that speech is made up of *intonational phrases* of various kinds which are separated by pauses of varying lengths [8]. Following existing work on predicting intonational phrasing [5,7] we make the simplifying assumption that there is a binary decision whether or not to include a pause between any two words in the output. Existing work is able to achieve impressive results at predicting where pauses occur in human speech (precision around 90% and recall around 80%) using information about, for instance, parts of speech, position of words in syntactic structure and distances between words and the start and end of the sentence. This gives an upper bound to what might be achieved by a TTS or CTS system. However, such work is judged by comparing with human intonational phrasing which, as discussed above, is complicated by various factors. It is therefore unclear to what extent these models get the intonation right *when it matters*, i.e. when a mistake would lead to a likely misinterpretation by the hearer.

The systems built by Stevens [15] and Fitzpatrick [3] for speaking algebra expressions to the blind both used pauses among other cues. In this domain, arguably, the only function of pauses in human speech is to convey structure. Unfortunately, Stevens devised special-purpose rules tailored to the particular set of expressions covered. Fitzpatrick use pauses (of 3 different lengths) to indicate the most prominent syntactic boundaries. Other work found evidence of a fine level of structure shown by pauses in algebra expressions read by a French speaker – basically every syntactic boundary was signalled by a proportional pause [6].

Whereas this work on intonation in artificial languages suggests a model where pauses follow syntax rather closely, experiments with natural language [12] suggest that major syntactic boundaries are not always signalled by pauses but that human speakers are more directed about where they choose to insert them. Indeed, intuitively this makes sense for artificial languages as well. For instance the Java expression `System.out.println(''hello'');` might be read aloud as:

```
system dot out dot println string hello
```

There is no potential ambiguity in this utterance and hence no need to design a clever sequence of appropriately sized pauses to indicate its nested structure.

On the other hand, it also seems plausible to provide help in some cases where there is no global ambiguity. For instance, the sentence *Wire A touches the diode, and the green selector switch is in the off position* could be hard to process in spoken form after:

---

[2] We acknowledge that other intonational mechanisms can play a role in structural ambiguity resolution and indeed may be essential in order to achieve naturalness in the output. However, it is relevant to explore to what extent an interface using pauses alone can achieve communicative effectiveness.

```
wire a touches the diode and the green selector switch...
```

because the sentence could end at this point. Some indication of structure corresponding to the written comma might well be useful.

Following these arguments, we hypothesise that a cooperative speaker will introduce pauses in such a way as to resolve parsing problems encountered by the hearer. Thus, for instance, if there is no local or global ambiguity, no special introduction of pauses is necessary. Crucially, this idea depends on the idea of modelling the interpretation processes of the hearer.

3   Modelling the Human Parser

There is an extensive literature on the characteristics of the human parser, and the current work is not attempting to make a new contribution in this area. Rather the intention is to build a simple model broadly compatible with current knowledge and suitable for building into a practical interface. To this end, we have done some preliminary work modelling the human parser as a shift-reduce mechanism. This is motivated by Pereira's demonstration [10] that such a parser can elegantly model certain human attachment preferences (specifically, right association and minimal attachment). Note that our current model takes no account of memory limitations [1,13]. Preliminary experiments using the parser design in [13] suggest, however, that there is not a great deal of difference in performance on our examples.

A shift-reduce parser can be characterised in terms of a *stack* and a sequence of *unseen words*. For simplicity here, we describe a shift-reduce *recogniser*. The presentation also assumes that the language grammar is a context-free grammar (whereas in fact our implementation uses a Definite Clause Grammar). The initial state of the parser is with an empty stack and the given input as the unseen words. At any point in time, the parser may be able to make either of the following moves (possibly in more than one way):

Shift. Look up the first unseen word in the lexicon. Remove this unseen word and push its syntactic category onto the stack.

Reduce. Find a sequence of syntactic categories at the top of the stack which matches the right hand side of a grammar rule. Replace this sequence by the left hand side of the rule.

A final successful state of the recogniser has on the stack just the distinguished symbol of the grammar ("S") and an empty sequence of unseen words.

Table 1 shows an example with two shift-reduce derivations for the sentence *Mary knows many languages you know* (corresponding to two possible structural interpretations). The two derivations share the initial 4 operations but diverge after that point (where a single line is shown). Each line shows the stack (with its top on the right), the unseen words, the operation that gave rise to this situation and the grammar rule used by that operation.

Table 1. Two shift-reduce derivations

Stack	Unseen words	Operation	Rule
	Mary knows many languages you know		
NP	knows many languages you know	Shift	NP → Mary
NP V	many languages you know	Shift	V → knows
NP V D	languages you know	Shift	D → many
NP V D N	you know	Shift	N → languages
NP V NP	you know	Reduce	NP → D N
NP VP	you know	Reduce	VP → V NP
S	you know	Reduce	S → NP VP
S NP	know	Shift	NP → you
S NP VP		Shift	VP → know
S S		Reduce	S → NP VP
S		Reduce	S → S S
	Mary knows many languages you know		
NP	knows many languages you know	Shift	NP → Mary
NP V	many languages you know	Shift	V → knows
NP V D	languages you know	Shift	D → many
NP V D N	you know	Shift	N → languages
NP V D N NP	know	Shift	NP → you
NP V D N NP VP		Shift	VP → know
NP V D N S		Reduce	S → NP VP
NP V D N		Reduce	N → N S
NP V NP		Reduce	NP → D N
NP VP		Reduce	VP → V NP
S		Reduce	S → NP VP

In shift-reduce parsing, the set of operations that are possible in a given state is further reduced by an *oracle*, a cheap test that looks ahead to eliminate obviously unproductive possibilities. In our implementation, an operation is only allowed if as a result the element on the top of the stack can participate in two levels of tree with the previous stack elements (or less if the stack is too short and a left corner of "S" is produced). (Local) ambiguity arises when more than one possible operation is allowed by the oracle. A shift-reduce parser encounters ambiguity in three possible places: shift/shift ambiguity arises when a word is lexically ambiguous, reduce/reduce ambiguity arises when more than one sequence of categories at the top of the stack can be reduced (or a sequence can be reduced in more than one way) and shift/reduce ambiguity arises when both a shift and a reduce are possible at some point. The divergence shown in the table occurs at a point where there is shift/reduce ambiguity.

Pereira showed that the human preference for right association could be modelled in a shift-reduce parser by having the parser always resolve a shift/reduce ambiguity in favour of a shift. Thus in some sense the human parser will always shift when it can and only reduce if there is no alternative. If comprehending the correct structure for a sentence would require a hearer to reduce when a shift is possible, the hearer needs some help at this point.

4 Resolving Shift-Reduce Conflicts

The general anatomy of a shift-reduce conflict can be shown through the above example (in which consistent differences in the pause structure of human readings, corresponding to the two interpretations, were reported by [12]):

<pre>
           A   C   B   D
           | | | |
Mary   knows | many| languages | you   know |
</pre>

Here B marks the actual point in the string that is reached when the shift/reduce ambiguity arises. A and D mark positions that are relevant if a reduce is chosen. A is the left end of the scope of the reduce (strictly speaking a reduce operates on a sequence of categories on the stack, but these correspond to words and phrases in the string). If the reduce is performed then the result is a phrase being recognised between A and B. This phrase may be at the right end of various larger phrases. Eventually one of these will combine with a phrase to the right of B. D marks the place where that other phrase would end. On the other hand, C marks a position relevant only if a shift is performed. If a shift takes place, this one-word phrase will eventually combine with a phrase to the left of it. C marks the rightmost start of a phrase (to the left of B) which will include this one-word phrase.

To force a reduce (not the preferred action, given the human strategy of right association), one could somehow emphasise points A, B and D, which correspond to boundaries that only make sense in this case. Correspondingly, to force a shift one might somehow emphasise point C. Intuitively, inserting pauses at the relevant points could be a plausible way of emphasising them. However, one could argue that highlighting C is unnecessary, since it only serves to reinforce the default shift strategy. Also, points A and D are only somewhat remotely connected to the actual shift/reduce decision. Therefore initially we adopt a strategy of inserting a pause only at point B if a reduce action is required.

For a longer utterance, several possible pauses may need to be introduced. Our strategy is to do this in a left-right manner. That is, first of all the first place where there might be a shift/reduce ambiguity (with a reduce required) is found. A pause is inserted at this point. The parser is then assumed to take the correct decision here and possible derivations continuing from this point are considered. Again the first possible shift/reduce ambiguity (with a reduce required) is found, and so on.

5 Preliminary Evaluation

The evaluation of a model of pause introduction should really involve an assessment of how well an interface using it manages to communicate and whether ambiguity really is avoided. We do not yet have a complete system to evaluate in this way and so have instead carried out a preliminary evaluation by comparing the results of the algorithm with two small sets of data about pauses in human reading reported in the literature. Both of these involved subjects reading small texts with known structural ambiguities in controlled conditions where the subjects were plausibly aware of at least some of the ambiguities.

The "English" Corpus

The study of [12] looked at seven types of structural ambiguities in English sentences (with 5 examples of each). For each sentence and each one of the two possible interpretations, they tested whether hearers could correctly determine the correct interpretation as intended by a human speaker (and generally they could). The example sentences were read in disambiguating contexts and were re-recorded if the experimenters judged from the speech that the context had been misinterpreted. Choosing the first example only for each ambiguity type and the two possible readings gives 14 sentences, with a total of 90 inter-word gaps where pauses could be inserted or not. It was not the main goal of [12] to report on the structure of pauses used by the human speakers, although the paper does give an overview of the main trends identified and we have used this as the basis of defining what the "correct" answer should be. This was the "English" corpus.

The "Maths" Corpus

In an appendix, [15] gives examples of mathematical equations spoken by humans with the main pauses identified (the exact criterion is not stated). Of these, 19 examples can be used directly, with a total of 103 inter-word gaps. Each equation is specified both in terms of words and in terms of standard mathematical notation, and so there is no doubt about the intended structure. This was the "Maths" corpus.

The Algorithms

We tested three different algorithms for pause insertion on the two corpora. SR is the algorithm based on shift-reduce parsing presented in this paper. Top is the algorithm that inserts a pause at the most significant syntactic boundary in a sentence (and nowhere else). Top2 is similar to Top except that it also marks the second most significant syntactic boundary. Thus Top and Top2 are approximations to the algorithm used by Fitzpatrick (who marks the top *three* most significant boundaries, though with the extra complication that his pauses are of different lengths). For the Maths corpus, three-part expressions arise from the use of infix operators and we gave the Top and Top2 algorithms the benefit of the doubt if they placed a pause correctly apart from possibly being on the wrong side of such an operator (we also assumed that repeated "-" and "+" expressions are left-branching, which was always to the benefit of these algorithms).

Table 2. Evaluation of Different Pause-Insertion Algorithms

Algorithm	Corpus	Precision	Recall	F	κ
SR	English	0.95	0.73	0.83	0.75
	Maths	0.83	0.48	0.61	0.48
Top	English	0.81	0.36	0.50	0.21
	Maths	0.83	0.52	0.64	0.48
Top2	Maths	0.74	0.76	0.75	0.41

6   Results

The results of this preliminary evaluation are shown in Table 2. For each algorithm/corpus combination, it shows precision, recall, an F-measurement and a κ value. The F-measurement is calculated as $\frac{2RP}{(R+P)}$. The κ value can be taken informally as something like the F-measurement, but taking into account that a certain number of correct pauses might be expected to be generated by chance.

The preliminary evaluation has many limitations and so its conclusions should not be taken too seriously. The amount of data is very small, it consists of examples devised by hand, and it is not clear what, if anything, it is representative of. We would expect human performance on this task to be somewhat variable, and so more data is required if we are to get really reliable indications. Furthermore, an additional stage of interpretation was required to translate the reported results into precise pause/no pause judgements that could be used as the "gold standard". Nevertheless, the following tendencies are worth noting and exploring in more extensive experiments.

- Precision is almost always better than recall. This could be explained by the human readers inserting pauses not required for ambiguity resolution, even in these carefully selected examples.
- It is interesting that SR performs much better on English than on Maths. It beats Top on the former, but not the latter. There could be some real differences in how people use pauses in the two domains.
- Recall of Top on English is very low, which suggests that for English sentences many pauses occur other than at the most significant syntactic boundary.
- Recall of Top on Maths is fairly low, and yet precision is good. This suggests that a method predicting *additional* pauses may be better. This is the reason why Top2 was attempted on Maths. However, Top2 gains extra recall only at the cost of reduced precision. On Maths, Top produces 6 false positives and 12 false negatives, whereas Top2 produces 21 false positives and 6 false negatives. Algorithms producing pauses additional to Top2 are unlikely to fare well because they will have at least these 21 false positives.
- Looking at the κ values for SR, the value of 0.75 for English ("substantial" agreement, according to some authorities) is encouraging, whereas the value of 0.48 for Maths ("moderate" agreement) is less encouraging.

7   Further Work

The preliminary results suggest that the SR method is worth investigating further, but an immediate priority is to obtain more reliable results about its comparative effectiveness. This will be done ideally through the evaluation of speech information interfaces using the different methods, though perhaps in the shorter term also through the study of larger and more representative corpora of human speech obtained when the goal is clearly that of achieving communicative success, rather than naturalness.

In the longer term, if naturalness of output is important, then a method of introducing pauses for structural ambiguity resolution needs to be integrated with, for instance, existing methods of signalling more detailed syntactic structure [5], information structure and contrast [11,18]. Of course, the information needed to drive such models is not always automatically available in a CTS system, especially if the object being conveyed is something artificial like an algebraic formula or part of someone's computer program. In this case, it needs to be investigated whether the combined method can gracefully degrade or whether completely different approaches have to be devised for the different situations.

References

1. Abney, S.,Johnson, M.: Memory Requirements and Local Ambiguities for Parsing Strategies. Journal of Psycholinguistic Research 20(3) (1991) 233–250
2. Cutler, A., Dahan, D., van Donselaar, W.: Prosody in the Comprehension of Spoken Language: A Literature Review. Language and Speech 20(2) (1997) 141–201
3. Fitzpatrick, D.: Towards Accessible Technical Documents: Production of Speech and Braille Output from Formatted Documents. PhD thesis, School of Computer Applications, Dublin City University (1999)
4. Hirschberg, J.: Communication and Prosody: Functional Aspects of Prosody. Speech Communication 36 (2002) 31–43
5. Hirschberg, J., Prieto, P.: Training Intonational Phrasing Automatically for English and Spanish Text-to-Speech. Speech Communication 18 (1996) 281–290
6. Holm, B., Bailly, G., Laborde, C.: Performance structures of mathematical formulae. Proceedings of the International Congress of Phonetic Sciences, San Francisco, USA (1999) 1297–1300
7. Koehn, P., Abney, S., Hirschberg, J., Collins, M.: Improving Intonational Phrasing with Syntactic Information. Proceedings of ICASSP-00 (2000)
8. Ladd, D.: Intonational Phonology. Cambridge University Press (1996)
9. Paris, C., Thomas, M., Gilson, R., Kincaid, J.: Linguistuc cues and memory for synthetic and natural speech. Human Factors 42(3) (2000) 421–431
10. Pereira, F.: A New Characterisation of Attachment Preferences. In Dowty, D., Karttunen, L., Zwicky, A.: Natural Language Parsing. Cambridge University Press (1985) 307–319
11. Prevost, S.: An Information Structural Approach To Spoken Language Generation. Proceedings of the 34th Annual Meeting of the Association for Computational Linguistics (1996) 294–301

12. Price, P., Ostendorf, M., Shattuck-Hufnagel, S., Fong, C.: The Use of Prosody in Syntactic Disambiguation. J of the Acoustical Society of America 90(6) (1991) 2956–2970
13. Pulman, S.: Grammars, Parsers and Memory Limitations. Language and Cognitive Processes 1(3) (1986) 197–225
14. Sanderman, A., Coller, R.: Prosodic Phrasing and Comprehension. Language and Speech 40(4) (1997) 391–409
15. Stevens, R.: Principles for the Design of Auditory Interfaces to Present Complex Information to Blind People. PhD thesis, University of York (1996)
16. Stevens, R., Edwards, A., Harling, P.: Access to Mathematics for Visually Disabled Students through Multimodal Interaction. Human-Computer Interaction 12 (1997) 47–92
17. Streeter, L.: Acoustic Determinants of Phrase Boundary Perception. J of the Acoustical Society of America 64(6) (1978) 1582–1592
18. Theune, M.: From Data to Speech: Language Generation in Context. PhD thesis, University of Eindhoven (2000)

A Framework for Stylistically Controlled Generation

Daniel S. Paiva[1] and Roger Evans[2]

[1] University of Sussex, Brighton, UK
danielpa@sussex.ac.uk
[2] University of Brighton, Brighton, UK
Roger.Evans@itri.brighton.ac.uk

Abstract. In this paper we describe a framework for stylistic control of the generation process. The approach correlates stylistic dimensions obtained from a corpus-based factor analysis with internal generator decisions, and uses the correlation to direct the generator towards particular style settings. We illustrate this approach with a prototype generator of medical information. We compare our framework with previous approaches according to how they define, characterise and specify style and how effective they are at controlling it, arguing that our framework offers a generic, practical, evaluable approach to the problem of stylistic control.

1 Introduction

One of the potential strengths of natural language generation (NLG) technology over simpler approaches to language production is the possibility of automatically varying the style of language generated. Simple canned text and templates deployed on a large scale can produce apparently quite sophisticated results in a fixed domain (as seen, for example, in sports commentaries in many popular computer games), but effective control over stylistic variation requires a more complex underlying model of the generation process. As attention in the NLG community turns towards wider coverage, more generic technology, research into stylistic control becomes more feasible and more pressing.

But a key hurdle standing in the way of progress towards controlling style is the lack of a clear notion of what style is. Although a number of theories have been developed in a range of subdisplines of linguistics (e.g. Enkvist (1973), Hudson (1980)), few of them offer precise, testable characterisations of style, or replicable experimental results to demonstrate that humans can reliably identify it, let alone algorithms that might allow a computer to do so. So NLG researchers are faced with a number of fundamental problems: there is no clear language for specifying the style desired; there is no clear model of what properties of the text contribute to the style, and hence no guidance as to what a system needs to do to achieve a certain style; and there is no reliable test for determining whether the system has achieved the desired result.

A. Belz et al. (Eds.): INLG 2004, LNAI 3123, pp. 120–129, 2004.

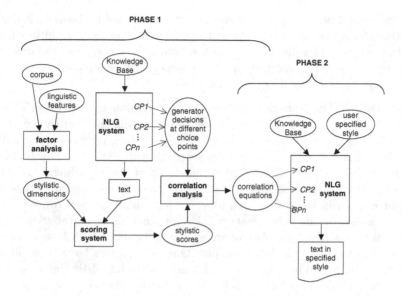

Fig. 1. The framework

In this paper, we present a framework for controlling style in an NLG system which finesses these problems by using statistical techniques. The starting point for the approach is Biber's method for determining dimensions of stylistic variation from a corpus of texts (Biber, 1988). These dimensions establish a multidimensional 'style space' of possible texts in which nearby texts are stylistically similar. We combine this with a generator capable of generating texts in a range of styles, in which a trace of the key decisions made during the generation process is recorded and returned with the text. By correlating the internal decisions of the generator with the stylistic factors associated with the resulting texts, across the whole range of generator outputs, we determine conditions on each choice point which can be used to guide the generator towards a particular target location in the style space. Success can be judged by measuring how close the actual output text score is to that target location.

2   The Framework

The overall architecture of the framework has two phases, as shown in figure 1. The goal of the first phase is to derive correlation equations relating internal generator decisions to surface stylistic features. We do this in three steps: (1) using a factor analysis to determine stylistic dimensions from a corpus of texts, which provides both a style space and a way of locating a given text within that space — by giving a text a style 'score' in each dimension; (2) free generation of texts (in the same domain as the corpus), recording a trace of the generator's decisions at key choice points $(CP1, \ldots, CPn)$ plus the style score for the resulting text; (3) finding a correlation between these two sets of data.

In the second phase the correlation equations are used in the same generation algorithm to control the behaviour at the choice points: each potential choice is scored according to its likely effect on the final style scores, and the one taking the generator closest to the user-specified target score is selected.

The key components of the framework are:

Factor Analysis The statistical factor analysis component uses Biber's method (1988)[3]. Each text in a corpus is analysed by counting the occurrence of easily detectable 'linguistic features', such as use of pronouns, passives and auxiliaries (Biber had 67 such features). These feature profiles are normalised for text length and used to derive 'factors'. Factors are made up of groups of linguistic features that are correlated (positively or negatively) with each other: each feature makes a weighted contribution to the overall score for the factor, according to its frequency relative to the other features. Factor analysis is a statistical method which seeks to derive a number of independent factors which best account for the variation found in the input corpus. Once the factors have been obtained, any text can be scored by counting occurrences of the linguistic features, normalising for text length and feeding into the factor definition equation. The scores for the texts in the original corpus give an indication of the overall extent of the style space in terms of factor scores.

Natural Language Generator The particular details of the generation algorithm are not critical for the framework as a whole. The key requirement is that the major choice points within the algorithm are clearly defined, since these are the points at which we control it. In any given generation instance, from input to a particular text, two sets of data can be produced — (1) a trace of the internal decisions the generator took, and (2) the set of linguistic feature counts of the resulting text, which in turn can be used to compute factor scores. It is these two sets of data, across a wide range of freely generated documents, that we correlate. We then run the generator in a more constrained mode, where its decision at the choice points is determined by the effect each choice has on the overall factor scores, with the goal of producing a single text with scores as close as possible to a user-supplied target[4].

Correlational Analysis This component is used to correlate generator's decisions and stylistic scores. Using a multivariate linear regression technique (although other techniques can be envisaged), we obtain correlation equations associated with each potential decision, indicating how making that choice is likely to affect the overall factor score of the resulting text.

It is important to realise that the choices made by the generator do not need to be directly associated with the linguistic features used to determine factor scores (although in some cases they may be, for example, the choice to

---

[3] The method has also been replicated with several other corpora (e.g. Sigley (1997), Lee (1999)).

[4] This is, of course, just a simple best-first search strategy which may not always reach the best overall solution.

select a passive grammar rule may well correlate with the presence of passive constructions in the text). The approach assumes only that these two ways of measuring the system's behaviour (choice point tracing and factor scores) can be statistically correlated, and hence that one can be used as a proxy measure of the other. A further important assumption is that the variation observed, both in the input corpus and the generator choice points, is *free* variation, unconstrained by functional requirements of the input or context. This does not preclude the generator from making such decisions, but the statistical correlation and control is only applied to the residual 'free choice' possibilities.

3   Example

We have implemented this framework in a proof-of-concept system which generates paragraph-length subsections of 'patient information leaflets'. In this section we provide an overview of the main features and results.

We used a corpus of just over 300 texts taken from proprietary patient information leaflets. These were part-of-speech tagged using Brill's tagger (Brill, 1994), counts for all of Biber's 67 linguistic features were obtained for each text, and the counts were normalised to a standard document length of 1000 words. A factor analysis over this data revealed two independent factors, each containing a subset of the original linguistic features[5]. The two factors determine a two-dimensional style space, and by scoring the original corpus against them, we get an idea of the extent of the overall style space. The factor analysis aims to give the best account of variability, rather than produce factors with intuitive interpretations. Nevertheless it is possible to interpret the factors approximately as follows:[6]

Factor 1 ranges from texts that try to be involved with reader (high positive score) to text that try to be distant from the reader (high negative score)

Factor 2 ranges from texts with pronominal reference and verbal style (high positive score) to text that use full nominal reference (high negative score)

The generator comprises six modules: input constructor, split network, network ordering, referring expression generation, NP pruning, and a sentence realiser (see figure 2[7]). Briefly, the input constructor creates a (paragraph-sized) semantic network representing the content of part of a patient information leaflet, using information from the medicine database. This network is split into sentence-sized subnetworks, which are then ordered. Referring expression generation extends the network by adding pronominal referents (using a module developed in the RICHES system (Cahill et al., 2001)), and the noun-phrase representations thereby made redundant are pruned. The realiser is a re-implementation

---

[5] Biber's original work on a more varied corpus produced seven factors, although in later publications the more minor dimensions were discarded.

[6] The results of our factor analysis and more detail about the corpus used in the study can be found in (Paiva, 2000).

[7] Dotted lines show the control flow and the straight lines show data flow.

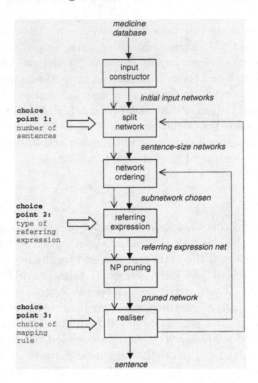

Fig. 2. Generator choice points

of Nicolov's algorithm (Nicolov, 1999) using the LEXSYS wide-coverage lexi-calised grammar (Carroll et al., 2000).

The choice points are the specific places in this architecture where non-determinism is present and, therefore, can have an impact in variation of the style of the texts produced. The choices available are related to: (1) the number of sentences into which an input network can be split, (2) the type of referring expression that is generated as the description of an object, and (3) the choice of final syntactic structure that will be associated with a piece of semantic representation (i.e., the choice of which mapping rule is used).

From a single input representation corresponding to three short paragraphs, we produced 600,000 different texts (with choice point traces) and from these we selected three random samples of respectively 1000, 1000 and 5000 instances to use in the correlation analysis. We used multivariate linear regression as our correlation technique and for each sample we obtained two equations, one for each stylistic dimension. Each equation has the form $SD^i = x^1GD^1 + \ldots + x^nGD^n$, where SD^i is the score in the stylistic dimension i, x^j's are weights for the counts of the respective generator decisions (GD^j's). These correlation equations were introduced into the generator in such a way that, at each choice point, all the possible generator decisions that could be applied would be used to calculate stylistic scores representing the possible next steps in the process

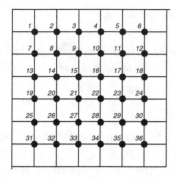

Fig. 3. Target style scores

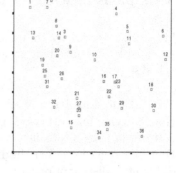

Fig. 4. Result style scores

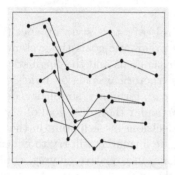

Fig. 5. Factor 1 fit

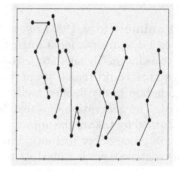

Fig. 6. Factor 2 fit

and these would be ordered with respect to their distance to the target scores (i.e., those specified by the user).

To test the framework, we ran the generator on a single input with thirty-six different target style settings, in a six-by-six grid spanning the whole style space (that is, the full range of variation observed in the generated corpus) – see figure 3. The resulting texts were scored to locate them in this style space, and the results are shown in figure 4. Figures 5 and 6 highlight these results for each factor separately — each line in figure 5 corresponds to a fixed setting of factor 1, and in a perfect system the lines would be the horizontal grid lines of figure 3 (and similarly in figure 6 for factor 2 and the vertical grid lines).

In general the results are fairly good: the system is able to generate across the whole range of the style space and guide its output to the target area of the style space in most cases. The correlation (R^2) of results with target values for factor 1 was 0.71, and for factor 2 was 0.95. The performance on factor 1 is not as good as on factor 2 because of non-linearity in the correlation which affected the margin of error considerably, but the factor 2 results are very encouraging[8]

---

[8] More advanced non-linear regression techniques may improve the results on factor 1.

4   Comparison with Other Approaches

In this section we briefly compare our approach to previous systems designed for, or capable of, controlling style. We consider the following issues in relation to each system:

1. What is the **definition** of style used by the system?
2. How is style **characterised**, for example, are there particular properties or features of texts which determine style?
3. How can style be **controlled** by the user, what is the language in which different stylistic options are specified?
4. How **effective** is the overall approach, how well can the system achieve the user's desired style?

Pauline (Hovy, 1988) offers the user control over text style by specifying values for 'conversational setting', and for the pragmatic goals the system will try to achieve. To mediate between the pragmatic goals and the linguistic features that could realise them, the system has 'rhetorical goals of style' which encode informally defined stylistic dimensions (e.g., formality, simplicity, detail, force). The generation of a text to realise a particular rhetorical goal of style is performed by taking the appropriate heuristic decisions at each point in the generation process. For instance, if a text needs to be formal, it will try to generate long sentences with causal or temporal relations, use relative clauses, conjoin sentences, include adjectives and adverbs, and use formal words. A monitoring module controls the achievement of the stylistic goals and the choice of the *least-satisfied* goal as the strategy for conflict resolution.

In terms of the questions specified above, the *definition* of style is informal, based on the researcher observation, and its *characterisation* is also informal, through its implementation in the generator heuristics. The *control* available to the user is in terms of the style definitions, plus the rather indirect notion of conversational setting, but use of discrete values for styles and the indirect link between goals and generator heuristics limit the *effectiveness* of the generator in achieving a particular desired style.

DiMarco (1990) manually constructed a stylistic grammar for sentences based on the notion of norm and deviation from the norm using a corpus of journalistic texts. In her three level grammar, the top level represented three stylistic dimensions: *clarity*, *concreteness*, and *staticness*, the middle level contained rules expressing the notions of *balance*, *dominance* and *position* of stylistic properties in a sentence, and the bottom level contained the *primitive elements* of the grammar, linking to concrete syntax. All of these levels were defined in terms of discrete graded values.

Green's generator (Green, 1992; Green and DiMarco, 1993) used DiMarco's grammar in a stylistic module to control the Penman realiser. For a given stylistic goal specified by the user, the system generates all possible realisations, represented as lists of primitive elements, according to the style grammar. It then realises elements sequentially, filtering and ranking the list of realisations in order to prefer continuations that are most compatible with what has already been realised.

In relation to our comparison criteria, the *definition* of style is again informal, based on a manual analysis of a corpus (and rather different to the previous case), and defined in terms of variance from a norm, which is likely to be genre-specific. The *characterisation* of style is quite well formalised in terms of the style grammar, so that in principle one can determine what features of a text determine or arise from a stylistic setting. The *control* is in terms of three high level, rather abstract, stylistic dimensions with discrete values, and the *effectiveness* of the system is probably somewhat limited by this.

Halogen (Langkilde-Geary, 2002) is a sentence realiser based on a two-stage architecture: the first module is a symbolic generator which produces a forest with all the possible realisations for a given input, and the second module is a filter, a statistical ranker, that uses n-gram language models (i.e., unigram, bigram and trigram models) to extract the top ranked phrases from a forest. Halogen is not designed with stylistic control particularly in mind: the main goal is to allow the core generator to overgenerate and then use a corpus-trained model to filter out unacceptable texts. However, by training the system on a corpus of a particular style, it seems likely that it would be able to effectively generate in that style, and so some degree of stylistic control is possible.

Halogen's *definition* of style is thus entirely corpus-based — it relies on being trained on a corpus in a single consistent style, as chosen by the trainer. Its *characterisation* of style is entirely incorporated into the language model it learns, and hence is an effectively computable characterisation, but not intuitively understandable. *Control* of the system is essentially through use of different language models, so the input style setting can be as varied as the corpora available for training. The *effectiveness* of the approach depends partly on the availability of good training data, but is also restricted by the statistical method used, which will provide a 'normalising' view of style — the system will tend towards producing 'average' texts, even if more deviant possibilities are also acceptable within the stylistic space.

The present framework also has a corpus-based *definition* of style, defined in terms of correlations of occurrences of primitive linguistic features. Thus the *characterisation* of style also is encapsulated in a statistical model, although the use of these features rather than n-grams does offer more scope for intuitive interpretations of the model. The *control* offered to the user is multidimensional and continuous, ranging over the evident variability in a single training corpus. Although there is no guarantee that the dimensions are intuitive, the system's behaviour can be understood in terms of the variability in its training corpus, and its *effectiveness* can be measured statistically with reference to that corpus.

5 Conclusion

In this paper, we have described a generic framework for controlling variation in an NLG system. The approach we have taken is generic in two significant ways.

First, it is generic in its approach to defining stylistic variation: it is trained by providing a corpus containing a range of styles and thereafter can be controlled to generate texts within the stylistic space implicitly defined by that corpus. This contrasts with approaches which use a pre-defined theoretical or informal notion of style, and also with approaches which train on a corpus defining a particular style — our corpus determines stylistic variation, not a single style. Furthermore it is not necessary to interpret the dimensions it uses as traditional 'styles' in order to evaluate the system, although it is possible and useful to do so for practical use. Second, the framework is in principle independent of the particular generation algorithm used, as long as it has the coverage to generate across the stylistic range, and identifiable decision points within its execution trace.

We illustrated the approach with a prototype implementation which provides stylistic variation in the generation of sections of medical leaflets, using a generator with limited domain coverage. In future work we aim to apply the approach to an existing wide-coverage realiser, with a view to exploring how well the framework scales to a more complex stylistic space and a different generation architecture. We are also interested in exploring the role of the particular language features used Biber's approach, and the extent to which such techniques can be used to control grammaticality and readability.

References

Biber, D. (1988), Variation across speech and writing. Cambridge University Press, Cambridge.

Brill, E. (1994) Some advances in rule-based part of speech tagging. In Proceedings of the AAAI'94 Conference, Seattle, USA.

Cahill, L., J. Carroll, R. Evans, D. Paiva, R. Power, D. Scott, and K. van Deemter (2001) From RAGS to RICHES: exploiting the potential of a flexible generation archi-tecture. In Proceedings of ACL/EACL 2001, Toulouse, France, pp. 98–105.

Carroll, J., N. Nicolov, O. Shaumyan, M. Smets, and D. Weir (2000) Engineering a wide-coverage lexicalized grammar. In Proceedings of the Fifth International Workshop on Tree Adjoining Grammars and Related Frameworks, Paris, France, pp. 55–60.

DiMarco, C. (1990) Computational Stylistics for Natural Language Translation. PhD Thesis, tech. rep. CSRI-239, University of Toronto, Canada.

Enkvist, N.E. (1973), Linguistic Stylistics. Mouton.

Green, S.J. (1992) A functional theory of style for natural language generation. MSc Thesis, University of Waterloo, Canada.

Green, S.J., and C. DiMarco (1993) Stylistic decision-making in NLG. In Proceedings of the 4th European Workshop on Natural Language Generation. Pisa, Italy.

Hovy, E. (1988) Generating natural language under pragmatic constraints. Lawrence Erlbaum Associates.

Hudson, R.A. (1980) Sociolinguistics. Cambridge University Press.

Lee, D. (1999) Modelling Variation in Spoken And Written English: the multi-dimensional approach revisited, PhD Thesis, University of Lancaster.

Langkilde-Geary, I. (2002) An Empirical Verification of Coverage and Correctness for a General-Purpose Sentence Generator. In Proceedings of the second International Conference on Natural Language Generation, New York, USA, pp. 17–24.

Nicolov, N. (1999) Approximate Text Generation from Non-hierarchical Representations in a Declarative Framework. PhD Thesis, University of Edinburgh.

Paiva, D.S. (2000) Investigating style in a corpus of pharmaceutical leaflets: results of a factor analysis. In Proceedings of the Student Workshop of the 38th Annual Meeting of the Association for Computational Linguistics (ACL'2000), Hong Kong, China..

Sigley (1997) Sigley, R. (1997) Text categories and where you can stick them: a crude formality index. International Journal of Corpus Linguistics, 2 (2), pp. 199–237.

SEGUE: A Hybrid Case-Based Surface Natural Language Generator

Shimei Pan and James Shaw

IBM T.J. Watson Research Center
19 Skyline Drive
Hawthorne, NY 10532
shimei@us.ibm.com, shawjc@us.ibm.com

Abstract. This paper presents SEGUE, a hybrid surface natural language generator that employs case-based paradigm but performs rule-based adaptations. It uses an annotated corpus as its knowledge source and employs grammatical rules to construct new sentences. By using *adaptation-guided retrieval* to select cases that can be adapted easily to the desired output, SEGUE simplifies the process and avoids generating ungrammatical sentences. The evaluation results show the system generates grammatically correct sentences (91%), but disfluency is still an issue.

1 Introduction

This paper presents an overview of SEGUE, a hybrid system that combines both case-based reasoning (CBR) and rule-based approaches for natural language generation (NLG). CBR is a machine learning paradigm that reuses prior solutions to solve new problems [1, 2]. It is closely related to instance-based learning where the representation of the instances is simpler (e.g. feature vectors).

There are several approaches to build a surface generator. Template-based systems are easy to develop, but the text they produce lacks variety. Rule-based systems, on the other hand, can produce more varied text, but developers with linguistic sophistication are required to develop and maintain the generators. Recently, statistics-based generation systems have achieved some success [3, 4, 5]. The main deterrent to the use of statistics-based generators is that they require a large training corpus. Without enough training instances, their performance degrades. A hybrid case-based generator can work with a relatively small annotated corpus. Because it uses rule-based adaptation to ensure the adapted sentences are grammatically correct, the hybrid generator is more accurate than statistical ones. More significantly, because CBR has learning capability, case-based generators can perform tasks more efficiently as they accumulate solutions.

This paper offers three significant contributions. First, we propose a case-based natural language generator with high accuracy that only requires a small corpus, thus easier to incorporate into applications than other corpus-based approaches. Second, We use rule-based adaptation operators to ensure that the

A. Belz et al. (Eds.): INLG 2004, LNAI 3123, pp. 130–140, 2004.

generated sentences are grammatically correct, a property that other corpus-based approaches cannot guarantee. Third, to our knowledge, our work is the first to incorporate *adaptation-guided retrieval* in a case-based NLG system. Case retrieval in SEGUE is not only based on a similarity measure, but also on how easily the retrieved cases can be adapted to the desired outputs.

In the remainder of the paper, Section 2 provides an overview of SEGUE's system architecture. Section 3 describes the representation of cases in the case repository. The details of the case-based generation process are described in Section 4. An evaluation experiment of the generator is described in Section 5. Related work is discussed in Section 6. Section 7 summarizes our results and discusses future work.

2   System Overview

SEGUE is a domain independent surface generator currently embedded in a multimodal dialogue system called RealHunter[6]. Users interact with the system to identify potential real estate they would like to purchase in a particular region. Below is an example of a user interacting with RealHunter:

> **User**: Show houses in the north.
>
> **RealHunter**: I found 145 houses in northern Westchester county. I cannot display all the houses at once. Please give me more constraints.
>
> **User**: Show houses along the Hudson River.
>
> **RealHunter**: I found 23 houses based on your criteria. I cannot display all the houses at once. Steve. You can specify more constraints using asking price.
>
> **User**: Just those with brick sidings.
>
> **RealHunter**: I found 2 houses in northern Westchester County with brick sidings next to the Hudson River Shore. The houses are a Colonial and a Cape cod. House features, such as asking price and city name, are displayed on the screen.

In the first and second responses, RealHunter's strategic component determined that there are too many houses to display on the screen, so it asks for more constraints to reduce the number of retrieved houses. In the third response, the first sentence is formulated by using revision operators described in Section 4.2. In the second sentence, a conjunction operator is used.

Figure 1 shows the architecture of SEGUE. Similar to the standard NLG architecture, the dialogue system has a content planner that creates semantic representations. SEGUE takes the specified semantic information and transforms it into sentences. Its knowledge resource is a case repository. In the repository, each training sentence is associated with a semantic representation of the sentence (SemGraph), and a realization tree (ReaTree), its corresponding syntactic lexical representation. Further details of the SemGraphs and ReaTrees can be found in [7]. Text generation in SEGUE has three phases: *retrieval, adaptation,* and *learning*. In the retrieval phase, the SemGraph$_I$[1] is compared with Sem-

---

[1] In the rest of the paper, we use SemGraph$_I$ for "input semantic graph", and SemGraph$_C$ for "semantic graphs in the case repository."

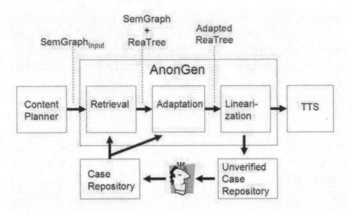

Fig. 1. Architecture of SEGUE

Graphs in the case repository to identify a ranked list of similar SemGraphs for later adaptation. In the adaptation phase, SEGUE applies one or more adaptation operators to the ReaTrees corresponding to the SemGraphs identified in the retrieval phase. After the adaptation, the adapted ReaTree is sent to a linearization module which handles subject-verb agreements and other boundary friction issues [8]. In the learning phase, the SemGraph$_I$, its corresponding adapted ReaTree, and the generated sentences are first stored in a temporary case repository. These new cases are manually verified before being incorporated into the main case repository for future reuse. Currently, SEGUE sends the generated sentences to a commercial TTS system to transform them into speech. SEGUE is implemented in Java. On a 1.8-GHz P4-M machine with 512 MB memory, it takes about 0.2 seconds to generate sentences with an average length of 23 words.

3   Case Repository

The corpus used to establish SEGUE's case repository is described in [7]. A Sem-Graph in the case repository contains a list of propositions. A proposition represents roughly a clause-sized information, as shown in Figure 2. Other information in a SemGraph includes speech act and theme/rheme information. The Sem-Graphs in the case repository support the computation of similarity measures in the retrieval phase.

The ReaTrees in the case repository are mainly used during the adaptation phase. A ReaTree contains a SemGraph ID and recursive phrase structures. The SemGraph ID establishes the correspondence between a SemGraph and a ReaTree. Because there can be several paraphrases for a particular SemGraph, multiple ReaTrees might have the same SemGraph ID. A ReaPhrase corresponds to a syntactic phrase that in turn contains recursive ReaPhrases and ReaWords, as shown in Figure 2. A ReaPhrase typically has 4 attributes, *reference, syntactic*

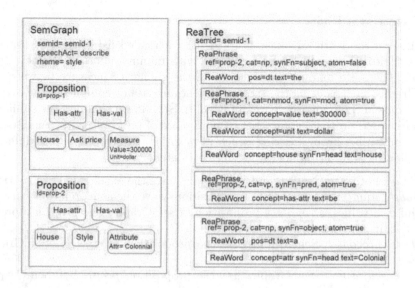

Fig. 2. The SemGraph and ReaTree for "The 300,000 dollar house is a Colonial."

category, syntactic function, and *atomicity.* The *reference* attribute points to a specific proposition in the corresponding SemGraph. The *syntactic category* attribute specifies whether a ReaPhrase is realized as a noun phrase, an adjective phrase, or etc. The *syntactic function* attribute specifies that either the phrase is a subject, predicate, object, complement, or modifier. The *atomicity* attribute indicates that either the phrase realizes only one proposition or it is a composition of multiple propositions. A ReaWord typically has the following attributes: *concept, syntactic function,* and *text.* The *concept* attribute points to a particular semantic relation or concept in the proposition. The *syntactic function* attribute specifies whether the ReaWord is the head of a ReaPhrase. The *text* attribute represents the surface string used to realize the *concept.*

Depending on the complexity of the desired output sentences, the number of instances needed varies widely for different applications. Furthermore, this number is greatly influenced by the type of information annotated in the case repository. Brown [9] demonstrated that by encoding more linguistic information into a machine translation system, he reduced the required number of instances by a factor of six or more while retaining comparable translation quality. Currently there are 210 instances in the repository for the real-estate application.

4   Algorithm

The generation process in SEGUE has three phases: *retrieval, adaptation,* and *learning.*

4.1   Retrieval Phase

The goal of the retrieval phase is to identify a ranked list of instances in the case repository that can later be adapted with minimal effort to the new Sem-Graph. There are many ways to compute the similarity measure between two SemGraphs, such as using the string-edit distance [10] or computing the overlap of concepts in the semantic representation. In SEGUE, we compute the similarity measure based on the distance between all pairs of propositions in SemGraph$_C$ and SemGraph$_I$. From knowing which propositions are the same and different, the following adaptation operators can be created:

- *null()*: both SemGraph$_C$ and SemGraph$_I$ have the exact same propositions.
- *substitution(prop$_C$,prop$_I$)*: the propositions have the same relation but with different values. *Prop$_C$* is a proposition in SemGraph$_C$ and *prop$_I$* is a proposition in SemGraph$_I$.
- *deletion(prop$_C$)*: SemGraph$_C$ has the proposition *prop$_C$*, but SemGraph$_I$ does not.
- *insertion(prop$_I$)*: SemGraph$_I$ has the proposition *prop$_I$*, but SemGraph$_C$ does not.

At this point in the retrieval process, even though which operation will be applied is known, whether it can be applied successfully is unknown. To retrieve cases with a high chance to be adapted successfully, we employ a technique known as *adaptation-guided retrieval* in CBR, where adaptation knowledge is integrated into the retrieval process. The rational behind this is that the most similar case may not be the most useful and easiest to adapt [11, 12]. As a result, we used the adaptation cost as the basis for case retrieval in SEGUE. The adaptation cost is estimated based on how likely an adaptation operator is to be successful. The cost for a *null* operator is zero. When applying a *substitution* operator, the overall sentence structure and the grammaticality of the final sentence are likely preserved. As a result, the cost of a *substitution* operator is relatively small. In contrast, the cost of applying *deletion* operators is higher because syntactic constituents are removed from the ReaTree$_C$ and might render the final sentences ungrammatical. The *insertion* operators have the highest cost because multiple sentences are involved and there are more opportunities for them to create ungrammatical sentences. By assigning lower cost to operators more likely to produce grammatically correct sentences, the retrieval in SEGUE is adaptation-guided.

Using only the adaptation operator cost described above, SEGUE sometimes still retrieves cases that are very similar at the semantic level, but are difficult to adapt at the syntactic level. This problem is particularly pronounced when the proposition realizing the main structure of the retrieved ReaTree is to be deleted. The following example illustrates the situation:

SemGraph$_I$: The {1995} house is a {Colonial}.

SemGraph$_C$: The {1995} {Colonial} house is {in Ardsley}.

In this example, SemGraph$_I$ is sent to SEGUE, and SemGraph$_C$ is retrieved for adaptation. Since the house attribute, *located-in-city*, does not exist in

SemGraph$_I$, the phrases that express this information will be deleted from the ReaTree$_C$. In this particular example, applying the *deletion* operator to ReaTree$_C$ will remove both the verb "is" and the complement "in Ardsley" and render the generated sentence incomplete: "*The 1995 Colonial house." To prevent deletion of main verbs, we assign high costs to SemGraph candidates that do not share the main syntactic structure. This is another case of adaptation-guided retrieval. Later we will show it simplifies the *deletion* operation during adaptation.

4.2   Adaptation Phase

After the retrieval phase, a short list of similar SemGraphs have been retrieved and the list of adaptation operators to be applied for each SemGraph is computed. Among all the adaptation operators, we apply *deletion* before *insertion*. Because the operators manipulate the intermediate ReaTree, reducing the size of ReaTree first also reduces the complexity.

We have explored both statistical and rule-based approaches for adaptation. Currently, the rule-based approach is used because it requires fewer instances.

Substitution Operator The *substitution* operator takes two parameters: the proposition *prop$_I$* from SemGraph$_I$ and its corresponding proposition *prop$_C$* from SemGraph$_C$. Using the *ref* attribute in the ReaTree$_C$, a list of ReaPhrases matching the proposition *prop$_C$* is retrieved. Then the operator goes through each ReaWord inside the retrieved ReaPhrases, verifying if the concept in each ReaWord is the same as those in the proposition *prop$_I$*. If they differ, a substitution appropriate for the particular concept is applied. After all ReaWords in the retrieved ReaPhrases are substituted, these ReaPhrases would convey the information expressed in the proposition, *prop$_I$*.

Deletion Operator In the retrieval phase, adaptation-guided retrieval is used to ensure that the proposition corresponding to the main structure of the retrieved ReaTree will not be deleted during the adaptation phase. This effort allows the *deletion* operators to be simple and ensures the soundness of the main sentence structure.

Deletion in SEGUE is basically a reverse-aggregation process. In the aggregation process, there are usually two ways to add new information into an existing sentence: *paratactic* or *hypotactic* transformations [13, 14]. Paratactic operators involve syntactically equivalent constituents, usually conjunctions. In contrast, hypotactic operators involve subordinate or modifying constructions, such as adjective or prepositional phrases. In SEGUE, there are two types of deletion: hypotactic and paratactic. For deleting hypotactic constructions, the *deletion* operator first recursively inspects all the ReaPhrases in the ReaTree$_C$ to retrieve those that express the propositions to be deleted. This is done through checking the *ref* attribute inside each ReaPhrase. If the *atomicity* attribute in the retrieved ReaPhrase is true, meaning it only expressed the proposition indicated in the *ref* attribute, then the ReaPhrase is removed from the ReaTree; otherwise, the system recursively inspects the subtree until an atomic ReaPhrase conveying the proposition is found. To delete constituents in paratactic constructions, a special procedure is used to ensure that the conjunctor "and" or "or" will be deleted or shifted to a grammatical correct position in the resulting phrase.

Insertion Operator *Insertion* operator is the most complex operator of all the adaptation operators. For propositions in the SemGraph$_I$ that do not exist in SemGraph$_C$, SEGUE incorporates ReaPhrases from various instances in the repository. In SEGUE, insertion is performed through two aggregation operations: *paratactic* and *hypotactic* operations.

Paratactic Operations. Without many training instances, conjunction is difficult to handle using pure case-based approaches. In SEGUE, paratactic operators use rules to avoid adding many instances. Currently, SEGUE supports two common types of paratactic operations: *quantification* ("**3** houses are Colonials. **1** is a Tudor."), and *simple conjunction* ("the names of the school districts are Lakeland School District **and** Panas School District.").

Both quantification and simple conjunction are performed mainly based on the semantic representations. When propositions from the SemGraph$_I$ are merged into the final ReaTree, the concepts in the new proposition are compared with the concepts in the final ReaTree. Depending on the results of the comparisons, the proposition is either merged into the final ReaTree using quantification or simple conjunction operator, or stored away, waiting to be realized as a part of a separate sentence. Currently, quantification and conjunctions in subject and object positions are implemented.

Hypotactic Operations. Hypotactic operators are the most used *insertion* operators in SEGUE. Applying hypotactic operators is a two-step process. In the first step, all the ReaTrees in the case repository are inspected to extract ReaPhrases that express the missing propositions. During this extraction process, the head modified by the extracted ReaPhrase is remembered, together with whether the ReaPhrase is used as a premodifier or post-modifier. In the second step, the extracted ReaPhrase is attached to the head constituent in the final ReaTree. Because SEGUE prefers ReaPhrases that can be realized in the shortest character length, a substitution operation (same as in Section 4.2) is performed on each of the extracted ReaPhrases to measure its length before selecting the shortest candidate. This heuristic results in the generation of concise sentences.

The hypotactic transformation operations in traditional rule-based generators also have these two similar steps [14]. In the first step, the rule-based system transforms the missing propositions into modifying constructions through a complex lexical process, which, in some cases, is domain dependent. In SEGUE, this transformation step is replaced by the extraction process to identify modifying constructions from the instances in the repository, which is much simpler and less error prone than the rule-based process. The second step in rule-based systems, attaching the modifying constructions to the final syntactic tree, is similar in SEGUE.

To ensure a variety of syntactic constructions in the generated sentence, we apply paratactic operators first because they have more restrictive preconditions. By applying them first, less restrictive hypotactic operators won't prevent paratactic operators from being applied. There are other ways to add new information into a sentence, such as through nominalization [13]. SEGUE currently generates these constructions by adding them into the case repository.

4.3   Learning Phase

If the operator applied in the adaptation phase is not trivial, the new SemGraph and adapted ReaTree are added to the case repository. For the purpose of text generation, an adaptation is considered non-trivial if either *deletion* or *insertion* operator is applied. If only *substitution* operator is applied, new case is not added to the case repository. Because not all the "learned" cases are fluent and grammatically correct, the "learned" cases are stored in a temporary case repository. Periodically, we manually run tests on those learned cases before integrating them into the repository.

Comparing to knowledge-intensive approaches, the CBR approach can learn from past experiences and become faster and more accurate over time. In rule-based generation systems [13, 14], however, a complex sentence is always built from scratch in a bottom-up manner – starting from a nucleus proposition and each satellite proposition is attached sequentially afterward. When a sentence is complex, such a revision process is inefficient. In SEGUE, once a solution is proposed and verified, it can be incorporated into the case repository. Next time the system encounters similar requests, it shortcuts the process and reuses the old solution. This speeds up the process tremendously and decreases the likelihood of making mistakes during the assembling of complex sentences from pieces.

5   Evaluation

This evaluation focuses on the generation of assertive sentences related to house attributes. SEGUE also generates sentences expressing other speech acts, such as expressive ones ("I am sorry."), questions, and commands. In this real-estate application, a typical house has about 20 main attributes (e.g., asking price, property tax, and city location). During evaluation, we created a repository of 20 SemGraphs, with each SemGraph expressing a different attribute of a house. Using these SemGraphs as candidates, we exhaustively generated all combinations with maximum 5 propositions[2]. 100 of the 21,699 synthesized SemGraphs

---

[2] Since generating all combinations in this setting is an exponential process, to make this possible, we restricted each sentence to have a maximum of 5 propositions. The number 5 is chosen because the number of propositions in a SemGraph from the content planner is almost always less than 5.

are randomly selected and sent to SEGUE to be transformed into sentences. Although the current setup led to empirically rare inputs, it gives an objective account of the generator's performance. If the semantic inputs are collected from natural interactions with users, SEGUE is likely to perform even better.

Two human evaluators graded the sentences using 3 ratings: **good** means all the sentences generated from a SemGraph are grammatical[3]; **minor grammatical error** indicates that some of the sentences have minor grammatical errors, such as subject-verb agreement; **major grammatical/pragmatic error** indicates that the sentences have major grammatical or pragmatic problems. Whenever there is a disagreement in the ratings, the evaluators reached an agreement after discussion. 91% of the generated cases were classified as **good**. There were no (0%) **minor grammatical errors**, and all the **major grammatical/pragmatic errors** (9%) involve multiple sentences and were caused by the lack of a referring expression module. For example, in the sentence "I found 3 Colonial houses with 0.2 acre of land. *The house* has an asphalt roof.", the subject in the second sentence should be a plural noun. For a baseline, we consider a substitution-only generator provided with the same input, using the same corpus instances as SEGUE. Under a best case assumption, each of the 210 corpus instances encodes a unique combination of propositions. Since only those input SemGraphs containing the identical set of propositions would be handled correctly by the baseline generator, this would result in a probability of less than 1% (210/21699) of the SemGraphs being generated correctly.

In our evaluation, we did find instances where the generated sentences are grammatically correct, but contained disfluencies. In addition to sentences that are too long, disfluencies are often caused by the lack of referring expression module and inadequate adaptation operators. An example of inadequate adaptation operator occurred in the sentence "?I found 2 2-bedroom houses" where the two numbers appeared consecutively and sounds quite strangely without proper prosody. A better sentence to be generated is "I found 2 houses with 2 bedrooms" Other disfluencies include awkward modifier ordering, such as "?a Colonial 1995 house" instead of "a 1995 Colonial house." We believe after adding a referring expression module and incorporating more corpus information to address disfluency issues, many of the major grammatical/pragmatic errors and disfluencies will be resolved.

6   Related Work

In recent years, researchers have successfully applied machine learning techniques to the generation task [3, 4, 5, 15, 16]. These works can be described as "overgeneration-and-ranking"[17]. In these works, a large number of candidates are first generated either using corpus information or rule-based transformations. Then, an evaluation function is used to rank these candidates to pick out the best one to realize the desired input. Except for IGEN [16], they required large

---

[3] Based on a sentence boundary determination algorithm, Segue may generate more than one sentence from a SemGraph$_I$.

corpora for training. If they use grammatical rules, these rules are used during the overgeneration stage and not in the ranking stage [3, 4]. In contrast, our work can be described as "retrieve-and-adapt". SEGUE retrieves grammatically correct sentences and adapts the retrieved sentences using grammatical rules. It can guarantee the generated sentences will be grammatically correct – a property that other machine learning approaches do not have.

Researchers have applied CBR techniques to example-based machine translation (EBMT) [8, 9, 18, 19]. Typical EBMT input representation is a sequence of words which is very different from the semantic representation in SEGUE. Furthermore in SEGUE, the examples consist of a semantic representation and a syntactic tree, but in EBMT systems, the examples consist solely of strings or syntactic trees of different languages. Due to this marked difference in the input and representation, the adaptation operations in SEGUE and EBMT systems are drastically different.

7   Conclusion

We have presented a hybrid surface natural language generator that uses a case-based paradigm, but performs rule-based adaptations. By combining the benefits of both approaches, we were able to implement a natural language generator that uses a small training corpus but is fast, accurate, and extensible. For developing a dialogue system in a new domain, the requirements of deploying our approach are more manageable than statistical approaches. By requiring only a small annotated corpus and using accurate rule-based adaptation operators, SEGUE can be customized for new application with less effort. To our knowledge, incorporating adaptation-guided retrieval into a generation system is the first of its kind. In the future, we want to build tools to facilitate annotation and demonstrate such a hybrid approach can significantly decrease the amount of effort needed to build NLG systems for different applications.

Acknowledgements

We would like to thank the anonymous reviewers for providing many useful suggestions. This material is based upon work supported by the Adventurous Research Program in IBM.

References

[1] Kolodner, J.: Case-Based Reasoning. Morgan Kaufmann (1993)
[2] Aamodt, A., Plaza, E.: Case-based reasoning; foundational issues, methodological variations, and system approaches. AI Communications **7** (1994)
[3] Lankilde, I., Knight, K.: Generation that exploits corpus-based statiscal knowledge. In: Proc. of the COLING and the ACL., Montreal, Canada (1998)
[4] Bangalore, S., Rambow, O.: Exploiting a probabilistic hierarchical model for generation. In: Proc. of the COLING. (2000)

[5] Ratnaparkhi, A.: Trainable methods for surface natural language generation. In: Proc. of the NAACL, Seattle, WA (2000)

[6] Chai, J., Pan, S., Zhou, M., Houck, K.: Context-based multimodal understanding in conversational systems. In: Proc. of International Conference on Multimodal Interfaces. (2002)

[7] Pan, S., Weng, W.: Designing a speech corpus for instance-based spoken language generation. In: Proc. of INLG, New York (2002)

[8] Somers, H.: EBMT seen as case-based reasoning. In: MT Summit VIII Workshop on Example-Based Machine Translation, Santiago de Compostela, Spain (2001)

[9] Brown, R.D.: Adding linguistic knowledge to a lexical example-based translation system. In: Proc. of the International Conference on Theoretical and Methodological Issues in Machine Translation, Chester, UK (1999)

[10] Ristad, E.S., Yianilos, P.N.: Learning string edit distance. IEEE Transactions on Pattern Analysis and Machine Intelligence **20** (1998)

[11] Smyth, B., Keane, M.T.: Experiements on adaptation-guided retrieval in case-based design. In: Proc. of the ICCBR. (1995)

[12] Leake, D.B.: Adaptive similarity assessment for case-based explanation. International Journal of Expert Systems **8** (1995)

[13] Robin, J., McKeown, K.R.: Corpus analysis for revision-based generation of complex sentences. In: Proc. of AAAI, Washington, DC (1993)

[14] Shaw, J.: Clause aggregation using linguistic knowledge. In: Proc. of the IWNLG. (1998)

[15] Walker, M., Rambow, O., Rogati, M.: SPot: A trainable sentence planner. In: Proc. of the NAACL. (2001)

[16] Varges, S., Mellish, C.: Instance-based natural language generation. In: Proc. of the NAACL, Pittsburgh, PA (2001)

[17] Oberlander, J., Brew, C.: Stochaastic text generation. Philosophical Transactions of the Royal Society **358** (2000)

[18] Collins, B., Cuningham, P.: Adaptation-guided retrieval in EBMT: A case-based approach to machine translation. In: Proc. of EWCBR. (1996)

[19] Somers, H.: Example-based machine translation. Machine Translation **14** (1999)

Modelling Politeness in Natural Language Generation

Kaśka Porayska-Pomsta[1] and Chris Mellish[2]

[1] University of Edinburgh, School of Informatics, 2 Buccleuch Place,
Edinburgh EH8 9LW, UK,
kaska@inf.ed.ac.uk,
http://www.hcrc.ed.ac.uk/~kaska/
[2] University of Aberdeen, Department of Computing Science, King's College,
Aberdeen AB24 3UE, UK,
cmellish@csd.abdn.ac.uk,
http://www.csd.abdn.ac.uk/~cmellish/

Abstract. One of the main objectives of research in Natural Language generation (NLG) is to account for linguistic variation in a systematic way. Research on linguistic politeness provides important clues as to the possible causes of linguistic variation and the ways in which it may be modelled formally. In this paper we present a simple language generation model for choosing the appropriate surface realisations of tutoring responses based on the politeness notion of face. We adapt the existing definition of face to the demands of the educational genre and we demonstrate how a politeness driven NLG system may result in a more natural and a more varied form of linguistic output.

1 Introduction

Generally natural language is characterised by enormous linguistic variation. Linguistic variation means that the same underlying message can be expressed by a multitude of different surface forms. As is well established in linguistics and Natural Language Generation (NLG), linguistic variation is determined by a number of well defined contextual factors [8,3]. It is one of the main challenges of research in NLG to account in a systematic way for linguistic variation. However, for such an account to be useful in constructing competent NLG systems, it needs to provide plausible answers as to what causes linguistic variation and how it is manifested through language.

The functional approach to language analysis [8], used in such important NLG systems as KPML [2], provides the field of NLG with some answers to these questions. Specifically, it provides a way in which to model peoples' linguistic behaviour as choice and a method for constructing formal systems (or grammars) which are used both for cataloguing the linguistic choices available and for explaining those choices in terms of their functional properties. In this approach the appropriateness of the possible choices is determined against both the contextual information and other linguistic possibilities available at the time

A. Belz et al. (Eds.): INLG 2004, LNAI 3123, pp. 141–150, 2004.

the linguistic decisions are made. However, while the functional approach accounts for linguistic variation on a general level (specifically through Halliday's language dimensions of *genre* and *register*), it does not explain in sufficient detail why the variation occurs on the contextual micro level, i.e., on the level of detailed situational circumstances and often within the linguistic repertoire of a single person. Furthermore, this theory does not provide a sufficiently detailed explanation of what such variation consists of in terms of concrete, if only prototypical, linguistic realisations.

Research on linguistic politeness, which is in line with the systemic functional theory, gives a more detailed account of linguistic variation. In particular, the model proposed by Brown and Levinson [3] (henceforth B&L) also treats language as a system of choices available to speakers with the appropriateness of those choices being judged based on socio-cultural factors and conventions established by a given speech community. However, crucially, the linguistic decisions of speakers are said in this theory to depend directly on the current *socio-psychological* demands of the people involved in a conversation. These demands mediate between different aspects of the situations and the language that is produced in those situations and they offer a basis for a model of a psychologically more plausible and varied NLG.

While on a general level we follow the systemic framework, we take the theory of linguistic politeness as the basis for explaining and ultimately for modelling linguistic variation on the level of the individual speakers. We demonstrate through our implemented model how politeness theory, if appropriately grounded in a particular linguistic genre, can be operationalised to allow for a more natural and more varied NLG. We do this in the context of the educational genre in which the modelled speaker is a teacher who needs to choose corrective feedback.

2   Politeness as the Basis for Linguistic Choice

B&L propose that all social activity including linguistic exchanges between people is motivated and controlled by *face* – a psychological dimension which applies to all members of society. Face is essentially a person's self-image which consists of **Negative face** (a person's need for autonomy from others), and **Positive face** (a person's need to be approved of by others). In addition to face, all members of society are equipped with an ability to behave in a rational way. On the one hand, the public self-image regulates all speakers' linguistic actions at all times in that speakers choose their language to minimise the threat to their own and to others' face, i.e., they engage in *facework*. On the other hand, the ability of speakers to behave rationally enables them to assess the extent of the potential threat of their intended actions and to accommodate (in various degrees) for others' face in the quest of achieving their own goals and face needs.

One of the main consequences of speakers engaging in facework is that they vary the levels of linguistic politeness in their utterances. In turn, varying levels of politeness lead to the varying levels of indirectness in the language produced, thus being one of the main causes of linguistic variation [9]. The most common occurrences of indirect use of language are found in the face threatening situations in which a speaker either needs to criticise the hearer, when he has to reject a hearer's previous act, or when he requires a favour from a hearer, for example, in the form of material goods, information or action. In order to achieve his communicative goal of rejecting a hearers previous action or to obtain the material goods or information, a speaker needs to design his language in a way that will manipulate the hearer into providing him with those goods or information, and/or that will make him receive the rejection without taking offence.

B&L propose three main strategies (Figure 1) which they say represent the social conventions that speakers use to make appropriate linguistic choices: the On-record, the Off-record and the Don't do FTA strategies. They further split the on-record strategy into a strategy which does not involve redressive language (the bald strategy), and two sub-strategies which do and which are aimed at accommodating the Positive and the Negative face respectively. In their system, each strategy leads to a number of different sub-strategies and to prototypical surface form realisations for each of those.

1.	On record strategy:
a.	Bald: To a perfect stranger: *Give me your money!*
b.	Redressive:
i.	To a friend: *Look I know youre broke just now, but I really need you to give me some money.*
ii.	To a stranger: *I am terribly sorry, sir, but I am short of 10p for my train ticket. Could you possibly help me out?*
2.	Off-record strategy: To a lunch partner after lunch: *I cant believe it! I left my purse at home.*
3.	Dont do FTA: do nothing.

Fig. 1. Examples of Brown and Levinson's strategies

B&L claim that the contextual information which is relevant to speakers' linguistic choices can be encapsulated as the sum of the current values of three social variables: (1) the power that the hearer has over the speaker, (2) the social distance between the hearer and the speaker, and (3) the rank of imposition for the linguistic act to be committed. The values of these variables are established by speakers on the basis of the current situation and the cultural conventions under which a given social interaction takes place. For example, power may depend on the interlocutors' status or their access to goods or information; distance depends on the degree of familiarity between the parties involved, while rank of imposition typically reflects social and cultural conventions of a given speech community which ranks different types of acts with respect to how much they interfere with people's need for autonomy and approval. A speaker's ability to assess the situation with respect to a hearer's social, cultural and emotional needs, i.e. his ability to produce polite language, constitutes a crucial facet of his social and linguistic competence.

3   Operationalising Politeness Theory for NLG

Few attempts to use linguistic politeness theory to inform the design of NLG systems have been made to date. Of those the most prominent is [17] and more recently [4]. Both systems combine B&L's theory with general approaches to speech act analysis (e.g., [16]) and with their AI interpretations [1,6]. The generative power of both systems is shown to be enhanced by the inclusion of the politeness dimensions which motivate a more human-like, user-sensitive and varied linguistic output. However, the applicability of the algorithms used in these systems to the linguistic genre of education is not immediate. This is primarily because B&L's work itself is not entirely applicable to teaching in that language produced in tutoring circumstances is governed by different conventions than that of normal conversations [15]. These differences have an impact on both the type of contextual information that is relevant to making linguistic choices and on the nature of the strategies and the corresponding surface choices. On the one hand, in the educational genre, in student-corrective situations, power and distance seem relatively constant rendering the rank of imposition the only immediately contextual variable relevant to teachers' corrective actions. On the other hand, while some of B&L's strategies apply to the educational genre, other ones require a more detailed specification or a complete redefinition. For example, conventionally, teachers do not offer gifts to students as a way of fulfilling their needs, nor do they apologise for requesting information from them.

In order to use the politeness theory in the context of generating teachers' language we had to determine a system of strategies representative of the linguistic domain under investigation. We then had to define face and facework for an educational context and define the strategies included in our system in terms of face. Furthermore, we had to identify the contextual variables which affect teachers' linguistic choices and relate them to the notion of face.

3.1   Determining the Strategic System

To establish a system of strategies applicable to the educational domain we examined two sets of human-human tutorial and classroom dialogues: one in the domain of basic electricity and electronics (BEE) [13] and one in the domain of literary analysis [18]. The resulting strategic system differs in a number of respects from that proposed by B&L. First, we established that unlike the strategies proposed by B&L in which there is a clear separation between those strategies which address Positive and Negative face respectively, all of the strategies used by teachers in our dialogues seem to address both face dimensions simultaneously. In our system this is reflected by all of the strategies being characterised in terms of the two face dimensions. While in B&L's model the selection of a strategy was based only on one number – the result of summing the three social variables – in our model two numbers are used in such a selection: one number referring to the way in which a given strategy addresses positive face and another to the way in which the strategy addresses negative face.

Second, following from our observations of the type of feedback that teachers provide in various situations, we split the strategies into two types: the main strategies which are used to express the main message of the corrective act, i.e., the teacher's rejection of the students previous answer, and the auxiliary strategies which are used to express redress. Unlike in B&L's model in which the strategies are rigidly assigned to a particular type of facework, in our approach the split between the strategies provides for a more flexible generative model which is not only in line with the more recent research on linguistic politeness (e.g., [7]), but more importantly reflects the way in which teachers tend to provide corrective feedback: in a single act a teacher can make use of several different strategies simultaneously. In our model then the strategies can combine with one another to form complex strategies. The individual ways in which these strategies can be used to address the two face dimensions are also combined using a simple weighted means function (for details on our system of strategies see [15]).

Third, although we observed that facework also seems to play a crucial role in education in that teachers tend to employ linguistic indirectness, we found B&L's definitions of the face dimensions not to be precise enough to explain the nature of face and facework in educational circumstances. The educational literature (e.g., [10]) suggests that indirect use of language by teachers is the result of them trying to allow their students as much freedom of initiative as possible (pedagogical considerations) while making sure that they do not flounder and become demotivated (motivational concerns). Our dialogue analysis confirms this and we found that all of teachers' corrective feedback, regardless of whether or not it is delivered through indirect language, can be interpreted in terms of both: differing amount of content specificity (how specific and how structured the tutors feedback is with respect to the answer sought from the student – compare: *No, that's incorrect* with *Well, if you put the light bulb in the oven then it will get a lot of heat, but will it light up?*) and illocutionary specificity (how explicitly accepting or rejecting the tutor's feedback is – compare: *No, that's incorrect* with *Well, why don't you try again?*). Based on these observations we defined the Negative and the Positive face directly in terms of:

- **Autonomy**: letting the student do as much of the work as possible (determination of the appropriate level of content specificity)
- **Approval**: providing the student with as positive a feedback as possible (determination of the appropriate level of illocutionary specificity).

These tightened definitions allowed us to characterise our strategies in terms of the *degree* to which each of them accommodates for the student's need for autonomy and approval respectively (henceforth <Aut, App>). The assignment of the two numbers, each between 0 and 1, to the individual strategies was done relative to other strategies in our system. For example when contrasting a strategy such as `give complete answer away` (e.g., *The answer is ...*) with a strategy such as `use direct hinting` (e.g., *That's one way, but there is a better way to do this*), we assessed the first strategy as giving lesser autonomy and lesser approval to the student than the second strategy. On the other hand, when compared with a third strategy such as `request self-explanation` (e.g., *Why?*), the hinting strategy seems to give less autonomy, but more approval. To make the assignment of the concrete numerical <Aut, App> values systematic involved three stages: (1) we classified the strategies intuitively into three types of autonomy as giving *plenty*, *medium* or *little* amount of guidance, and three types of approval: no approval, implicit approval and explicit approval, (2) we then translated these types into fuzzy linguistic ranges, for example, *low-medium*, *medium* and *medium-high* for autonomy, and (3) into proper numerical ranges such as 0–0.45, 0.45–0.55, and 0.55–1 respectively. Based on our dialogues, for each strategy we compiled a list of its possible surface realisations and we also ordered them according to the degrees of <Aut, App> that they seem to express. We used the numerical ranges associated with a given strategy to assign the <Aut, App> values to the concrete surface forms. The full set of surface forms which are coded for <Aut, App> values are stored in a case base (CB2 in Figure 3) which we use in our system to provide us with the different feedback alternatives using a standard Case Based Reasoning technique.

3.2 Determining the Relevant Contextual Variables

To determine the contextual variables affecting teachers feedback we relied on the relevant educational literature [5,11,12], our dialogue analysis as well as on informal interviews with a number of teachers [14,15]. From these, we compiled a list of situational factors which seemed important to teachers' choices.

Student-oriented factors
— student confidence
— student interest (bored/motivated)
Lesson-oriented factors
— time left for lesson
— amount of material left to be covered
— difficulty of material
— importance of material
Performance-oriented factors
— correctness of students previous answer(s)
— ability of student

Fig. 2. Situational Factors

In order to (1) validate the situational factors, (2) relate the individual factors to the <Aut, App> dimensions and (3) calculate the degree of <Aut, App> based on specific situations, we performed a study in which teachers were given situations as characterised by combinations of the factors in Figure 2 and their values. The factor-values in our current model are binary, e.g., the possible values of the factor *student confidence* are *confident* or *not confident*. While in reality the situational factors may have more continuous values, such simplified definitions allowed us to reduce significantly the cognitive load on the teachers during data collection, as well as reducing the complexity of this initial model. For each combination of factors, the teachers were asked to rate every factor-value according to how important they thought it to be in affecting the form of their feedback. The results of the study were used to inform the design and the implementation of the situational model. Specifically, the results of Principal Component Analysis allowed us to group the factors according to how they relate to one another, while teachers' written comments and post-hoc interviews allowed us to determine their possible relation to the <Aut, App> dimensions. For example, while the student-oriented-factors seem to be most closely related to approval, the lesson-oriented-factors seem to affect the autonomy dimension. We also derived the means from teachers' ratings for each situation given in the study. We used these means to represent the relative importance (salience) of each factor-value in a given combination. Based on the groupings of factors along with their salience we derived rules which (1) combine situational factor-values, (2) relate them to either guidance or approval goals in terms of which the two face dimensions are defined, (3) calculate <Aut, App>. For example, the effect of the rule with preconditions *little time left* and *high student ability* is a numerically expressed degree of guidance calculated using a weighted means function from the salience of the two contributing factors. We built a Bayesian network (BN) which combines evidence from the factors to compute values for <Aut, App> for every situational input. The structure of the network reflects the relationship of factors as determined by the study, and the individual nodes in the network are populated with the conditional probabilities calculated using the types of rules just described.

4   Generating Corrective Feedback

To generate feedback recommendations (Figure 3), the system expects an input in the form of factor-values. The factor-values are passed to the Pre-processing unit (PPU) which interprets the input in terms of the evidence required by the BN. The evidence consists of the relative salience of each factor-value in the input and it is either retrieved directly from the Case Base 1 (CB1) which stores all the situations seen and ranked by the teachers in the study, or if there is no situation in the CB1 that matches the input, it is calculated for each factor-value from the mean salience of three existing nearest matching situations. A K-nearest neighbour algorithm (KNN1) performs the search for the nearest matching situations. When the evidence is set, the BN calculates <Aut, App>. These are then passed to the linguistic component. KNN2 finds N closest matching pairs of <Aut, App> (N being specified by the user) which are associated with specific linguistic alternatives in CB2 and which constitute the output of the system.

5   Evaluation and Conclusions

We performed an evaluation of our model focusing on (1) the performance of the situational component responsible for calculating the <Aut, App> values, and

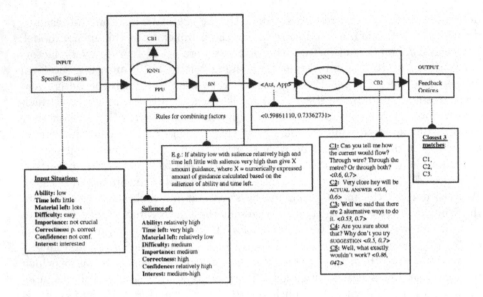

Fig. 3. The structure of the system with an example

(2) the overall appropriateness of the model's linguistic recommendations for specific situations. To evaluate the performance of the situational component, we wrote a program which automatically input all possible factor-value combinations into the system and recorded the output. Given the 256 combinations of the eight situational factors used in our model, each having two possible values, we expected a variety of <Aut, App> output values across the 0 to 1 range in order that the situational component's output would lead to varied linguistic responses. The results show that for Autonomy the average value is 0.53, with values ranging from 0.28 to 0.8. For Approval, the average is 0.59, with values between 0.2 and 0.89. This is encouraging, showing that while the lowest and the highest possible values in the range are never reached – a consequence of a relatively limited range of importance ratings assigned by teachers in the first study to the individual factor-values – the spread of Autonomy and Approval values is large enough to lead to a reasonably wide linguistic coverage. This is further confirmed by the results of the second part of the evaluation.

To assess the appropriateness of the linguistic output, we carried out a study in which four experienced BEE tutors took part. Each tutor was presented with twenty different situations in the form of short dialogues between a student and a tutor (Figure 4). Each interaction ended with either incorrect or partially correct student answer. For each situation, the participants were provided with three possible tutor responses to the student's answer and were asked to rate each of them on a scale from 1 to 5 according to how appropriate they thought the response was in the given situation. The tutors were asked to pay special attention to the manner in which each response attempted to correct the student.

The three types of responses rated included: a response that a human made to the given situation, the response recommended by the system, and a response that the system was less likely to recommend for the same situation.

Teacher: You're doing really well, we still need to clarify a few simple things which are nevertheless important.

Teacher: Since we're running out of time, can you briefly explain how to observe polarity?

Student (*interested*): Yes, thats just making sure the positive wire is connected to the positive side and vice versa. (CORRECT)

Teacher: OK, then, if the red lead were connected to the tab number 3 and the black lead to number 4, which tab positions would be included in the negative side of the circuit?

Student (*confident*): the number 4 tab, of course. (PARTIALLY CORRECT: the negative side of the circuit would span from tab 3 to 6).

CHOICE 1: You are right that tab 4 would be on the negative side of the circuit, but is it the only one? **CHOICE 2**: What gives you the idea that tab 4 is on the negative side of the circuit? **CHOICE 3**: That's true. Are there any other tabs in the negative side of the circuit?

Fig. 4. Example dialogue and three possible responses used in the evaluation study.

We performed a t-test to determine whether there was a significant difference between the three types of responses. The analysis revealed a significant difference between human follow-up responses and the system's less preferred responses ($t(19) = 4.40$, $p < 0.001$), as well as a significant difference between the system's preferred and the system's less preferred responses ($t(19) = 2.72$, $p = 0.013$). Finally, and most encouraging, there was no significant difference between the ratings of the human responses and the system's preferred responses, ($t(19)=1.99$, $p=0.61$). Although encouraging, the current evaluation was done on a small scale which may have impacted the results. Specifically, the average across all dialogues of the difference between the mean score for the human response and the mean score for the system's preferred response was 0.48. Assuming the use of two-tailed t-test with the standard deviation being the same as that observed, the average difference would have had to be 0.51 or larger to be statistically significant at p < 0.05. Thus, the observed result although definitely not significant is fairly close to significance which means that given a larger subject pool and more situations, the outcome may have been less positive. Nevertheless, the available results suggest that the model's choices are in line with those made by a human tutor in identical situations: while the situational component manages to produce plausible <Aut, App> values for the various situations, the <Aut, App> values assigned to the surface forms correspond broadly to the judgements of experienced tutors. Although a larger scale evaluation is needed, the preliminary results bode well for the role of politeness theory in NLG, showing that when appropriately formalised, it may lead to a more varied and more human-like linguistic output.

References

1. Allen, J. F., Perrault, C. R.: Analyzing intention in utterances. Artificial Intelligence 15 (1980) 143–178.
2. Bateman, J. A.: Enabling technology for multilingual natural language generation: the KPML development environment. Natural Language Engineering 3(1) (1997) 15–55.
3. Brown, P., Levinson, S.: Politeness: Some Universals in Language Use. Cambridge University Press (1987).
4. Cassell, J., Bickmore, T.: Negotiated collusion: Modeling social language and its relationship effects in intelligent agents. User Modeling and Adaptive Interfaces (2002).
5. Chi, M. T. H., Siler, S. A., Jeong, H., Yamauchi, T., Hausmann, R. G.: Learning from human tutoring. Cognitive Science (25) (2001) 471–533.
6. Cohen, P. R.: On knowing what to say: Planning speech acts. Technical Report 118, University of Toronto (1978).
7. Fetzer, A.: 'No Thanks': a socio-semantic approach. Linguistik (14) (2003) 137–160.
8. Halliday, M. A. K.: An Introduction to Functional Grammar. Edward Arnold (1985).
9. Leech, G.N.: Language and tact. Amsterdam (1980).
10. Lepper, M.R., Chabay, R.W.: Socializing the intelligent tutor: Bringing empathy to computer tutors. In Mandl and Lesgold (Eds.), Learning Issues for Intelligent Tutoring Systems (1988) 114–137, Springer.
11. Lepper, M. R., Woolverton, M., Mumme, D. L., Gurtner, J.: Motivational Techniques of Expert Human Tutors: Lessons for the Design of Computer-Based Tutors. (1993) Chapter 3, 75–107. Lawrence Erlbaum Associates, Hillsdale, NJ.
12. Malone, T. W., Lepper, M. R.: Making learning fun: A taxonomy of intrinsic motivations for learning. In R. E. Snow and M. J. Farr, editors, Aptitude, Learning and Instruction: Conative and Affective Process Analyses, (1987) vol. 3, 223-253. Hillsdale, NJ: Lawrence Erlbaum Associates.
13. Penstein-Rose, C., Di Eugenio, B., Moore, J.D.: A dialogue based tutoring system for basic electricity and electronics. In V. M. Lajoie editor, Artificial Intelligence in Education (1999), p.759, IOS Press.
14. Porayska-Pomsta, K., Mellish, C. S., Pain, H.: Aspects of speech act categorization: Towards generating teachers language. International Journal of Artificial Intelligence in Education 11(3) (2000) 254–272.
15. Porayska-Pomsta, K.: Influence of situational context on language production: Modelling teachers corrective responses. PhD thesis, University of Edinburgh (2003).
16. Searle, J.: Speech Acts. Cambridge University Press (1969).
17. Walker, M.A., Cahn, J.E., Whittaker, S. J.: Improvising Linguistic Style: Social and Affective Bases for Agent Personality. Proc. of the First International Conference on Autonomous Agents (1997).
18. Wojtczuk, K.: Zachowania jezykowe nauczycieli w sytuacji lekcji szkolnej. PhD thesis, Uniwersytet Siedlecki (1996).

Context-Based Incremental Generation for Dialogue

Matthew Purver[1] and Ruth Kempson[2]

Departments of [1]Computer Science and [2]Philosophy,
King's College London, Strand, London WC2R 2LS, UK
{matthew.purver, ruth.kempson}@kcl.ac.uk

Abstract. This paper describes an implemented model of context-based incremental tactical generation within the Dynamic Syntax framework [1] which directly reflects dialogue phenomena such as alignment, routinization and shared utterances, problematic for many theoretical and computational approaches [2]. In Dynamic Syntax, both parsing and generation are defined in terms of *actions* on semantic tree structures, allowing these structures to be built in a word-by-word incremental fashion. This paper proposes a model of dialogue context which includes these trees and their associated actions, and shows how alignment and routinization result directly from minimisation of lexicon search (and hence speaker's effort), and how switch of speaker/hearer roles in shared utterances can be seen as a switch between incremental processes directed by different goals, but sharing the same (partial) data structures.

1 Introduction

Study of dialogue has been proposed by [2] as the major new challenge facing both linguistic and psycholinguistic theory. Several phenomena common in dialogue pose a significant challenge to (and have received little attention in) theoretical and computational linguistics; amongst them *alignment, routinization, shared utterances* and various *elliptical* constructions. Alignment describes the way that dialogue participants mirror each other's patterns at many levels (including lexical choice and syntactic structure), while routinization describes their convergence on set descriptions (words or sequences of words) for a particular reference or sense. Shared utterances are those in which participants shift between the roles of parser and producer:[1]

(1)
Daniel: Why don't you stop mumbling and
Marc: Speak proper like?
Daniel: speak proper?

(2)
Sandy: if, if you try and do enchiladas or
Katriane: Mhm.
Sandy: erm
Katriane: Tacos?
Sandy: tacos.

These are especially problematic for approaches in which parsing and generation are seen as separate disconnected processes, even more so when as applications of a grammar formalism whose output is the set of wellformed strings:[2]

---

[1] Examples from the BNC, file KNY (sentences 315–317) and KPJ (555–559).
[2] Although see [3] for an initial DRT-based approach.

A. Belz et al. (Eds.): INLG 2004, LNAI 3123, pp. 151–160, 2004.
© Springer-Verlag Berlin Heidelberg 2004

The initial hearer B must parse an input which is not a standard constituent, and assign a (partial) interpretation, then presumably complete that representation and generate an output from it which takes the previous words and their syntactic form into account but does not produce them. The initial speaker A must also be able to integrate these two fragments.

In this paper we describe a new approach and implementation within the Dynamic Syntax (DS) framework [1] which allows these phenomena to be straightforwardly explained. By defining a suitably structured concept of context, and adding this to the basic word-by-word incremental parsing and generation models of [1, 8, 9], we show how otherwise problematic elliptical phenomena can be modelled. We then show how alignment and routinization result directly from minimisation of effort on the part of the speaker (implemented as minimisation of lexical search in generation), and how the switch in roles at any stage of a sentence can be seen as a switch between processes which are directed by different goals, but which share the same incrementally built data structures.

2   Background

DS is a parsing-directed grammar formalism in which a decorated tree structure representing a semantic interpretation for a string is incrementally projected following the left-right sequence of the words. Importantly, this tree is not a model of syntactic structure, but is strictly semantic, being a representation of the predicate-argument structure of the sentence. In DS, grammaticality is defined as parsability (the successful incremental construction of a tree-structure logical form, using all the information given by the words in sequence), and there is no central use-neutral grammar of the kind assumed by most approaches to parsing and/or generation. The logical forms are lambda terms of the epsilon calculus (see [4] for a recent development), so quantification is expressed through terms of type e whose complexity is reflected in evaluation procedures that apply to propositional formulae once constructed, and not in the tree itself. The analogue of quantifier-storage is the incremental build-up of sequences of scope-dependency constraints between terms under construction: these terms and their associated scope statements are subject to evaluation once a propositional formula of type t has been derived at the topnode of some tree structure.[3] With all quantification expressed as type e terms, the standard grounds for mismatch between syntactic and semantic analysis for all NPs is removed; and, indeed, all syntactic distributions are explained in terms of this incremental and monotonic growth of partial representations of content, hence the claim that the model itself constitutes a NL grammar formalism.

Projected trees are, in general, simpler than in other frameworks, because adjunct structures (e.g. for relative clause construal) are constructed as paired "linked" structures. Such structures may be constructed in tandem, with evaluation rules then determining that these independent structures, once completed,

---

[3] For formal details of this approach to quantification see [1] chapter 7.

are compiled together via conjunction.[4] So the overall construction process involves constructing predicate-argument structures, in tree format.

Parsing [1] defines parsing as a process of building labelled semantic trees in a strictly left-to-right, word-by-word incremental fashion by using computational and lexical actions defined (for some natural language) using the modal tree logic LOFT [5]. These actions are defined as transition functions between intermediate states, which monotonically extend tree structures and node decorations. Words are specified in the lexicon to have associated lexical actions: the (possibly *partial*) semantic trees are monotonically extended by applying these actions as each word is consumed from the input string. Partial trees may be underspecified: tree node relations may be only partially specified; node decorations may be defined in terms of unfulfilled requirements and metavariables; and trees may lack a full set of scope constraints. Anaphora resolution is a familiar case of update: pronouns are defined to project metavariables that are substituted from context as part of the construction process. Relative to the same tree-growth dynamics, long-distance dependency effects are characterised through restricted licensing of partial trees with relation between nodes introduced with merely a constraint on some fixed extension (following D-Tree grammar formalisms [6]), an underspecification that gets resolved within the left-to-right construction process.[5] Once all requirements are satisfied and all partiality and underspecification is resolved, trees are *complete*, parsing is successful and the input string is said to be grammatical. For the purposes of the current paper, the important point is that the process is monotonic: the parser state at any point contains all the partial trees which have been produced by the portion of the string so far consumed and which remain candidates for completion.

Generation [8, 9] give an initial method of context-independent tactical generation based on the same incremental parsing process, in which an output string is produced according to an input semantic tree, the *goal tree*. The generator incrementally produces a set of corresponding output strings and their associated partial trees (again, on a left-to-right, word-by-word basis) by following standard parsing routines and using the goal tree as a subsumption check. At each stage, partial strings and trees are tentatively extended using some word/action pair from the lexicon; only those candidates which produce trees which subsume the goal tree are kept, and the process succeeds when a complete tree identical to the goal tree is produced. Generation and parsing thus use the same tree representations and tree-building actions throughout.

---

[4] The difference between restrictive and nonrestrictive relative construal turns on whether the LINK transition is defined from an epsilon term variable (as in the restrictive *"The man who I like smokes"*) leading to conjunction of the restrictor for the term under construction, or from the constructed term itself (as in *"John, who I like, smokes"*) in which case the result is conjunction of formulae.

[5] In this, the system is also like LFG, modelling long-distance dependency in the same terms as *functional uncertainty* [7], differing from that concept in the dynamics of update internal to the construction of a single tree.

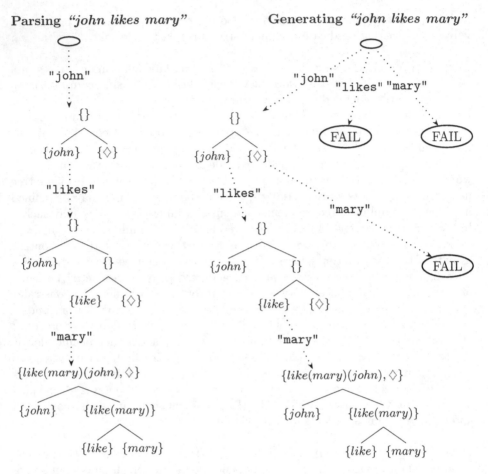

The current model (and implementation) is based on these earlier definitions, but modifies them in several ways, most significantly by the addition of a model of context as described in full in Sections 3 and 4; here we briefly describe two other departures. Firstly, we do not adopt the proposal of [8, 9] to speed up generation by use of a restricted multiset of lexical entries (word/action pairs), selected from the lexicon on the basis of goal tree features. Such a strategy assumes a global search of the goal tree prior to generation, preventing subsequent modification or extension, and so is not strictly incremental.

Secondly, the implementation has been extended to allow linked structures as input: the generation of a relative-clause containing sequence *"John, who Sue likes, smokes"*, following the subsumption constraint that the partial tree(s) subsume the goal tree, may involve at any step a partial tree that subsumes a pair of trees, associated with a compound propositional formula $Smoke(John) \land Like(John)(Sue)$. Generation of a sentence involving quantification can now also take a goal tree with evaluated formula, so a sentence such as *"A man smokes"* would be generated from a tree whose top node is assigned a formula $Smoke(\epsilon, x, Man(x))$, evaluated as $Man(a) \land Smoke(a)$, where $a = (\epsilon, x, Man(x)$

$\wedge Smoke(x)$). As with relative clauses, given the entailment relation between a conjunctive formula and each of its conjuncts, the subsumption constraint on generation may be met by a partial tree in the sequence of developed trees, despite the compound formula assigned to the goal tree, given that the concept of growth is defined over the parse process leading to such a result.[6]

3   Modelling Context

The basic definitions of parsing and generation [1, 8, 9] assume some notion of context but give no formal model or implementation. For a treatment of dialogue, of course, such a model is essential, and its definition and resulting effects are the subject of this paper. This section defines the model and redefines the parsing and generation processes to include it. Section 4 then describes how the resulting framework allows a treatment of dialogue phenomena.

Context Model NLG systems often assume models of context which include information about both semantic representation and surface strings. [13, 14] both describe models of context which include not only entities and propositions, but also the sentences and phrases associated with them, for purposes of e.g. information structure and subsequent clarificational dialogue. The model of context we require here adds one further element: not only semantic trees (propositional structures) and word strings, but the sequences of lexical actions that have been used to build them. It is the presence of, and associations between, all three that allow our straightforward model of dialogue phenomena, together with the fact that this context is equally available to the parsing and generation processes, as both use the same lexical actions to build the same tree representations.

For the purposes of the current simple implementation, we make a simplifying assumption that the length of context is finite and limited to the immediately previous sentence (although as information that is independently available can be represented in the DS tree format, larger and only partially ordered contexts are no doubt possible in reality): context at any point in either parsing or generation is therefore made up of the trees and word/action sequences obtained in parsing or producing the previous sentence and the current (incomplete) sentence.

Parsing in Context A parser state is therefore defined to be a set of triples $\langle T, W, A \rangle$, where T is a (possibly partial) semantic tree, W the sequence of words and A the sequence of lexical and computational actions that have been used in building it. This set will initially contain only a single triple $\langle T_a, \emptyset, \emptyset \rangle$ (where T_a is the basic axiom taken as the starting point of the parser, and the

---

[6] In building n-tuples of trees corresponding to predicate-argument structures, the system is similar to LTAG formalisms [10]. However, unlike LTAG systems (see e.g. [11]), both parsing and generation are not head-driven, but fully (word-by-word) incremental. This has the advantage of allowing fully incremental models for all languages, matching psycholinguistic observations [12] irrespective of the position in the clausal sequence of the verb.

word and action sequences are empty), but will expand as words are consumed from the input string and the corresponding actions produce multiple possible partial trees.

At any point in the parsing process, the context for a particular partial tree T in this set can then be taken to consist of: (a) a similar triple $\langle T_0, W_0, A_0 \rangle$ given by the previous sentence, where T_0 is its semantic tree representation, W_0 and A_0 the sequences of words and actions that were used in building it; and (b) the triple $\langle T, W, A \rangle$ itself. Once parsing is complete, the parser state will again be reduced to a single triple $\langle T_1, W_1, A_1 \rangle$, corresponding to the final interpretation of the string T_1 with its sequence of words W_1 and actions A_1.[7] This triple will now form the new starting context for the next sentence, replacing $\langle T_0, W_0, A_0 \rangle$.

Generation in Context A generator state is now defined as a pair (G, X) of a goal tree G and a set X of pairs (S, P), where S is a candidate partial string and P is the associated parser state (a set of $\langle T, W, A \rangle$ triples). Initially, the set X will (usually) contain only one pair, of an empty candidate string and the standard initial parser state, $(\emptyset, \{\langle T_a, \emptyset, \emptyset \rangle\})$. However, as both parsing and generation processes are strictly incremental, they can in theory start from *any* state – this will be required for our analysis of shared utterances.

In generation, the context for any partial tree T is defined exactly as for parsing: the previous sentence triple $\langle T_0, W_0, A_0 \rangle$; and the current triple $\langle T, W, A \rangle$. As generation and parsing use the same parsing actions, they make parallel use of context. Thus the generation of *He smiled* in *"John came in. He smiled"* is licensed not simply because the metavariable lexically provided by the pronoun allows the structure induced by the string to (trivially) subsume the goal tree, but because, following the parsing dynamics, a value for this metavariable must be identified from context, and the parse of the previously uttered string provides such a value *john* which (less trivially) allows subsumption. Generation and parsing are thus very closely coupled, with the central part of both processes being a parser state: a set of tree/word-sequence/action-sequence triples. Essential to this close correspondence is the lack of construction of higher-level hypotheses about the state of the interlocutor. All transitions are defined over the context for the individual (parser or generator). In principle, contexts could be extended to include high-level hypotheses, but these are not essential and are not implemented in our model (see [15] for justification of this stance).

4   Modelling Dialogue

Anaphora & Ellipsis This model, with its inclusion of action sequences, now allows a full analysis of anaphora and ellipsis. Pronouns and strict readings of VP ellipsis are formally defined as decorating tree nodes with metavariables, to be updated using terms established in context, i.e. by copying a suitably typed

---

[7] This formalisation assumes all ambiguity is removed by inference etc. If not, the final parser state, and thus the initial context for the next sentence, will contain more than one triple.

semantic formula which decorates some tree node $n \in (T_0 \cup T)$. The analysis of sloppy readings of VP ellipsis instead defines this update as achieved by action re-use: any contextual sequence of actions $(a_1; a_2; \ldots; a_n) \in (A_0 \cup A)$ which causes a suitably typed formula to be derived can be re-used. This allows generation of a range of phenomena, including those which are problematic for other (e.g. abstraction-based) approaches [19], such as cases in which the interpretation of a pronoun to be reconstructed in the elliptical fragment must involve binding not by the subject, but by some term contained within it:

(3)   *A:* A policeman who arrested Bill said he was speeding.
     B: The policeman who arrested Harry did too.

The actions associated with *said he was speeding* in (3) include the projection of a metavariable associated with the pronoun which is updated from context (in *A*'s utterance, taking *Bill* as antecedent). Re-using the actions in *B*'s utterance allows *Harry* to be selected from the new context as antecedent, leading to the desired sloppy reading.

The incremental nature of the generation process and its ability to start from any state also licenses other forms of ellipsis such as bare fragments as taking a previous structure from context as a starting point (4). Here *wh*-expressions are analysed as particular forms of metavariables, so parsing *A*'s question yields an open formula; *B* can then begin generation from a resulting partial tree which the fragment updates and completes (rather than having to postulate a separate grammar rule to license fragments as complete utterances):

(4)   *A:* What did you eat for breakfast?
     B: Porridge.

Minimizing Lexicon Search The context model and notion of action re-use now also allows the minimisation of lexical search, as proposed by [8, 9] (though without formal definitions or implementation). At each stage, the generation process must extend the current partial tree using a lexical action, then check for goal tree subsumption. In principle, this is a computationally expensive process: the lexicon must be searched for all possible word/action pairs, the tree extended and the result checked – and this performed at every step i.e. for each word. Any strategy for minimising this task (reflecting the psychological concept of minimizing speaker's effort) will therefore be highly preferred.[8] The apparently high frequency of elliptical constructions is expected as ellipsis minimises lexical lookup by re-use of structure or actions from context; the same can be said for pronouns, as long as they (and their corresponding actions) are assumed to be pre-activated by default; and as suggested by [8, 9], this makes possible a model of alignment.

---

[8] Even given a more complex model of the lexicon which might avoid searching all possible words (e.g. by activating only certain subfields of the lexicon based on the semantic formulae and structure of the goal tree), searching through the immediate context will still minimise the task.

Alignment & Routinization Alignment is now characterisable as follows. If there exists some action $a \in (A_0 \cup A)$ which is suitable for extending the current tree, full lexical search can be avoided altogether by re-using a and generating the word w which occupies the corresponding position in the sequence W_0 or W. This results in lexical alignment – w will be repeated rather than choosing an alternative but as yet unused word from the lexicon. Alignment of syntactic structure in which participants mirror syntactic choices (e.g. preserving double-object or full PP forms in the use of a verb such as *give* rather than shifting to the semantically equivalent form [16]) also follows in virtue of the procedural action-based specification of lexical content. A word such as *give* has two possible sequences of lexical actions a' and a'' despite semantic equivalence of output, corresponding to the two alternative forms. A previous use of a particular form will cause either a' or a'' to be present in $(A_0 \cup A)$, and re-use of this action will cause the form to be repeated.[9] This can be extended to sequences of words – a sub-sequence $(a_1; a_2; \ldots; a_n) \in (A_0 \cup A)$ can be re-used, generating the corresponding word sequence $(w_1; w_2; \ldots; w_n) \in (W_0 \cup W)$. This will result in sequences or phrases being re-used whenever the same sense or reference is to be conveyed, modelling the semantic alignment described by [17], and resulting in what [2] call *routinization* (construction and re-use of word sequences with consistent meanings).

Shared Utterances [8, 9] also suggest that shared utterances as in examples (1) and (2) should be easy to analyse. The definitions of Section 3 now provide a formal basis for allowing the switch of speaker/hearer roles as follows, given that the generation and parsing processes can start from any state, and share the same lexical entries, context and semantic tree representations. We take in order transition from hearer to speaker, transition from speaker to hearer.

Transition from Hearer to Speaker: Normally, the generation process begins with the initial generator state as defined above: $(G, \{(\emptyset, P_0)\})$, where P_0 is the standard initial "empty" parser state $\{\langle T_a, \emptyset, \emptyset \rangle\}$. As long as a suitable goal tree G is available to guide generation, the only change required to generate a continuation from a heard partial string is to replace P_0 with the parser state (a set of triples $\langle T, W, A \rangle$) as produced from that partial string: we call this the *transition state* P_t. The initial hearer A therefore parses as usual until transition,[10] then given a suitable goal tree G, forms an initial generator state $G, \{(\emptyset, P_t)\}$, from which generation can begin directly. Note that the context does not change between processes.

For generation to begin from this transition state, the new goal tree G must be subsumed by at least one of the partial trees in P_t (i.e. the proposition to

---

[9] Most frameworks would have to reflect this via activation of syntactic rules, or preferences defined over parallelisms with syntactic trees in context, both problematic. Though lexical alignment effects might be modelled via a context which includes only semantic referents and associated strings (as used by [18] to echo NPs), independent characterisation will be essential to model syntactic effects and routinization.

[10] We have little to say about exactly *when* transitions occur. Presumably speaker pauses and the availability to the hearer of a possible goal tree both play a part.

be expressed must be subsumed by the incomplete proposition that has been built so far by the parser). Constructing G prior to the generation task will often be a complex process involving inference and/or abduction over context and world/domain knowledge – [3] give some idea as to how this inference might be possible – for now, we make the simplifying assumption that a suitable propositional structure is available.[11]

Transition from Speaker to Hearer: At transition, the initial speaker B's generator state contains the pair (S_t, P'_t), where S_t is the partial string output so far, and P'_t is the corresponding parser state, the transition state for B.[12] In order for B to interpret A's continuation, B need only use P'_t as the initial parser state which is extended as the string produced by A is consumed.

As there will usually be multiple possible partial trees at the transition point, it is possible for A to continue in a way that differs from B's initial intentions – i.e. that does not match B's initial goal tree. For B to be able to understand such continuations, it is important that the generation process preserves all possible partial parse trees (just as the parsing process does), whether they subsume the goal tree or not, as long as at least one tree in the current state *does* subsume the goal tree. A generator state must therefore rule out only pairs (S, P) for which P contains no trees which subsume the goal tree, rather than thinning the set P directly via the subsumption check as proposed by [9].

5   Summary

The close coupling of parsing and generation processes, and in particular their sharing of a suitable model of context, allow shared utterances and various ellipsis and alignment phenomena to be modelled in a straightforward fashion. A prototype system has been implemented in Prolog which reflects the model given here, demonstrating all the above phenomena in simple dialogue sequences.

Acknowledgements

This paper builds on, and is indebted to, earlier work on the DS framework with Wilfried Meyer-Viol and on generation with Masayuki Otsuka. Thanks are also due to the anonymous INLG reviewers. This work was supported by the ESRC (RES-000-22-0355) and (in the case of the second author) the Leverhulme Trust.

---

[11] Assuming the goal tree as input raises logical-form equivalence problems [20]. Investigation of the degree to which this affects the current approach must be left for further work, but some points are worth noting: the goal tree is semantic, reflecting predicate-argument structure not that of a NL string, so its construction will not require detailed consultation of a grammar; as the language of inference (and tree decoration) is presumed to be the epsilon calculus (not FOL), structural representations will reflect NL structures relatively closely; and we assume that use of context will help determine not only mode of expression but also the goal tree itself.

[12] Of course, if both A and B share the same lexical entries and communication is perfect, $P_t = P'_t$, but we do not have to assume that this is the case.

References

[1] Kempson, R., Meyer-Viol, W., Gabbay, D.: Dynamic Syntax: The Flow of Language Understanding. Blackwell (2001)

[2] Pickering, M., Garrod, S.: Toward a mechanistic psychology of dialogue. Behavioral and Brain Sciences **forthcoming** (2004)

[3] Poesio, M., Rieser, H.: Coordination in a PTT approach to dialogue. In: Proceedings of the 7th Workshop on the Semantics and Pragmatics of Dialogue (DiaBruck). (2003)

[4] Meyer-Viol, W.: Instantial Logic. PhD thesis, University of Utrecht (1995)

[5] Blackburn, P., Meyer-Viol, W.: Linguistics, logic and finite trees. Bulletin of the IGPL **2** (1994) 3–31

[6] Marcus, M.: Deterministic parsing and description theory. In Whitelock, P., Wood, M., Somers, H., Johnson, R., Bennett, P., eds.: Linguistic Theory and Computer Applications. Academic Press (1987) 69–112

[7] Kaplan, R., Zaenen, A.: Long-distance dependencies, constituent structure, and functional uncertainty. In Baltin, M., Kroch, A., eds.: Alternative Conceptions of Phrase Structure. University of Chicago Press (1989) 17–42

[8] Otsuka, M., Purver, M.: Incremental generation by incremental parsing. In: Proceedings of the 6th CLUK Colloquium. (2003)

[9] Purver, M., Otsuka, M.: Incremental generation by incremental parsing: Tactical generation in Dynamic Syntax. In: Proceedings of the 9th European Workshop in Natural Language Generation (ENLG-2003). (2003)

[10] Joshi, A., Kulick, S.: Partial proof trees as building blocks for a categorial grammar. Linguistics and Philosophy **20** (1997) 637–667

[11] Stone, M., Doran, C.: Sentence planning as description using tree-adjoining grammar. In: Proceedings of the 35th Annual Meeting of the ACL. (1997) 198–205

[12] Ferreira, V.: Is it better to give than to donate? syntactic flexibility in language production. Journal of Memory and Language **35** (1996) 724–755

[13] van Deemter, K., Odijk, J.: Context modeling and the generation of spoken discourse. Speech Communication **21** (1997) 101–121

[14] Stone, M.: Specifying generation of referring expressions by example. In: Proceedings of the AAAI Spring Symposium on Natural Language Generation in Spoken and Written Dialogue. (2003)

[15] Millikan, R.: The Varieties of Meaning: The Jean-Nicod Lectures. MIT Press (2004)

[16] Branigan, H., Pickering, M., Cleland, A.: Syntactic co-ordination in dialogue. Cognition **75** (2000) 13–25

[17] Garrod, S., Anderson, A.: Saying what you mean in dialogue: A study in conceptual and semantic co-ordination. Cognition **27** (1987) 181–218

[18] Lemon, O., Gruenstein, A., Gullett, R., Battle, A., Hiatt, L., Peters, S.: Generation of collaborative spoken dialogue contributions in dynamic task environments. In: Proceedings of the AAAI Spring Symposium on Natural Language Generation in Spoken and Written Dialogue. (2003)

[19] Dalrymple, M., Shieber, S., Pereira, F.: Ellipsis and higher-order unification. Linguistics and Philosophy **14** (1991) 399–452

[20] Shieber, S.: The problem of logical-form equivalence. Computational Linguistics **19** (1993) 179–190

Contextual Influences on Near-Synonym Choice

Ehud Reiter and Somayajulu Sripada

Dept of Computing Science, University of Aberdeen, UK
{ereiter,ssripada}@csd.abdn.ac.uk

Abstract. One of the least understood aspects of lexical choice in Natural Language Generation is choosing between near-synonyms. Previous studies of this issue, such as Edmonds and Hirst [4], have focused on semantic differences between near-synonyms, as analysed by lexicographers. Our empirical analysis of near-synonym choice in weather forecasts, however, suggests that other factors are probably more important than semantic differences. These include preferences and idiosyncrasies of individual authors; collocation; variation of lexical usage; and position of a lexeme in a text. Our analysis also suggests that when semantic differences do influence near-synonym choice, they may do so in an author-dependent manner. Thus, at least in our domain, 'context' (including author) seems to be more important than semantics when choosing between near-synonyms.

1 Introduction

Natural Language Generation (NLG) systems must choose the words used in a generated text. This task is called *lexical choice*. Lexical choice can be an especially difficult task when the NLG system wishes to communicate a meaning that can be expressed by several synonyms or near-synonyms; which of these should be used? For example, if the system wishes to communicate the time 1200, should it express this as *midday, noon, 1200, late morning* or *early afternoon*?

In this paper we describe our work on near-synonym choice, which (unlike most previous work in this area) is based on corpus analysis and other empirical work. This work was motivated by a desire to develop more sophisticated representations of lexical meanings which could capture fine semantic nuances. In fact, though, our strongest finding is that the choice between near-synonyms is mostly determined by non-semantic factors, including the preferences and 'idiolect' of individual authors (which in some cases change over time); collocation; which words were previously used for similar concepts in the text; and the position of a lexeme in a text and sentence. At least in our domain, these 'contextual' factors seem to have more impact than subtle semantic differences on near-synonym choice.

A. Belz et al. (Eds.): INLG 2004, LNAI 3123, pp. 161–170, 2004.
© Springer-Verlag Berlin Heidelberg 2004

2   Background

2.1   Lexical Choice

Lexical choice is the task of choosing words; it obviously is a key task in NLG. In this paper we focus on the choice of content (open-class) words. We also assume the three-stage pipeline architecture of Reiter and Dale [10], where lexical choice is part of the middle stage, *microplanning*. This means that the lexical choice module is given as input some specification of the information the NLG system wishes to communicate (this comes from content determination in the first pipeline stage); and produces as output a word or set of words in their root forms (morphology is done during the third stage, realisation). Finally, we assume that lexical choice is carried out on small chunks of information; that is, the lexical choice module is given information in small chunks, and is expected to choose a small number of words (often just one) for each chunk.

In summary, the task of lexical choice as we define it is to select a word or a small set of words that communicate a small piece of content information; for example, choosing *midday* to express the meaning 1200, as described above. For other perspectives on lexical choice, see Fawcett et al. [5], who integrates lexical choice with realisation; Reiter [9] and Stone et al. [17], who treat lexical choice as a pragmatic process of satisfying communicative goals; and Robin and McKeown [13], who treat lexicalisation as an optimisation process which chooses many words simultaneously.

Lexical choice from this perspective has two aspects, search and choice. Search is the task of finding those lexemes (or sets of lexemes) that communicate the desired information; choice is the task of choosing which of these candidates to actually use. Our focus here is on choice, and in particular the choice between near-synonyms.

Perhaps the best known previous work on choosing between near-synonyms is Edmonds and Hirst [4]. They assume that words are grouped into 'clusters' of near-synonyms. Each cluster has a core meaning or denotation, which all words in the cluster communicate. Near-synonyms in a cluster are distinguished by further 'peripheral' distinctions, which indicate fine shades of meaning or connotation which are compatible with the core meaning. These distinctions are based on a standard synonym dictionary [6]. Actual lexical choice is based on a matching and optimisation process, which searches for the near-synonym which most closely matches the current situation.

Edmonds and Hirst's work is impressive, but it is not empirically based in the sense that they did not themselves perform corpus analysis or psycholinguistic experiments (although presumably the definitions in the synonym dictionary they used had some empirical basis). They also did not look at the influence of the kind of contextual effects we discuss in this paper, probably because this information was not present in their synonym dictionary.

In an earlier paper [11], we discussed the fact that different people may associate different meanings with words. For example, our data showed that some people interpret *by evening* to mean 1800 (6PM), while others interpret

FORECAST 00-24 GMT, 18-Sep 2000 MONDAY
WIND(10M): SSE 10-14 RISING 24-28 IN THE MORNING THEN VEERING
          SSW EARLY AFTERNOON AND EASING 16-20 LATER
   (50M): SSE 12-18 RISING 30-35 IN THE MORNING THEN VEERING
          SSW EARLY AFTERNOON AND EASING 20-25 LATER
 SIG WAVE: 1.0-1.5 RISING 2.0-2.5, LOCALLY 2.5-3.0 FOR A TIME
MAX WAVE: 1.5-2.5 RISING 3.0-4.0, LOCALLY 4.0-5.0 FOR A TIME
 WEATHER: RAIN CLEARING BY EVENING. CONTINUING RISK OF MIST
          AND FOG

Fig. 1. Extract from 5-day human-authored forecast issued on 16-Sep-00

Table 1. Wind (at 10m) extract from 16-Sep-00 NWP data file

day	hour	wind dir	wind speed
18-09-00	0	SSE	10
18-09-00	3	S	13
18-09-00	6	S	18
18-09-00	9	S	22
18-09-00	12	S	26
18-09-00	15	SSW	25
18-09-00	18	SW	23
18-09-00	21	SW	19
19-09-00	0	SSW	17

it to mean 0000 (midnight). This paper in part continues our exploration of individual differences in language usage, but it focuses on near-synonym choice instead of semantic interpretation.

2.2   SumTime-Mousam

Our empirical work was carried out using data from SUMTIME-MOUSAM [14]. SUMTIME-MOUSAM is an NLG system that produces textual weather forecasts from numerical weather prediction (NWP) data (that is, numerical predictions of wind speed, precipitation, temperature, and other meteorological parameters). SUMTIME-MOUSAM is currently being operationally used by Weathernews (UK) Ltd, whose forecasters manually post-edit the computer generated forecasts before releasing them to the ultimate users.

The analysis presented here is mostly based on two corpora created for SUMTIME-MOUSAM:

– A corpus of 1045 human-written forecasts, together with corresponding NWP data [15]. An extract from this corpus is shown in Figure 1; the NWP data corresponding to the WIND (10M) statement of Figure 1 is shows in Table 1.

From SumTime-Mousam
FORECAST 00-24 UTC Fri 4-Jul 2003
WIND(10M): NW 15-20 INCREASING 21-26 BY MIDDAY THEN EASING 18-23
     BY MIDNIGHT.
SIG WAVE: 1.5-2.0 MAINLY NW SWELL RISING 2.5-3.0 BY AFTERNOON
     THEN FALLING 2.0-2.5 BY MIDNIGHT.

Post-edited
FORECAST 00-24 UTC Fri 4-Jul 2003
WIND(10M): NW 15-20 INCREASING 21-26 BY MIDDAY THEN **DECREASING**
     18-23 **IN THE EVENING**.
SIG WAVE: 1.5-2.0 RISING 2.5-3.0 THEN FALLING 2.0-2.5.

Fig. 2. Extract from post-edit corpus, for forecast issued on 30-Jun-03 (near-synonym changes in **BOLD**)

- A corpus of 2728 post-edited forecasts: this includes the forecast produced by SUMTIME-MOUSAM from this data, the forecast actually sent to clients after human post-editing, and the source NWP data. An example of a computer-generated and post-edited forecast is shown in Figure 2. A smaller version of this corpus is described by Sripada et al. [16].

The post-edit example of Figure 2 illustrates some of the near synonym choices that SUMTIME-MOUSAM must make. In this case, the forecaster has replaced *easing* by its near-synonym *decreasing*, and has also replaced *by midnight* by its near-synonym *in the evening*.

3   Analysis of Human Written Forecasts

We analysed near-synonym choice in wind statements in our corpus of manually written forecasts. To do this, we manually grouped words into near-synonym clusters, each of which had a core meaning (similar to Edmonds and Hirst [4]). If a word's meaning was context dependent or otherwise varied, we attempted to disambiguate each usage of the word (for example, time phrases were disambiguated as described in Reiter and Sripada [12]); clusters only contained instances instances where the word was used with the cluster's meaning. Examples of clusters include

- *easing, decreasing, falling*: verbs indicating wind speed is decreasing
- *by midnight, by late evening, later-0000* (that is, *later* used to mean 0000), *by-end-of-period-0000, by-evening-0000, in-the-evening-0000*: time phrases meaning 0000.
- *then, before, and-SEQ*: connectives used to mean temporal sequence.

There were 14 clusters in all.

For each cluster, we extracted from our corpus all wind statements which used the words in that cluster. This resulted in an average of 449 instances of each cluster (individual cluster size ranged from 61 instances to 1106 instances). We then used Ripper [2] and C4.5 [8] (as implemented in Weka's [19] J4.8 classifier) to learn classification rules that predicted which near-synonym in a cluster was used in each text. We experimented with different feature sets to determine which information was most useful in predicting near-synonym choice:

- *semantic* features: change in wind direction, change in wind speed, amount of time over which this change took place, and several derived features (such as the change in wind direction divided by the change in wind speed).
- *author* feature: which forecaster wrote the text.
- *collocation* features: the preceding and subsequent words in the text (numbers and directions were replaced by generic NUMBER and DIRECTION symbols).
- *repetition* feature: the previous word of this type (e.g., verb) in the text.
- *surface* features: the number of words in the sentence, the number of words in the phrase that contained the near-synonym, and the position of the word and phrase in the sentence.
- *temporal* features: the day and hour the forecast was issued on, and how far in the future the prediction was from the forecast issue date.

The above features were chosen on the basis of knowledge acquisition activities with forecasters and small-scale pilot experiments. For the purposes of this paper, all feature sets except 'semantic' are considered to be contextual.

Ripper and C4.5 gave very similar results, below we report only the ones for C4.5. All error rates are computed with 10-fold cross-validation.

3.1   Verbs

Our analysis of the impact of different feature sets in predicting verb near-synonym choice is shown in Table 2. We show the error rates of classifiers built with no features (baseline), each individual feature set, each combination of author (best individual feature set) with another feature set, and all features. In this analysis we have ignored conjoined verbs, such as *backing and easing*.

Author is clearly the most powerful feature set; it halves classification error, from 16% to 8%. For example, some forecasters preferred to use *rising* as a wind-speed-increase verb, and others preferred to use *increasing*; this simply reflects personal idiosyncrasies and writing styles.

Semantic features by themselves were of no help, but when added to the author feature the error rate went down a bit, from 8% to 7%. For example, again looking at wind-speed-increase verbs, one forecaster preferred *freshening* if the wind speed was still moderate (20 knots or less) even after it increased, and *increasing* otherwise. No other forecaster did this. In other words, while individual authors sometimes associated fine-grained semantic connotations with words, these seemed to be idiosyncratic and not shared by the group as a whole.

Table 2. Verb classifier error rates, by feature sets used

features used	error
none (baseline)	16%
author	8%
collocation	14%
repetition	16%
semantic	16%
surface	16%
temporal	15%
author, collocation	8%
author, repetition	8%
author, semantic	7%
author, surface	8%
author, temporal	8%
all	6%

3.2   Connectives

We analysed connectives in a similar fashion to verbs, but due to space limitations we cannot present detailed results here. The baseline (no feature) connective classifier had a 22% error rate. The most useful single feature set was collocation; a classifier based on collocation had a 16% error rate (for example, *and* is strongly preferred for a sequence connective if the subsequent word is *later*). Adding the repetition feature set improved error rate to 14%; essentially forecasters like to vary the connectives used in a sentence.

Adding further feature sets did not significantly improve classification performance. We did note some cases of individual preferences; for example, when authors needed an alternative to *then* to avoid repetition, most used *and* but one used *before*. However, such cases were not common enough to significantly influence overall classification accuracy.

We also attempted to learn a classifier that predicted the punctuation associated with a connective. The baseline classifier (just connective) had a 30% error rate; a classifier based on connective and author had a 5% error rate; and a classifier based on connective, author and surface features had a 4% error rate.

3.3   Time Phrases

The baseline (no feature) classifier for time phrases had a 67% error rate. The most useful single feature for classification was again author; this reduced error rate to 52%. Adding information about the position of a phrase in a sentence further reduced error rate to 48%; for example, one author used *by midnight* to refer to 0000 in the middle of a sentence, but *later* to refer to this time at the end of a sentence.

Adding semantic information did not further improve the error rate. We did notice a few cases where semantics seemed to play a role; for instance one forecaster seemed to prefer *by afternoon* for 1500 when the wind was changing slowly, but *by mid afternoon* when it was changing rapidly. But as with the impact of author on connective choice (see above), these effects were small and had no significant impact on overall error statistics.

The classifier error rate was 46% with all the features sets included.

3.4 Discussion

Our analysis suggests that the author feature is overall the most powerful predictive feature in our set. In other words, the idiosyncrasies and preferences ('idiolect') of individual authors has a strong influence on near-synonym choice. Semantics plays little role except in verb choice, but even here its effect is author-dependent. Other contextual features also play a role, including collocation, lexical repetition, and the position of the phrase in the sentence.

Of course, our classifiers still have a high error rate, and it is possible that this is due to a semantic feature which we have omitted from our feature set; in other words, perhaps semantics would be more significant if we used a different feature set. We also of course are working in a single domain (and in a sublanguage), and perhaps different results would be obtained in other domains.

4 Post-edit Analysis

Our post-edit corpus shows how forecasters have edited computer generated texts. These texts were generated using a version of SUMTIME-MOUSAM that always chooses the same member of a near-synonym cluster, usually the one that was most common in our corpus analysis. We are currently analysing cases where forecasters have replaced a word by one of its near-synonyms. This work is not complete, but we present some initial results for verb choice below. As above, all figures cited below are for wind statements.

4.1 Verbs

The only case where forecasters regularly post-edited a verb into another verb in the same cluster was changing *easing* to *decreasing*. This happened in 15% of cases. Individual differences are very striking. Of the 9 forecasters for which we have post-edit data, 5 changed *easing* to *decreasing* less than 5% of the time, 2 made this change over 90% of the time, with the remaining two in between (30% and 75%). A classifier (which predicts when *easing* is changed to *decreasing*) built on the author feature has a 5.5% error rate.

We were especially surprised by forecaster F5, who changed *easing* to *decreasing* in 92% of cases. We have data from him in our manual corpus, and in this corpus he used *easing* 69% of the time, and *decreasing* only 30% of the time. However, as noted in Reiter and Sripada [12, Figure 2], F5's behaviour in this respect may have changed over time. The manual corpus was collected from July 2000 to May 2002, and while at the beginning of this period F5 preferred *easing*, at the end of this period he preferred *decreasing*. Since the post-edit corpus was collected in 2003, this behaviour change may explain the above discrepancy. In other words, not only do individuals have idiosyncratic preferences about near-synonym choice, but these preferences may change over time.

We also asked the forecasters (anonymously) about the *easing* vs *decreasing* choice. The comments received included

1. "Personally I prefer *decreasing* to *easing*"
2. "I tend to think of *easing* being associated with a slower decrease and or perhaps with lower wind speeds or heights"
3. "*Easing* is used when trying to indicate a slight decrease when condition are bad ... it is not used when conditions are quiet"
4. (from forecast manager) "On the whole it seems safer to say *decreasing*"

Note that (2) and (3), which are exactly the sort of subtle semantic differences we expected to find between near-synonyms, are in fact contradictory. The forecaster who said (3) associated *easing* with bad weather, which generally means high wind speeds; while the forecaster who said (2) associated *easing* with low wind speeds. This supports the evidence from Section 3 that subtle semantic differences can be idiosyncratic.

Comment (4), that *decreasing* is the safest choice, presumably because it has the fewest connotations, is interesting. This is supported by another puzzling fact, which is that the *increasing* was edited into a near-synonym (*rising* or *freshening*) in only 1% of cases. Yet in the manually written forecasts, *increasing* was less dominant in its cluster than *easing*; *increasing* was used in 58% of cases for wind-speed-increase, whereas *easing* was used in 71% of cases for wind-speed-decrease. One explanation is that *increasing* (unlike *easing*) is 'safe' in the sense of comment (4), and hence there is no need to change it. Safety is perhaps another factor that should be considered in near-synonym choice.

4.2   Other Types of Words

We have not yet analysed our post-edit data for the other types of near-synonym choices. However, when we asked forecasters in general about problems with SumTime-Mousam's output texts, the only other comment relevant to near-synonym choice was variation in connectives (Section 3.2).

We have not noticed such variation in any other type of word, in either the manual corpus or the post-edit corpus. So variation (at least in this domain) seems important in connectives, but not other types of words.

5   Future Work

Our work to date has focused on understanding how writers choose between near-synonyms. We hope in the future to investigate how the near-synonym choice affects readers. For example, it may make sense to prefer high-frequency words, because such words are usually read faster [7]. This may be especially important in texts intended for poor readers [3,18]. It may also make sense to prefer words which mean the same thing to all readers; for example to express 0000 as *by midnight* (which means 0000 to everyone) instead of *by evening* (which means 0000 to some people and 1800 to others) [12]. This is related to the idea of choosing 'safe' words mentioned in Section 4.1.

We also plan to empirically analyse lexical choice in other domains, in particular textual descriptions of medical data (using the corpus from Alberdi et al. [1]), in a similar manner. We would also like to empirically investigate other types of microplanning choices, such as aggregation.

6 Conclusion

When we started this work, we expected to find that near-synonym choice was mostly determined by semantic details and connotations, along the lines of the comments about *easing* and *decreasing* made in comments (2) and (3) of Section 4.1. In fact, however, our empirical work suggests that near-synonym choice is mostly influenced by contextual information, especially author. Furthermore, when semantics does play a role in near-synonym choice, it often does so in a highly author-dependent way; in other words, semantic connotations often seem to be idiosyncratic and not shared by a linguistic community. Of course we have only looked at one domain, perhaps other domains are different.

From a practical NLG system-building perspective, our current thinking is that in general it probably is not worth trying to choose between near-synonyms on the basis of semantic differences. Instead, the system-builder's priority should be a good understanding of the impact of contextual factors such as collocation, repetition, and individual preferences on near-synonym choice; he or she may also wish to consider safety (chance of misinterpretation). At least in the short term, we believe that a better understanding of these factors may be the best way to improve near-synonym choice in NLG systems.

Acknowledgements

Our thanks to the many individuals who have discussed this work with us, of which there are too many to list here. Special thanks to the forecasters and meteorologists at Weathernews, without whom this work would have been impossible! This work was supported by the UK Engineering and Physical Sciences Research Council (EPSRC), under grant GR/M76881.

References

1. Alberdi, E., Becher, J., Gilhooly, K., Hunter, J., Logie, R., Lyon, A., McIntosh, N., Reiss, J.: Expertise and the interpretation of computerized physiological data: implications for the design of computerized monitoring in neonatal intensive care. International Journal of Human-Computer Studies 55 (2001) 191–216

2. Cohen, W.: Fast effective rule induction. In: Proc. 12th International Conference on Machine Learning, Morgan Kaufmann (1995) 115–123
3. Devlin, S., Tait, J.: The use of a psycholinguistic database in the simplification of text for aphasic readers. In Nerbonne, J., ed.: Linguistic Databases. CSLI (1998)
4. Edmonds, P., Hirst, G.: Near-synonymy and lexical choice. Computational Linguistics (2002) 105–144
5. Fawcett, R., Tucker, G., Lin, Y.: How a systemic functional grammar works: the role of realization in realization. In Horacek, H., Zock, M., eds.: New Concepts in Natural Language Generation. Pinter (1993) 114–186
6. Gove, P., ed.: Webster's New Dictionary of Synonyms. Merriam-Webster (1984)
7. Harley, T.: The Psychology of Language. second edn. Psychology Press (2001)
8. Quinlan, J.R.: C4.5: Programs for Machine Learning. Morgan Kaufmann (1992)
9. Reiter, E.: A new model of lexical choice for nouns. Computational Intelligence 7 (1991) 240–251
10. Reiter, E., Dale, R.: Building Natural Language Generation Systems. Cambridge University Press (2000)
11. Reiter, E., Sripada, S.: Human variation and lexical choice. Computational Linguistics 28 (2002) 545–553
12. Reiter, E., Sripada, S.: Learning the meaning and usage of time phrases from a parallel text-data corpus. In: Proceedings of the HLT-NAACL 2003 Workshop on Learning Word Meaning from Non-Linguistic Data. (2003) 78–85
13. Robin, J., McKeown, K.: Empirically designing and evaluating a new revision-based model for summary generation. Artificial Intelligence 85 (1996) 135–179
14. Sripada, S., Reiter, E., Davy, I.: SumTime-Mousam: Configurable marine weather forecast generator. Expert Update 6 (2003) 4–10
15. Sripada, S., Reiter, E., Hunter, J., Yu, J.: Exploiting a parallel text-data corpus. In: Proceedings of Corpus Linguistics 2003. (2003) 734–743
16. Sripada, S., Reiter, E., Hunter, J., Yu, J.: Generating English summaries of time series data using the Gricean maxims. In: Proceedings of KDD-2003. (2003) 187–196
17. Stone, M., Doran, C., Webber, B., Bleam, T., Palmer, M.: Microplanning with communicative intentions: The SPUD system. Computational Intelligence 19 (2003) 311–381
18. Williams, S., Reiter, E., Osman, L.: Experiments with discourse-level choices and readability. In: Proceedings of the 2003 European Workshop on Natural Language Generation. (2003) 127–134
19. Witten, I., Frank, E.: Data Mining: Practical Machine Learning Tools and Techniques with Java Implementations. Morgan Kaufmann (2000)

Overgenerating Referring Expressions Involving Relations and Booleans

Sebastian Varges

Information Technology Research Institute,
University of Brighton, UK
Sebastian.Varges@itri.brighton.ac.uk

Abstract. We present a new approach to the generation of referring expressions containing attributive, type and relational properties combined by conjunctions, disjunctions and negations. The focus of this paper is on generating referring expressions involving positive and negated relations. We describe rule-based overgeneration of referring expressions based on the notion of 'extension', and show how to constrain the search space by interleaving logical form generation with realization and expressing preferences by means of costs. Our chart-based framework allows us to develop a search-based solution to the problem of 'recursive' relations.

1 Introduction

The task of generating referring expressions (GRE) can be characterized by the following question: given a domain model and a set of referents, how can we uniquely identify the referent(s) using natural language? This task has often been combined with the requirement to be minimal, i.e. to use only a minimal number of properties, and with considerations of computational complexity. Earlier work often centered around the 'incremental algorithm' [3] which originally dealt with selecting attributive properties but which can also be taken as a processing framework for selecting relations [2] and Boolean combinations of attributes for reference to sets [13]. A separate strand of recent work originates from the graph-based approach to GRE which provides an elegant treatment of relations [9] and which has also been extended to deal with Boolean combinations [14]. These approaches see GRE as a task separated from surface realization.

Previously, overgeneration has mostly been explored in the context of surface realization [10,1,15]. In this work, we apply it to the generation of referring expressions including both logical form construction (or 'description building', as we call it) and realization. First, we make sure that we can actually handle all the types of properties (attributes, relations, types) and their combinations (conjunction, disjunction, negation) we want to cover, and only then do we start weeding out unwanted solutions and address efficiency issues. Thus, at first we overgenerate vastly, giving priority to completeness of coverage over efficiency and correctness of all outputs. The advantage of this methodology is a separation of concerns: we can first concentrate on giving a consistent treatment to a wide

A. Belz et al. (Eds.): INLG 2004, LNAI 3123, pp. 171–181, 2004.
© Springer-Verlag Berlin Heidelberg 2004

range of phenomena without worrying about efficiency and algorithmic complexity. After that we can concentrate on defining constraints and preferences, and search for 'good' solutions. At the implementation level, some of these constraints are applied in the rule-based part, some are implemented as filters on the output of the rule system.

In the next section, we introduce the general processing framework and the three levels of representation of our approach: domain representation, description building and realization. In section 3, we examine the output of a first version of the system and introduce a constraint designed to prevent the inclusion of 'redundant' information. In section 3.1 we address the issue of search for optimal referring expressions, followed by a discussion of the problem of 'recursive' relations. In section 4 we compare our work to previous work on GRE and in section 5 we discuss possible extensions of our approach.

2   Processing Framework and Representations

Overgeneration requires a flexible processing framework that allows one to produce a large number of candidate outputs and experiment with different search strategies. Chart-based algorithms offer just this: different agenda orderings can be used to model different search strategies, and intermediate results can be reused in order to avoid unnecessary recomputations. Chart generation algorithms [8] have often been applied to surface realization. We apply them to description building as well: starting from a domain specification, we first derive basic description edges, and then recombine these bottom-up using logical connectives. Employing overgeneration at the level of description building can lead to the generation of vast numbers of descriptions that cannot be realized. As a consequence, we closely couple description building with surface realization. Such a coupling has previously been advocated in [12]. In the context of our approach, this means that the chart algorithm attempts to immediately realize new description edges. Only descriptions that have been successfully realized can be used in further rule applications. Surface realizations of partial referring expressions are always combined compositionally (see section 2.3).

2.1   Domain Representation

Domain objects are defined by means of three types of properties: attributes, types and relations. A domain D contains a set of domain objects $\{o_1, o_2, ..., o_n\}$. As in [3], every domain object is required to have exactly one type t (e.g. $t(o_1) =$ cup) and has zero or more attributes and relations. Types can be arranged in a subsumption hierarchy, e.g. artifact $\succ$ cup. Attributes are defined by attribute value pairs where both attributes and values are atomic (e.g. $attr(o_1) =$ colour:red). Similar to the graph representation language of [9], relations are directed arcs between domain objects (e.g. $rel(o_1, o_2) =$ in). In the following, we illustrate our approach with an example domain similar to the one in [2]. It contains three cups (c_1, c_2, c_3), three bowls (b_1, b_2, b_3), a table (t_1) and a floor (f_1).

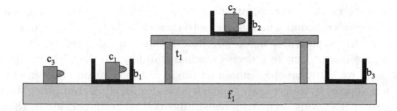

Fig. 1. Example domain

Cups c_1 and c_2 are 'in' b_1 and b_2, respectively. b_1, b_3 and c_3 are 'on' the floor but b_2 is 'on' the table which in turn is 'on' the floor. c_1 and c_2 are red, c_3 is blue and all other objects are black. All these objects are subtypes of `artifact` which in turn is a subtype of `domain_object`. Figure 1 shows the relative positions of the domain objects in the example domain (colours are not depicted).

2.2 Description Building

We regard constructing descriptions of domain objects as an inference process working over the domain model. Descriptions are represented as pairs of logical form and their extension which is defined as the set of domain objects for which the description is true. Logical forms contain the properties of the domain model, combined by conjunction, disjunction and negation.

The first step in building up increasingly complex descriptions is to determine the extension of the explicitly defined domain properties excluding relations, for example $<type(cup), \{c_1, c_2, c_3\}>$ or $<attr\_val(colour : red), \{c_1, c_2\}>$. The subsumption hierarchy is used to compute the extension of the supertypes of the domain objects as well, for example $<type(artifact), \{c_1, c_2, c_3, b_1, b_2, b_3, t_1, f_1\}>$. This allows us to deal with all types in a uniform way.

The main description building phase takes the basic description edges and recursively generates new description edges. We employ the following rules:

1. Conjunction: given two description edges d_1 and d_2, generate a new edge d_3 whose extension ext_{d_3} is the intersection $ext_{d_1} \wedge ext_{d_2}$, for example
   $<(type(artifact) \wedge attr\_val(colour : blue)), \{c_3\}>$.
2. Disjunction: given two description edges d_1 and d_2, generate a new edge d_3 whose extension ext_{d_3} is the union $ext_{d_1} \vee ext_{d_2}$, for example $<(type(floor) \vee type(table)), \{f_1, t_1\}>$.
3. Negation: given a description edge d_1, generate a new edge d_2 whose extension ext_{d_2} is the complement $\overline{ext_{d_1}}$, for example
   $<\neg attr\_val(colour : black), \{c_1, c_2, c_3\}>$.

Relations are introduced in a separate rule. Generally, we see relations as combining two existing descriptions. For example, *the cups* can be combined with *the bowls* through relation *in* into *the cups in the bowls*. Thus, we define a rule that takes two description facts and establishes whether a given relation holds between them. This allows us to introduce both positive and negated relations in the same rule. Since our descriptions are defined by exactly one extension, we have to make a decision when building up descriptions involving relations: do we focus on the domain or range of the relation? (Given our over-generation approach, we generate relation edges for all cases, but other strategies are possible.) Relations seem to have similarities to conjunctions in that they add constraints to the description. In the above example, extending *the cups* to *the cups in the bowls* reduces the size of the focus extension of 'cups' from three to two elements. Introducing negative relations has the same constraining effect: the focus extension of *the cup not in the bowl* leaves only one element, c_3. We define the following relation introducing rule:

4. Given two description edges d_1 and d_2 and a relation name rel:

- let extension $ext_{dom,pos}$ contain all $o_i \in ext_{d_1}$ that are in domain of rel with at least one member of ext_{d_2} in its range.
- let extension $ext_{dom,neg}$ contain all $o_{ii} \in ext_{d_1}$ that are *not* in domain of rel with any member of ext_{d_2} in its range.
- let extension $ext_{ran,pos}$ contain all $o_j \in ext_{d_2}$ that are in range of rel with at least one member of ext_{d_1} its domain.
- let extension $ext_{ran,neg}$ contain all $o_{jj} \in ext_{d_2}$ that are *not* in range of rel with any member of ext_{d_1} in its domain.

4.1 generate a new description edge d_3 with extension $ext_{dom,pos}$ and focus on domain of rel, for example $<in(FOCUS(type(cup)), type(bowl)), \{c_1, c_2\}>$.

4.2 generate a new description edge d_5 with extension $ext_{dom,neg}$ and focus on domain of rel, for example $<\neg in(FOCUS(type(cup)), type(bowl)), \{c_3\}>$.

4.3 generate a new description edge d_4 with extension $ext_{ran,pos}$ and focus on range of rel, for example $<in(type(cup), FOCUS(type(bowl))), \{b_1, b_2\}>$.

4.4 generate a new description edge d_6 with extension $ext_{ran,neg}$ and focus on range of rel, for example $<\neg in(type(cup), FOCUS(type(bowl))), \{b3\}>$.

Since relations are represented by *directed* arcs, relation rule 4 needs to test d_1 and d_2 at both domain and range of a relation. The relation rule introduces positive relations if the relation holds for at least one pair of domain objects. Negated relations use the complements of the extension of the positive cases at the respective relation 'ends', i.e. $ext_{dom,neg} = \overline{ext_{dom,pos}}$ and $ext_{ran,neg} = \overline{ext_{ran,pos}}$.

Description building using relation rule 4 (and also rules 1-3) is subject to the constraint that the (focus) extension should not be the empty set. For example, let us assume a domain consisting of two bowls containing a cup each. We should be able to generate *the cups in the bowls* but we should not produce *the cup not in the bowl* as there is none. Rule 4 computes an empty focus extension in this case and we 'block' the resulting description. However, if we add another empty bowl, we can generate *the bowl not containing the cup* while still excluding *the cup not in the bowl*. Requiring description extensions to be non-empty seems a reasonable restriction for GRE since in the end we want to refer to at least one domain object. Due to the availability of a single extension in descriptions involving relations, the results of the relation rule can be combined further in rules 1-3 like all other descriptions.

2.3 Realization

Grammar rules and lexicon map description facts to surface forms. Basic description edges for types and attributes are realized by means of a phrasal lexicon. Complex descriptions are realized by collecting the realizations of the component descriptions and combining them bottom-up. The derivation structure of descriptions resulting from rules 1-4 is mirrored by the syntactic structure of the realizations. For example, when we conjoin attribute value edge `colour:red` with type edge `cup` into a new conjunction edge in the description builder, this is mirrored in the realizer by combining the realizations of the two descriptions, adjective edge *red* and Nbar edge *cup*, into Nbar *red cup*. Every realized description contains at least one type for the head noun of the top-level NP. In contrast to the incremental algorithm [3], this is a result of the grammar rules and the close coupling of description building and realization rather than a hard-wired constraint.

Relations are realized by combining already realized NPs for domain and range of the relation with a verb or preposition provided by the lexicon, possibly introducing a negation, for example *the cup + not + in + the bowl*. The same relation can be realized by different syntactic categories depending on the focus of the description. For example, relation 'in' is realized as verb gerund *containing* rather than a preposition if the focus is on the range of the relation.

3   Overgeneration and Search

The currently implemented system uses 34 description building rules (distinguishing between negation of different description types, amongst others) and 21 rules for NP generation. The rules are expressed as productions in a production system [4], the knowledge base of which serves as the chart. In the following, we first look at the output of the system using bottom-up breadth-first search without specific referents in mind. After that we define goal referents and refine the search strategy.

Figure 2 shows some output NPs generated from the example domain of section 2.1. The last column ('complexity') measures the number of description rules involved. Introducing a negated relation increases the complexity by 2. The first 3 NPs in figure 2 are realizations of basic descriptions. The following NPs are complex descriptions. 4 is an example of a disjunction. 5 and 6 exhibit negations which, as 6 shows, can be applied repeatedly. 7 and 8 use adjectives and 9-15 use relations of increasing complexity.

One problem of the generated NPs involves 'redundant' information. This is most obvious in cases of direct repetitions, for example NP 7. Moreover, in

	Realization	Extension	Complexity
(1)	the cups	c1 c2 c3	1
(2)	the bowls	b1 b2 b3	1
(3)	the artifacts	c2 c3 b2 b3 c1 b1 t1 f1	1
(4)	the table or the cups	t1 c1 c2 c3	3
(5)	the non-blue domain objects	c1 c2 b1 b2 b3 t1 f1	4
(6)	not not a cup	c1 c2 c3	3
(7)	the black black bowls	b1 b2 b3	5
(8)	the black non-blue table	t1	6
(9)	the bowl on the table	b2	3
(10)	the table under the bowl	t1	3
(11)	the cups in the bowls	c1 c2	3
(12)	the bowls containing the cups	b1 b2	3
(13)	the bowl not containing the cup	b3	4
(14)	the cups in the bowls containing the cups in the bowls containing the cups	c1 c2	9
(15)	the bowls containing the cups in the bowls containing the cups in the bowls	b1 b2	9

Fig. 2. Some realized NPs of overgeneration experiment

10 *the table* would have been sufficient to describe the referent. As Dale and Reiter [3] point out, 'redundant' information may violate the Gricean maxim of quantity, leaving the reader wondering why information such as *under the bowl* (NP 10) was included. Since description building is extension-based, it is quite natural to require description building rules to reduce the extension size. This only applies to operations that are intersective in nature, i.e. conjunctions and relations. Concerning relations, additional information should constrain the focus extension, preventing, for example, NP 10 because *under the cup* does not reduce the extension of *the table*. Conjunctions of descriptions, apparently symmetric, also seem to have a focus extension when we consider how they are realized: in *the red cups*, *red* should only constrain the number of cups. If we also require the extension of 'red' to be reduced, we cannot generate *the red cups* in our example domain because all red objects are cups. This observation again points to a close coupling of content determination and realization: the syntactic head corresponds to the focus extension used in the description builder. Applying the extension-reducing constraint prevents the generation of NPs 7, 8 and 10.

3.1   Filtering and Search for Optimal Referring Expressions

Our bottom-up breadth-first chart algorithm generates referring expressions in order of increasing complexity. Thus, it can stop as soon as the system has generated a description for some *intended* referent(s), knowing that there cannot be a less complex one. This is essentially the 'full brevity' algorithm described by Dale and Reiter [3]. What, however, if we want to use a different cost metric? For example, integration with surface realization allows one to define costs based on

c	NO CONSTRAINTS			EXT. CONSTR.			EXT. CONSTR. + EQUI.		
	edges	realizations	secs	edges	realizations	secs	edges	realizations	secs
1	33	21	1	33	21	1	33	21	1
2	51	32	2	51	32	1	51	32	2
3	128	78	3	112	67	3	96	54	3
4	272	158	6	219	122	6	155	76	4
5	887	443	37	521	261	19	277	128	9
6	2042	979	189	1073	504	64	372	169	15

Table 1. Performance figures for different levels of NP complexity ('c')

the number of words. These alternative metrics can be incorporated by making costs explicit and ordering the agenda in terms of increasing cost. Under the assumption of monotonically increasing costs, we know that a current best NP describing the intended referent(s) is indeed the optimal one according to the cost metric once all other descriptions on the agenda have a higher cost. This is similar to the branch-and-bound algorithm used in graph-based GRE [9]. We can reduce the search space further by defining an admissible heuristic for estimating the minimal additional cost of the descriptions on the agenda. For example, we may know that further rule applications will add at least one more word to the realizations. We then use the increased minimal cost to compare descriptions on the agenda to the cost of the current best solution. The result is A^* search [11] for intended referents.

In addition, we can filter descriptions by means of equivalence classes. These are defined by the extension of the descriptions and the syntactic features of their realization. For example, an equivalence class for c_3 and syntactic category NP may contain descriptions realized as *the blue cup* and *the blue artifact*, amongst others. Dropping one of these will not reduce the referential capabilities of the generator since the alternatives are substitutable. Which one is dropped depends on the cost metric: for example, if costs reflect the distance from 'basic level types' [3], we can eliminate *the blue artifact*.

Table 1 shows some performance figures for the example domain for different levels of NP complexity ('c'). The number of edges includes both description and realization edges. Up to a complexity of 5 the simplest version of the implemented system ('NO CONSTRAINTS') generates 443 realizations within 37 seconds. The constraint that requires extensions to be reduced ('EXT. CONSTR.') decreases the number of realizations to 261 in 19 seconds. Adding filtering based on equivalence classes ('EXT. CONSTR. + EQUI.') leads to a further reduction to 128 realizations in 9 seconds. The system generates *the table or the floor* for goal referents t_1 and f_1 in 2 seconds, and finds *the cup in the bowl on the floor* for referent c_1 within 10 seconds. We believe that there is a lot of room for further efficiency gains which, as we argued earlier, should be seen as a separate issue from the generative capabilities of the system. For example, when referring to an individual, we can disable the disjunction rule. This reduces generation time for referent c_1 from 10 to 4 seconds. Furthermore, the use of a rule system that runs on top of Java involves considerable overhead that could be removed by employing a lower-level implementation language.

3.2   The 'Recursion' Problem for Relations

Dale and Haddock [2] describe a problem of infinite regress or 'recursion' that occurs when extending the incremental algorithm to relations. The problem can be recreated in our example domain. Let us assume that our goal is to describe the cup that is in the bowl on the table, i.e. c_2. An infinite regress occurs because the system can always prefix *the cups in* to a description of the bowls containing the cups (like 12 and 15 in figure 2) and *the bowls containing* to a description of the cups in the bowls (like NPs 11 and 14). This is possible because in each case the focus extension is reduced from 3 to 2 domain objects so that the extension-reduction constraint defined earlier is not violated.

The fact that the recursion problem can be re-created in our approach shows its generality. However, in a breadth-first style algorithm like ours, the problem is less severe because a solution is found in one of the parallel branches of the search tree, after which search can stop, knowing that the infinite recursive branch will result in a higher cost than some alternative solution obtained already. This search-based solution to the recursion problem is different from the proposal of Dale and Haddock in that it does not require any form of check for structural repetitions.

4   Comparison to Previous Work on GRE

Our domain representation language bears similarities to the graph approach of Krahmer et al. [9], the major difference being the addition of a subsumption hierarchy and a different representation of attributes. In contrast to the graph approach, we separate descriptions (logical forms) and domain model. This has the advantage of not having to express logical formulae in the domain representation language where graphs encounter problems when it comes to representing disjunctions, for example. A further difference is the integration with surface realization: this makes surface-based costs available for decisions about referring expressions. In contrast, the graph approach requires costs to be attached to the edges of the domain graph. Arguably, these costs are more difficult to obtain. Using the number of words as a cost metric as we did in this work is just a simple illustration of the possibilities of this integration.

Gardent [5] integrates logical form construction and surface realization in a constraint-based approach. Search finds solutions in 'increasing order of size'. Other search strategies and cost functions are not discussed. Gardent observes that the graph-based approach to domain representation becomes less intuitive when applied to relations of arity higher than two. This also applies to our domain representation language. However, propositional nodes may offer a way out. For example, we could use ternary 'in-between' and 'give' nodes.

In contrast to the incremental algorithm [3] and its extensions, our approach crucially involves search. It finds globally best solutions and can correct local decisions rather than cutting off choices. A further difference is the notion of 'distractors' used in the incremental algorithm, which in our terminology corresponds to the extension set minus any referents it contains.

Horacek [7] describes a best-first search algorithm that works by expanding a tree structure representing the state of the search. The algorithm uses an A^*-style notion of future minimum costs. However, it is not entirely clear if choosing the locally best expansion point can lead to globally non-optimal results. Integration with realization is not described.

5   Discussion and Future Work

The work presented in this paper is limited to the generation of purely referential expressions, ignoring attributive descriptions [6]. However, it should be possible to incorporate goals such as motivating somebody to make a purchase into the computation of preference scores, allowing for trade-offs between the preference for least complexity and other goals.

Furthermore, scalability is an important issue. Using larger domain models and additional grammar rules will increase the search space. However, we believe that these issues can be solved in practical applications for all cognitively plausible levels of NP complexity. On the other hand, we freely acknowledge that this has to be demonstrated in an implementation.

Costs such as NP complexity and surface length do not take the extension size or the presence of intended referents in the extension set into account. It could be argued that negation constitutes an 'indirect' way of arriving at a description of intended referents: the system first aims to describe the complement of the intended referents (or at least a subset of these), and then negates it. Incorporating search strategies that take these considerations into account is left to future work.

In ongoing work we address remaining errors of the output candidates. For example, when edges are combined, their extension changes. This in turn can result in the apparent need for non-monotonic changes of the corresponding realizations, for example trying to re-use the bowls to generate the bowl (on the table). One technique to prevent such non-monotonic changes is to delay morphological realization [16]. Our current implementation uses shallow methods to 'adjust' morphology.

Another problem is ambiguity of surface forms, in particular when using logical connectives. For example, in the musicians holding the drum or the instrument, the musicians can 1) only hold the drum or 2) hold the drum or the instrument. In our current implementation, we introduce a comma before or to at least enforce one of the readings in such cases. This may not be a very principled approach but it should be noted that ambiguity from a parsing (reader) perspective is a general issue for NLG systems which is not confined to GRE or overgeneration approaches.

6   Conclusions

We presented a new approach to the generation of referring expressions. By using overgeneration, we can focus on how to consistently treat a wide range of phenomena rather than trying to prematurely optimize or restrict our algorithm. We found that at the level of logical form construction (description building), using the extension as the main 'interface' between descriptions results in a consistent treatment of arbitrarily complex descriptions involving positive and negated relations. Our search algorithm can be seen as a generalization of the full-brevity algorithm to arbitrary monotonic cost functions. We offer an alternative solution to the 'recursion' problem for relations identified by Dale and Haddock.

Acknowledgements

Our thanks go to Kees van Deemter and Richard Power for very helpful discussions on the topics of this paper. The presented research has been conducted as part of the TUNA[1] project funded by EPSRC (grant number GR/S13330/01).

References

1. Bangalore, S., Rambow, O. 2000: Exploiting a probabilistic hierarchical model for generation. Proceedings of COLING-00.
2. Dale, R., Haddock, N. 1991: Generating referring expressions involving relations. Proceedings of EACL-91.
3. Dale, R., Reiter, E. 1995: Computational interpretations of the gricean maxims in the generation of referring expressions. Cognitive Science, 19:233-263.
4. Friedman-Hill, E. 2004. JESS - the Java Expert System Shell, Version 6.x. Sandia National Laboratories.
5. Gardent, C. 2002: Generating minimal definite descriptions. Proceedings of ACL-02.
6. Green, N., Carenini, G., Moore, J. 1998: A principled representation of attributive descriptions for generating integrated text and information graphics presentations. Proceedings of IWNLG-98.
7. Horacek, H. 2003: A best-first search algorithm for generating referring expression. Proceedings of EACL-03 (research notes).
8. Kay, M. 1996: Chart generation. Proceedings of ACL-96.
9. Krahmer, E., Verleg, A., van Erk, S. 2003: Graph-based generation of referring expressions. Computational Linguistics, 29(1):53-72.
10. Langkilde, I., Knight, K. 1998: Generation that exploits corpus-based statistical knowledge. Proceedings of COLING/ACL-98.
11. Pearl, J. 1984: Heuristics: intelligent search strategies for computer problem solving. Addison-Wesley.
12. Stone, M., Doran, C. 1997: Sentence planning as description using Tree-Adjoining Grammar. Proceedings of ACL-97.
13. van Deemter, K. 2002: Generating referring expressions: Boolean extensions of the incremental algorithm. Computational Linguistics, 28(1):37-52.

---

[1] Towards a UNified Algorithm for the Generation of Referring Expressions.

14. van Deemter, K., Krahmer E. to appear: Graphs and Booleans: on the generation of referring expressions. Kluwer Academic Publishers.
15. Varges, S., Mellish, C. 2001: Instance-based natural language generation. Proceedings of NAACL-01.
16. Wilcock, G. and Matsumoto, Y. 1996: Reversible delayed lexical choice in a bidirectional framework. COLING-96.

Reining in CCG Chart Realization

Michael White

School of Informatics, University of Edinburgh
Edinburgh EH8 9LW, UK
http://www.iccs.informatics.ed.ac.uk/~mwhite/

Abstract. We present a novel ensemble of six methods for improving the efficiency of chart realization. The methods are couched in the framework of Combinatory Categorial Grammar (CCG), but we conjecture that they can be adapted to related grammatical frameworks as well. The ensemble includes two new methods introduced here—feature-based licensing and instantiation of edges, and caching of category combinations—in addition to four previously introduced methods—index filtering, LF chunking, edge pruning based on n-gram scores, and anytime search. We compare the relative contributions of each method using two test grammars, and show that the methods work best in combination. Our evaluation also indicates that despite the exponential worst-case complexity of the basic algorithm, the methods together can constrain the realization problem sufficiently to meet the interactive needs of natural language dialogue systems.

1   Introduction

Chart realization algorithms [1, 2, 3, 4, 5, 6] perform the inverse task of chart parsing algorithms: that is, rather than transducing strings to logical forms (LFs), they transduce logical forms to strings, a task often called surface (or linguistic or syntactic) realization. As Kay [2] explains, chart realization algorithms are generally exponential in the worst case, though in practice their behavior can vary greatly depending on the specific algorithm and grammar. In this paper, we address the question whether chart realization using Steedman's [7, 8] Combinatory Categorial Grammar (CCG)—with its theoretically attractive accounts of coordination and intonation—can be practically employed in natural language dialogue systems, even in the presence of mild overgeneration. In a case study, we show for the first time that by employing a novel ensemble of methods for improving the efficiency of CCG chart realization, one can reliably realize sentences in a dialogue system fast enough for interactive use.[1]

The methods have been implemented in the OpenCCG[2] open source CCG realizer, which takes advantage of the multi-modal extensions to CCG developed

---

[1] Though the amount of time that can be allocated to realization without introducing undue response latencies varies for different dialogue systems, as a rule of thumb, we have been aiming to keep realization times under a second.

[2] http://openccg.sourceforge.net/

A. Belz et al. (Eds.): INLG 2004, LNAI 3123, pp. 182–191, 2004.

by Baldridge and Kruijff [9, 10]. It has also been deployed in two prototype dialogue systems, COMIC [11] and FLIGHTS [12]. Initial experience with these systems suggests that realization times are satisfactory.

2   Efficiency Methods

In this section, we review the methods for improving the efficiency of CCG chart realization described in [6, 13], then introduce two new methods here. For space reasons, we omit a description of the chart realization algorithm itself.

Index Filtering In the OpenCCG realizer, an *edge* is a CCG sign (string-category pair) plus various bookkeeping data structures. These include two bit vectors that make it possible to instantly check whether two edges cover disjoint parts of the input LF, and whether they have any indices in common. Both of these tests must succeed in order for the algorithm to attempt to create new edges by combining the pair using the combinatory rules.

Our approach to index filtering essentially follows Kay [2] and Carroll et al. [4]. The twist with CCG [6] is that a check must be made for paired indices in the input LF in order to handle argument cluster coordination, since the type-raised NPs which need to compose into an argument cluster do not have any indices in common. If index filtering is turned off, the search space can quickly become unmanageable [6, 13].

Anytime Search The anytime search method [6] involves integrating n-gram scoring of possible realizations into the chart realization algorithm, as proposed by Varges and Mellish [14], rather than ranking all complete realizations by their n-gram score as a post-process, as in the pioneering work of Knight and Hatzivassiloglou [15] and their successors. With this method, the search is formulated as a best-first anytime algorithm that can return the best available realization (according to its n-gram score) at "any time." Implementing this method simply requires treating the agenda as a priority queue sorted by n-gram scores, and adding a protocol for time-outs.

The anytime search method partially addresses the problem that the grammar may license an exponential number of possible realizations for a given input. This method is particularly appropriate for the needs of natural language dialogue systems, where response times must be kept short in order to achieve sufficient interactivity.

LF Chunking The LF chunking method [13] addresses the problem, noted by Kay [2], that chart realization algorithms can waste a great deal of time on generation paths containing semantically incomplete phrases. As Kay observes, chart realization in its naive form generates sentences for all subsets of the predicates corresponding to syntactically optional modifiers, only one of which is semantically complete. For example, with an input LF for Kay's sentence *Newspaper reports said that the tall young Polish athlete ran fast*, a naive chart realizer produces syntactically complete sentences for all subsets of the modifiers *newspaper*, *tall, young, Polish,* and *fast,* yielding a grand total of 32 strings, 31 of which are useless.

Our approach to this problem is to make use of a small set of rules, written by the grammar author, for chunking input logical forms into sub-problems to be solved independently prior to further combination, thereby avoiding a proliferation of semantically incomplete edges. The default rule is to chunk sub-trees in the input LF. With Kay's sentence, this rule would ensure that the edges for the two NPs are semantically complete before allowing them to combine with the verb, thus avoiding unwanted edges such as *the athlete ran.*

A handful of exceptions to the default rule are generally required. For example, an exception must be made for negation, since the syntactic position of *not* is incompatible with chunking the negated proposition. If no exception were made, the chunking constraint would force the edges for the subject and verb phrase that realize the proposition to combine before allowing combinations with the edge for *not,* effectively blocking all desired derivations.

An advantage of Kay's original approach to avoiding semantically incomplete phrases over the present one is that his solution is fully automatic, and does not require the insights of the grammar author. On the other hand, the LF chunking method is more flexible than Kay's solution, and also extends to cases not considered by Kay. In particular, it can help to more efficiently realize non-standard coordinated constituents [13].

As an alternative to Kay's approach, Carroll et al. [4] propose to delay the insertion of all intersective modifiers until the rest of the chart has been completed, and then to add them via adjunction. An advantage of their solution over Kay's is that it further reduces unwanted edges by avoiding extra intermediate results. However, it is unclear how well delaying the handling of intersective modifiers until the end would fit with our anytime approach to realization, and for this reason we have not pursued their solution.

N-Best Edge Pruning While the chunking rules cut down the search space by keeping semantically incomplete phrases from proliferating, a grammar may still license an exponential number of phrases for a given input—especially when the grammar is intentionally allowed to overgenerate, in order to take advantage of an n-gram scoring function's ability to select preferred word orders. The n-best edge pruning method [13] is designed to help keep the realizer from getting bogged down in the face of cases where the grammar leaves word order relatively free. It does so by limiting the number of edges in the chart that can have equivalent categories (but different strings), removing the edge whose string has the lowest n-gram score when the limit is exceeded. Note that since edge pruning only takes place within groups of edges sharing the same syntactic and semantic category, there is no way that edge pruning can prevent the search from turning up any complete realizations. However, as a heuristic method, n-best edge pruning can prevent the realization with the best n-gram score from ever being found, if applied too aggressively.

Caching of Category Combinations To efficiently implement pruning, a hash map is used to group edges together with equivalent categories. This same hashing strategy can be reused to cache the results of the combinatory rules when applied to an edge or pair of edges, according to the categories involved. In this way, the application of the combinatory rules can be short-circuited when an edge or pair of edges is encountered whose categories have been seen before. Instead of applying the combinatory rules as usual, the previous results of applying the rules are adapted to create new edges; the resulting edges share the same category, but have different strings appropriate to the current edge or pair of edges. Using cached category combinations achieves some of the same improvements in efficiency as using packed representations, as in [3, 16], since both methods serve to group edges with equivalent combinatory potential. The advantage of caching category combinations is that it fits better with the anytime search approach.

Feature-Based Licensing and Instantiation As Carroll et al. [4] point out, semantically null words such as case-marking prepositions or particles, complementizers, and infinitival *to* (depending on the grammar) can significantly worsen performance, since the edges for these words do not have indices to constrain their potential combinations. To lessen the problem they pose, Carroll et al. suggest using ad hoc filters to avoid using edges for semantically null words, in cases where the input semantics contains no evidence that they are needed.

Pursuing a similar idea, we have devised a systematic way to use features to license semantically null categories, as well as to instantiate the indices on these categories where possible. Our method involves having the grammar author concisely specify which features—of those found on the initial categories, accessed during lexical lookup—should be used for licensing and instantiation. For example, the grammar author can specify that the `inf` value of the `vform` feature should be used for both licensing and instantiation.[3] As a result, the category for infinitival *to* will only be licensed if there is an initial category that subcategorizes for an infinitival verb phrase; furthermore, the index on this category will be instantiated with the index of the infinitival verb phrase.[4]

By default, the `lex` feature is used to license subcategorized case-marking prepositions or particles. It also receives special treatment, in that it is used to instantiate the indices on the semantically null edges with new pseudo-indices created for each value of the `lex` feature found in the initial categories. For example, with the phrasal verb *pick up*, an initial edge is created for the verb *pick*, which subcategorizes for a particle where `lex=up`; thus, an edge for the particle *up* will be licensed, which gets instantiated with a new pseudo-index so that it will combine only with the *pick* edge.

We have also extended the approach to include the licensing of "marked" categories, such as inverting categories for auxiliaries which are used in questions,

---

[3] It is also possible to specify that the feature value must appear only on the target category, or only on an argument category. Features may also be specified as relevant for licensing only or instantiation only.

[4] Multiple edges are created if the relevant index is not unique.

but not ordinary declaratives. Though such marked categories are not semantically null, in our approach they similarly require licensing by other initial edges. In this way, some of the benefits of the top-down constraints used in semantic head–driven approaches to realization [17] become available, without changing the essentially bottom-up nature of the chart realization algorithm.

3   Case Study

To compare the contributions of the different methods for improving efficiency, we measured the realizer's accuracy and speed, under a variety of configurations, on test suites for two small but linguistically rich grammars:

COMIC The COMIC grammar covers sentences in the domain of bathroom redesign and has been deployed in the COMIC (COnversational Multimodal Interaction with Computers) prototype dialogue system. The grammar partially implements Steedman's [7] theory of information structure and prosody in CCG, and the core of the grammar is shared with the one deployed in the FLIGHTS system. The test suite contains 549 unique pairs of logical forms and target sentences, out of which 219 are unique after replacing certain words with semantic classes (e.g., replacing *Armonie* by *SERIES*). The test suite was derived by running the system through a range of simulated dialogues; deduplicating the generated logical forms; realizing the logical forms using a language model derived from a smaller regression test suite for the grammar; and manually correcting the resulting realizations to obtain the desired target sentences. The target sentences average 13.1 words in length, with a minimum of 6 and a maximum of 34 words. In these sentences, pitch accents such as H* and L+H* are considered integral parts of words, whereas boundary tones such as LH% and LL% are treated as separate words, like punctuation marks. The input logical forms range from 2 to 20 nodes and have 8.4 nodes on average.[5] An example sentence is *once_again_L+H* LH% there are floral_H* motifs_H* LH% and geometric_H* shapes_H* on the decorative_H* tiles LL% , but L here_L+H* LH% the colours are off_white_H* LH% and dark_red_H* LL%* .

Worldcup The Worldcup grammar is from a linguistic study of extraction and coordination, and covers heavy NP shift, non-peripheral extraction, parasitic gaps, particle shift, relativization, right node raising, topicalization, and argument cluster coordination. The test suite contains five additional invented variants for each of the 46 phrases discussed in [9], for a total of 276 unique pairs of logical forms and target phrases, half of which are unique after semantic class replacement. The phrases average 9.2 words in length, and vary from a minimum of 4 words to a maximum of 18 words. The number of nodes in the input logical forms averages 6.8, and ranges from 3 to 13. Example phrases include *game that John watched without enjoying* and *John knew that Brazil would defeat and Bill predicted that China would tie with Turkey.*

---

[5] The number of nodes essentially corresponds to the number of content words.

While these two grammars use unification in the usual way to handle phenomena such as person, number and case agreement, they still overgenerate to varying extents. In particular, neither grammar sufficiently constrains modifier order, which in the case of adverb placement especially can lead to a large number of possible orderings. Additionally, the COMIC grammar allows for a one to many mapping from themes or rhemes [7] to boundary tones, yielding many variants that differ only in boundary tone type or placement. This flexibility makes it possible to handle discontinuous themes or rhemes, but it does so at the expense of making the grammar considerably more challenging for the realizer to process efficiently. Nevertheless, in comparison to most previous work on using n-gram scoring in realization (going back to [15]), our grammars are narrower in coverage and only mildly overgenerate; as a result though, our approach is the only one capable of achieving near perfect quality, which we consider more important in dialogue systems than wide coverage. Another difference is that our approach currently leaves very little lexical choice to the realizer, though in future work, we plan to investigate allowing the input logical forms to underspecify lexical choice in a flexible way.

Using these two test suites, we timed how long it took on a 2.2 GHz Linux PC to realize each logical form using various realizer configurations.[6] Before examining the relative contributions of the efficiency methods, we first assessed the effect of n-gram scoring on accuracy and search times. To do so, we counted the number of times the best scoring realization exactly matched the target, and also computed a simplified version of the Bleu n-gram precision metric [18] employed in machine translation evaluation. To rank candidate realizations, we used 5-gram backoff models with semantic class replacement, created using the SRI language modeling toolkit [19] in a 25-fold cross-validation setup. We then compared the realization results using the n-gram scorers with two baselines and one topline. The first baseline assigns all strings a uniform score of zero, and adds new edges to the end of the agenda, corresponding to breadth-first search. The second baseline uses the same scorer, but adds new edges at the front of the agenda, corresponding to depth-first search. The topline uses the modified Bleu score, computing n-gram precision against just the target string, a technique which we have found to be very useful for regression testing the grammar.

The results of this comparison appear in Table 1. Since the COMIC grammar is more challenging to process, we employed 3-best edge pruning with the COMIC test suite, as 3 was the smallest value that allowed the topline method to achieve perfect accuracy. For both suites, all other efficiency methods were turned on. With the COMIC test suite, the n-gram scorer succeeded in ranking the target realization as the best one in all but one case—*there is also_H* artwork on the decorative tiles LL%*—where it mistakenly preferred *also_H* fronted*, due to the trigram *there is also_H** appearing in just this example. With the World-cup test suite, the n-gram scorer did less well in ranking the target realization as best, achieving exact matches in only 250 out of 276 cases. However, with the

---

[6] Running the tests under different Linux and Windows Java virtual machines did not appear to change the relative timings.

COMIC				
			Mean (±σ) Time 'til	
	Accuracy	Score	First	Best
Baseline 1	284/549	0.78	497 (±380)	497 (±380)
Baseline 2	41/549	0.38	400 (±286)	400 (±286)
Topline	549/549	1	152 (±93)	154 (±95)
CV-25	**548/549**	**0.99**	**206 (±138)**	**206 (±138)**

Worldcup				
			Mean (±σ) Time 'til	
	Accuracy	Score	First	Best
Baseline 1	70/276	0.55	181 (±198)	181 (±198)
Baseline 2	67/276	0.53	133 (±152)	133 (±152)
Topline	276/276	1	54 (±36)	55 (±37)
CV-25	**250/276**	**0.93**	**93 (±60)**	**93 (±60)**

Table 1. Effect of n-grams on accuracy and search times (in ms.), with the COMIC test suite and 3-best pruning, and with the Worldcup test suite and no pruning.

exception of a couple of topicalization[7] choices, the 26 non-matching realizations appear to represent cases of acceptable free variation. Moreover, the scorers managed to avoid many dispreferred variants allowed by the mildly overgenerating grammar, such as *easily Brazil defeated Germany and *Marcos picked up it. In regard to realization times, the n-gram scorers also yielded substantial speedups over the baselines in the time to find the first complete realization. What was somewhat surprising to observe was that the best scoring realizations nearly always appeared first, or soon after, with a neglible effect on the average time.

Turning now to the contributions of the various efficiency methods, the realizer configurations we compared are as follows. The **Baseline** configuration corresponds to the realizer version described in [6], and uses the index filter plus "quick-and-dirty" licensing of semantically null edges, where the lex feature is used to license, but not instantiate, some semantically empty function words. The **All** configuration uses the index filter plus LF chunking, caching of category combinations, and systematic licensing and instantiation of edges. The **No Chunking**, **No Licensing** and **No Caching** configurations are like the **All** configuration, except with the method in question turned off. Under all configurations, we imposed a time limit of 10 seconds on the search, considering times over 10 seconds to be clearly too slow for dialogue systems. Had we not imposed this time limit, the observed improvements would have been more dramatic.

The realizer timings for the efficiency comparisons appear in Figures 1-3. Figure 1 shows the amount of time until the first realization is found for input logical forms of different sizes, averaged across inputs with the same number of nodes. Figure 2 shows the amount of time until all realizations are found for inputs of different sizes, on a logarithmic scale. Finally, Figure 3 compares the amount of time until the first realization is found to the amount of time until all realizations are found, both on average and in the worst case.

Reviewing the results in turn, Figure 1 shows that as the inputs get larger, chunking becomes essential to keep the time until the first realization is found reliably short, while licensing can contribute a sizeable speedup. Caching only

---

[7] With the Worldcup grammar, topicalization has no semantic reflex in the logical form; in contrast, with the COMIC grammar, topicalization choices in the realizer are determined by a feature in the input logical form, rather than being left for the n-grams to try to decide.

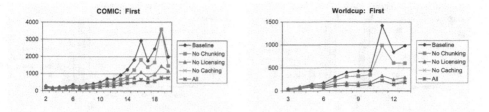

Fig. 1. Mean time until first realization is found for inputs of different sizes.

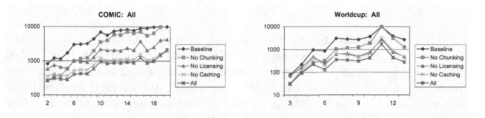

Fig. 2. Mean time until all realizations are found for inputs of different sizes.

offers a tiny improvement though, at least with 3-best pruning in use with the
COMIC test suite. All improvements were statistically significant using paired t-
tests, except with caching on the Worldcup test suite. Note that with the largest
input sizes, there are relatively few test cases per size, which is why the curves
become jagged; also, the time scales for the two suites are different, reflecting
the greater difficulty in processing the COMIC grammar.

Figure 2 shows how the various efficiency techniques combine to reduce the
time until all realizations are found: caching yields a small improvement, licensing
a larger one, and chunking a substantial one; and with none of these methods in
operation (the baseline configuration), the time to completion is often an order
of magnitude worse. Note that these curves actually understate the differences
between the configurations, since the 10-second cutoff reduces the average times
when some test cases fail to complete within the time limit. Specifically, with
the COMIC test suite, 87 cases failed to finish within 10 seconds in the baseline
configuration, while 40 cases did not complete in the no chunking configuration;
in the baseline configuration, there was even one case when the first realization
was not found within the time limit. With the Worldcup test suite, 20 cases
failed to complete within 10 seconds in the baseline configuration, and 10 cases
did not finish in the no chunking configuration.

Figure 3 shows that the time until the first realization is found can be much
less than the time until all realizations are found, both on average and in the
worst case, thereby showing the potential for anytime search to yield much more

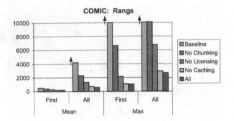
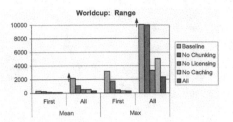

Fig. 3. Comparison of time until first realization is found vs. time until all realizations are found, on average and in the worst case.

reliably fast realization times.[8] For example, with the COMIC grammar in the baseline configuration, the average time until the first realization is found is 500 ms, while the average time until all realizations are found is more than eight times longer; and in the all methods configuration, the average time until the first realization is found is 207 ms, while the average time until all realizations are found is 568 ms, more than two and a half times longer. In the worst case, the situation is more dramatic. For example, with the Worldcup test suite, even in the all methods case, the maximum time until all realizations are found (2327 ms) is more than eight times longer than the maximum time until the first realization is found (286 ms).

4   Conclusion

In this paper, we have presented a novel ensemble of methods for improving the efficiency of chart realization, including two new methods, feature-based licensing and instantiation of edges, and caching of category combinations. The methods are couched in the framework of Combinatory Categorial Grammar (CCG), but we conjecture that they can be adapted to related grammatical frameworks as well. In particular, since the anytime search method requires only that the agenda be treated as a priority queue sorted by n-gram scores, it should be directly applicable to other grammatical frameworks.

In evaluating the impact of these methods, we have shown that together they can enable CCG realization to be practically employed for the first time in natural language dialogue systems, even in the presence of mild overgeneration. While we expect that performance may vary substantially with different grammars, the empirical observation that the best scoring realizations appear first or soon after suggests that one could reliably realize sentences fast enough for interactive use even with wider coverage grammars. Whether the approach will continue to work equally well when faced with more underspecified input logical forms, however, remains a topic for future research.

---

[8] The upward arrows indicate configurations where the times would have been worse had all cases been allowed to run to completion.

Acknowledgements

Thanks to Mark Steedman, Jason Baldridge, Geert-Jan Kruijff, Johanna Moore, Jon Oberlander, Mary Ellen Foster, and the anonymous reviewers for helpful discussion. This work was supported in part by the COMIC (IST-2001-32311) and FLIGHTS (EPSRC-GR/R02450/01) projects.

References

[1] Shieber, S.: A uniform architecture for parsing and generation. In: Proc. of the 14th International Conference on Computational Linguistics. (1988) 614–619

[2] Kay, M.: Chart generation. In: Proc. of the 34th Annual Meeting of the Association for Computational Linguistics. (1996) 200–204

[3] Shemtov, H.: Ambiguity Management in Natural Language Generation. PhD thesis, Stanford University (1997)

[4] Carroll, J., Copestake, A., Flickinger, D., Poznański, V.: An efficient chart generator for (semi-) lexicalist grammars. In: Proc. of the 7th European Workshop on Natural Language Generation. (1999) 86–95

[5] Moore, R.C.: A complete, efficient sentence-realization algorithm for unification grammar. In: Proc. of the 2nd International Natural Language Generation Conference. (2002)

[6] White, M., Baldridge, J.: Adapting Chart Realization to CCG. In: Proc. of the 9th European Workshop on Natural Language Generation. (2003)

[7] Steedman, M.: Information structure and the syntax-phonology interface. Linguistic Inquiry **31** (2000) 649–689

[8] Steedman, M.: The Syntactic Process. MIT Press (2000)

[9] Baldridge, J.: Lexically Specified Derivational Control in Combinatory Categorial Grammar. PhD thesis, School of Informatics, University of Edinburgh (2002)

[10] Baldridge, J., Kruijff, G.J.: Multi-Modal Combinatory Categorial Grammar. In: Proc. of 10th Annual Meeting of the European Association for Computational Linguistics. (2003)

[11] den Os, E., Boves, L.: Towards ambient intelligence: Multimodal computers that understand our intentions. In: Proceedings of eChallenges e-2003. (2003)

[12] Moore, J., Foster, M.E., Lemon, O., White, M.: Generating tailored, comparative descriptions in spoken dialogue. In: Proceedings of FLAIRS-04. (2004)

[13] White, M.: Efficient Realization of Coordinate Structures in Combinatory Categorial Grammar. Research on Language and Computation (2004) To appear.

[14] Varges, S., Mellish, C.: Instance-based natural language generation. In: Proc. of the 2nd Meeting of the North American Chapter of the Association for Computational Linguistics. (2001) 1–8

[15] Knight, K., Hatzivassiloglou, V.: Two-level, many-paths generation. In: Proc. ACL. (1995)

[16] Langkilde, I.: Forest-based statistical sentence generation. In: Proc. NAACL. (2000)

[17] Shieber, S., van Nord, G., Pereira, F., Moore, R.: Semantic-head–driven generation. Computational Linguistics **16** (1990) 30–42

[18] Papineni, K., Roukos, S., Ward, T., Zhu, W.J.: Bleu: a Method for Automatic Evaluation of Machine Translation. Technical Report RC22176, IBM (2001)

[19] Stolcke, A.: SRILM — An extensible language modeling toolkit. In: Proceedings of ICSLP-02. (2002)

Categorization of Narrative Semantics for Use in Generative Multidocument Summarization

David K. Elson

Columbia University
450 Computer Science Building
1214 Amsterdam Avenue
New York, NY 10027-7003
delson@cs.columbia.edu

Abstract. The generative summarization of textual stories has been one of the goals of computational narratology since attempts at full semantic NLU in the '70s. Our NLP group has recently created several systems for multidocument news summarization, but using purely statistical methods. Between these poles, there may be an unexplored avenue where knowledge of story structure can give partial, yet useful semantic understanding to a news reader. Such knowledge can then lead to summaries more informed than those based on solely statistical means. This student paper represents work in progress on a two-module system: The first module categorizes news articles into their underlying dramatic structures; the second will attempt to use this understanding to create and execute a generative plan, concisely retelling the story to form a surface-level summary.

1   Introduction

Content selection is a limiting factor in many generation systems, especially those intended for summarization. Statistical summarizers that rely purely on sentence extraction, while practical on unrestricted texts, often produce summaries too "close" to the sources. Without any semantic insight into the gist of the text, a statistical summarizer can favor sentences with nonessential details over those that tell salient events.

While full semantic understanding of an arbitrary text is not a practical goal, the domain of news summarization imposes a restriction on many of its texts that one may be able to exploit: news is, at its core, an act of storytelling. If a news event does not arouse fear, or compassion, or a laugh, or some other emotional response to the dramatic underpinnings of the story, it does not make the pages of a broadsheet.

In this paper, we describe the initial stages of a project to create a new model of the rhetorical structure of textual stories and apply it to the content selection piece of a generative multidocument news summarizer.

A. Belz et al. (Eds.): INLG 2004, LNAI 3123, pp. 192–197, 2004.

2   Related Work

The link between news and storytelling has been investigated before, originally by those attempting full semantic understanding in the '70s [17]. More recently, researchers such as Power [13], Mann and Thompson [9] have developed rhetorical structure theory as a more practical, high-level representation of a general text's structure. Plans have been used by Hovy [7], Moore and Paris [12] to improve text generation for expert systems, as have schemas by McKeown [11].

In parallel with this work, computational narratology has aimed to capture the essence of drama for both story understanding and generation. The different approaches vary widely: Some place the notion of conflict between characters at the atomic center of their models [18]; others prefer surface-level syntactic structure [16], the autonomy of self-determining characters [15], the human process of storytelling [8] or even the reader's emotional response to a story [2].

Computational narratology has experienced a revival in recent years, by both theorists and those bringing practical applications to bear. The introductory paper by Mateas and Sengers [10] from the 1999 AAAI Fall Symposium gives an excellent overview, as does the summary of the MIT Media Lab's reading group on narrative intelligence by Davis and Travers [4]. The potential for a fusion with rhetorical structure theory for summarization has been little explored.

3   System Design

Telling interesting narratives is a skill that journalists and writers of fiction alike are trained to do. They each look for the best "angle" with which to cast the events of their worlds into a dramatic mold.

One of the motifs in the heritage of literary theory, where computational limitations are not even considered, has been the idea that there are only so many stories that *can* be told ([1], [14]). Within the news domain, there are even fewer, as journalists strive to sell their stories to the public by invoking plots, characters, and themes that have been shown to generate interest in the past (e.g., the *death of the unsuspecting innocent*; the *fall from power*; the *personal attack*; the *rich magnate*; the *comeback* or *recovery*; *justice for the evil*; *new technology for old wants*).

Each of these plots, characters and themes are metadata for a story that carry certain narrative connotations. For example, a *fall from power* article probably describes the person in question, portrays the person as a villain brought to justice or a hero wrongfully hindered, exposits the reason for the fall, and characterizes the opposing force. As these are the essentials of the *fall from power* story, they represent the facts most important to the reader, and as such, they are the best facts to portray in a summary. If, by contrast, an article tells of the *death of the unsuspecting innocent*, the corresponding content selection problem is slightly different.

In other words, by categorizing an article into one or several of a reasonably small number of plot elements, we can invoke a generative plan that is customized for retelling that particular story. Such a system would combine the knowledge-based and the statistical: each of the possible stories would be coded *a priori* with its structural properties, but the content planner and surface-level generator would be statistical, using extant tools such as FUF/SURGE [6]. This approach would create summaries more informed than those by pure sentence extraction, while avoiding the rigidness of complete semantic understanding and working for real texts in an online environment.

Our system will execute such a process by using two modules: a **story categorizer** and a **plan generator**.

3.1   Story Categorizer

The categorizer, partially implemented, determines the narrative backbone of a story, choosing the plot elements that most closely apply to the text. There are several intersecting categorization problems that lie at this stage.

For one, not all news articles are stories in the straightforward sense, declaratively describing events unknown to the reader. The categorizer uses syntactic and lexical features to distinguish between several structural patterns of news articles:

1. Articles that tell a highly narrative story ("hard news")
2. Articles that are more digressive than "hard news," such as:
   - Articles that provide an analysis, historical perspective, or opinion/editorial
   - Character studies or articles that identify an emerging trend

Once the categorizer can isolate the highly narrative portions of a set of documents, it will more accurately be able to make further distinctions to determine the participating plot elements, such as:

- Is the protagonist **losing something, gaining something, fighting to reclaim something lost**, or **fighting to gain something new**?
- Does that goal take the form of **romance, freedom, privacy, peace, security, power, recuperation** or **survival**?
- Does the protagonist face competition from **a rival, an enemy, an authority, nature** or **limitations of a social class**?

We are continuing to develop our narrative model (i.e., the story elements available to the categorizer), and plan on utilizing statistical categorization techniques over large training sets to achieve this step. There may, for example, be a particular set of words or syntactic relationships that identify a *redemption from past mistakes* story, or one about *family bonding*.

Our current progress in implementing the categorizer is described below.

3.2   Plan Generator

Once the narrative elements of a news article are identified, content selection and regeneration will be able to capitalize upon the limited semantic knowledge.

Each story element will have an associated set of "arguments": names of people, places, and other details that concretize the abstract narrative pieces. These arguments will be essential for the generative piece of the summarizer; working from the output of a high-accuracy statistical parser [3], the categorizer will also perform knowledge acquisition as it goes. Other statistical content selection will be performed in methods similar to those in related studies [5]. The plan generator will then perform sentence planning, also in ways that are specific to the associated story elements. For instance, the "root" event might be explicated first, followed by details and complications.

Finally, the generative plan will be executed by a surface-level lexical chooser [6], which will produce a final summary.

4   Initial Results

As we have mentioned, the initial step in this project has been the development of a model of common plots, characters, and themes of which most news articles are instances. Several examples have already been given, such as *the fall from power*. The challenge at this stage is to identify elements that are general enough to be complete and enumerable, yet specific enough to be useful. For example, almost all news can fall into the plot *a character wants something but has difficulty in getting it*; such a model would be complete, but too vague to be useful. Yet once plots get too specific, they become too knowledge-dependent, and the data are too sparse to train for them.

Simultaneously, we have implemented a prototype for the first task of the categorizer, as described above. Working from a statistical parse, it uses syntactic rules to decide whether a sentence is one of declarative, highly narrative "hard news," or a more digressive detail. (We don't yet distinguish between the subtypes of digressive sentences.) The features include:

– Whether a sentence is attributed, or is a direct quotation of some source
– Whether there is a clear subject-action pattern
– Whether the subject is in the first or third person
– Whether the subject is a noun phrase or a pronoun

We are testing the categorizer on a collection of over 350 first sentences of articles, which are manually labeled as either "narrative" or "digressive." (We hypothesize that the first sentence of an article will be the richest source for key words and phrases for story categorization, as it is good form for journalists to summarize the narrative essence of their stories in their leads.) Initial results indicate that the categorizer achieves 78% precision and 78% recall for the task of identifying narrative sentences from digressive ones.

5 Conclusion

In this paper, we have described a project in an intermediate stage that seeks to use high-level narrative semantics as a means for generating news summaries more informed than those that operate on purely statistical means. We have identified several of the plot elements we plan to encode, and implemented a prototype for the categorizer that distinguishes highly narrative sentences from more digressive ones. In the near future, we will continue to implement the categorizer, and the plan generator to follow.

References

1. Aristotle. *Poetics*. Available at http://www.gutenberg.net/etext99/poetc10.txt, 350 B.C.E.
2. P. Bailey. Searching for storiness: Story-generation from a reader's perspective. In Mateas and Sengers [10].
3. M. Collins. A new statistical parser based on bigram lexical dependencies. In Arivind Joshi and Martha Palmer, editors, *Proceedings of the Thirty-Fourth Annual Meeting of the Association for Computational Linguistics*, pages 184–191, San Francisco, 1996. Morgan Kaufmann Publishers.
4. M. Davis and M. Travers. A brief overview of the narrative intelligence reading group. In Mateas and Sengers [10].
5. P. Duboue and K. McKeown. Statistical acquisition of content selection rules for natural language generation. In *2003 Conference on Empirical Methods for Natural Language Processing (EMNLP 2003)*, Sapporo, Japan, July 2003.
6. M. Elhadad and J. Robin. An overview of surge: A reusable comprehensive syntactic realization component, 1996.
7. E. Hovy. Automated discourse generation using discourse structure relations. *Artificial Intelligence*, 1993.
8. M. Lebowitz. Story telling and generalization. *Proceedings of the Seventh Annual Conference of the Cognitive Science Society, (Berkeley, California), pp. 100-109, 1985*, 1995.
9. W.C. Mann and S.A. Thompson. Rhetorical structure theory: Toward a functional theory of text organization. *Text*, 8(3):243 – 281, 1988.
10. M. Mateas and P. Sengers, editors. *Narrative Intelligence*. Carnegie Mellon University / Media Arts Research Studies, Sankt Augustin, Germany; Cornell University, 1999.
11. K. McKeown. *Text Generation: Using Discourse Strategies and Focus Constratins to Generate Natural Langauge Text*. Cambridge University Press, 1985.
12. J. D. Moore and C. L. Paris. Planning text for advisory dialogues: Capturing intentional and rhetorical information. *Computational Linguistics*, 19(4):651–695, 1993.
13. R. Power. Planning texts by constraint satisfaction. In *Proceedings of the 18th International Conference on Computational Linguistics (COLING-2000), Saarbruecken, Germany*, pages 642–648, 2000.
14. V. Propp. *Morphology of the Folktale*. Trans. Laurence Scott. Ed. Louis A. Wagner. 2nd edition. Univ of Texas Press, 1969.
15. M. Riedl. Actor conference: Character-focused narrative planning. In Mateas and Sengers [10].

16. D. Rumelhart. Notes on a schema for stories. In *Representation and Understanding: Studies in Cognitive Science, Bobrow, D.G. and Collins A., eds*, pages 211–236. New York: Academic Press, Inc., 1975.

17. R. Schank and C. Riesbeck, editors. *Inside Computer Understanding: Five Programs Plus Miniatures*. Hillsdale, New Jersey: Lawrence Erlbaum Associates, 1981.

18. N. Szilas. Interactive drama on computer: beyond linear narrative. In Mateas and Sengers [10].

Corpus-Based Planning of Deictic Gestures in COMIC

Mary Ellen Foster

School of Informatics, University of Edinburgh
2 Buccleuch Place, Edinburgh EH8 9LW
http://www.iccs.informatics.ed.ac.uk/~mef/

Abstract. We describe the recording and annotation of a corpus of role-playing dialogues in the domain of the COMIC multimodal dialogue system. We give some generalisations about the use of deictic gesture in this task, and show how those findings are currently used in the presentation-planning module of the dialogue system prototype. Finally, we describe how the use of gestures in the system will be evaluated, and outline the next steps in the development of the module.

1   Introduction

When producing multimodal output, an important task is deciding what content should be produced on each of the output channels, and then controlling the output on those channels; this task is sometimes called *fission*. In this paper, we describe how the fission component plans deictic gestures in the COMIC demonstrator. The COMIC demonstrator is a multimodal dialogue system in which a virtual sales consultant presents a range of options to a client, in a guided-browsing scenario. A particular goal for COMIC is to base the system output as far as possible on the features of human-human dialogues in the same domain.

To get a better overview of the features of multimodal dialogue—in particular, of the distribution of deictic gestures—in this domain, we recorded a number of interactions in which the participants played the roles of consultant and client, and annotated and analysed those features of the recordings that are particularly relevant to the COMIC demonstrator. We are now using the results of this analysis to guide the choices made in the COMIC fission module.

2   The COMIC Demonstrator

COMIC ("COnversational Multimodal Interaction with Computers") [1,2] is an ongoing project investigating multimodal dialogue systems. The project demonstrator system adds a spoken-language dialogue interface to a CAD-like application used in bathroom sales situations to help clients redesign their rooms. The input to the system includes speech, handwriting, and pen gestures; the output

A. Belz et al. (Eds.): INLG 2004, LNAI 3123, pp. 198–204, 2004.

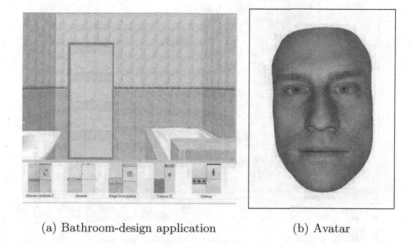

(a) Bathroom-design application   (b) Avatar

Fig. 1. Components of the COMIC demonstrator

combines synthesised speech, a "talking head" avatar, and control of the underlying application. Figure 1 shows screen shots of the bathroom design application and the avatar.

The interaction with the demonstrator has four main steps. First, the user specifies the floor-plan of their bathroom. Next, the system helps the user to choose a layout for the sanitary ware in that room. Then, the system describes and compares a number of tiling options for that bathroom, guiding the user as they browse through the range of possibilities. Once the user has selected a design, the system gives a three-dimensional virtual tour of the finished room.

Output is produced on the following channels: synthesised speech; expressions, gazes, and lip movements of the avatar; direct commands to the underlying design application; and deictic gestures at objects on the screen, using a simulated mouse pointer. In this paper, we will concentrate on the deictic gestures produced during the third phase of the interaction, in which the system describes and compares options for tiling the bathroom.

There are three decisions that must be made when planning deictic gestures. Firstly, we must decide where gestures should occur at all. Once we have decided to include a gesture, we must choose the specific type of that gesture. Finally, we must decide on the exact time that the chosen gesture should take place in relation to other parts of the output. To help make these decisions in the fission module, we gathered and analysed the corpus described in the following section.

3   Creating the Corpus

To determine the features of deictic gestures in this specific domain, we recorded a number of role-playing interactions, with the participants taking the roles of

Fig. 2. Annotating a video with ANVIL

a sales consultant and a client. We then annotated and analysed the deictic gestures and spoken references occurring in the relevant parts of these interactions. This section gives an overview of how these interactions were recorded and annotated; full details are provided in [3].

The subject playing the consultant was given five to seven possibilities for each choice that the client could make in designing a bathroom, and was instructed to help the client to explore this range of possibilities. Each of the design possibilities was presented on an individual sheet of paper. Seven dialogues were recorded, making a total of two and a half hours of video. About 20% of this time contained descriptions and comparisons from the consultant that were similar to those that COMIC can generate.[1] For example, (1) is a comparison produced by one of our subjects, while (2) is a similar comparison generated by COMIC:

(1)   This is a very kind of traditional design, just having them lined up down the wall, whereas this, this is kind of ... a bit more audacious perhaps.
(2)   This design features terracotta and dark-red in the colour scheme, while this one has a blue and beige colour scheme.

These relevant descriptions and comparisons were annotated (Figure 2) using ANVIL [4], as follows. First, we marked the onset and duration of each deictic gesture and spoken reference made by the consultant in the relevant sections. For each gesture, we then indicated whether it referred to an entire image or to a part of that image, and put it into one of five categories: pointing, waving (repeated pointing), circling, tracing the edges of the referent, or physically moving the

---

[1] The other 80% consisted mainly of times when the client spoke, and discussion of real-world issues outside the scope of the COMIC demonstrator.

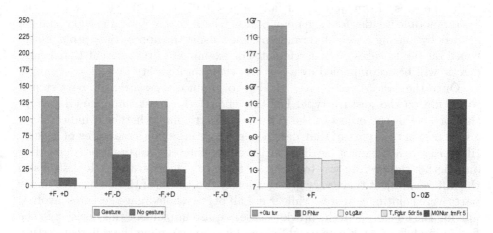

(a) Gesture counts by speech feature   (b) Gesture counts by object type

Fig. 3. Graphs of gesture counts

entire image. In addition, we created links between the spoken and gestural references to the same object, and among the different references to the same objects.

4   Using the Corpus Data in the Fission Module

The annotated corpus provides information that can be used to influence all three of the necessary decisions in planning deictic gestures. The current fission module makes weighted random choices using weights based on the corpus results, as described below. Section 5 describes how this version of the module will be evaluated, and also outlines our plans to make more sophisticated use of data in future versions.

In current implementation of the fission module, deciding where to put a deictic gesture is a two-phase process. When the text is created, every noun phrase that could have an associated gesture is marked in the plan; examples of such phrases are *this design* and *the decorative tiles*. Then the gesture-planning component considers all of the possible gesture referents and decides which of those should have an associated gesture. The relevant information from the corpus is therefore the circumstances under which a spoken reference did or did not have an accompanying gesture. We consider two features of a speech reference at this stage: whether it was the first reference to a given entity in the dialogue (F), and whether it was deictic (D). Figure 3(a) shows the influence of these features on the occurrence of gestures. Note that both had an influence on the probability of a gesture occurring: 92% of all first, deictic references had a gesture, while only 61% of follow-up, non-deictic references had one. An ANOVA found that all of the differences shown were significant at $p < 0.05$. In the implementation, the fission module decides for each noun phrase whether to include an accompanying gesture by making a weighted random choice, using the appropriate probabilities based on the features of that referent. For example, a first referent that is also deictic will be accompanied by a gesture with a probability of 0.92.

Once the fission module has decided to produce a gesture, the next step is to decide on the gesture type. For this choice, the most important factor in the corpus was the object of the gesture—in particular, whether it indicated an entire design or a part of that design (e.g., pointing out the features of specific tiles). Figure 3(b) shows the distribution of the different gesture types depending on whether the gesture was to a part or a whole. The characteristic gestures to the different object types vary greatly: nearly two-thirds of the gestures to image parts were pointing gestures, while over half of the whole-image gestures involved moving the image. As in the previous case, we also implement this decision in the fission module by making a weighted random choice among the different gesture types, using the weights from the corpus. The animated mouse pointer cannot reproduce all of the observed gesture types, so waving and edge-tracing are both mapped to circling, while image-moving is realised by instructing the bathroom application to show the selected design in its main window (Figure 1(a)).

The final stage of gesture planning is to decide on the timing of the gesture with respect to other parts of the presentation. For deictic gestures, the most relevant timing point is the spoken reference to the same object that caused the gesture to be included in the first place. In the recordings, the mean time between the onset of a deictic gesture and the onset of a spoken reference to the same object was 0.83 seconds, with a standard deviation of 1.3; that is, a gesture began on average 0.83 seconds before the corresponding speech, although there were some gestures that began a short time after the speech. These findings are consistent with previous work on gesture-speech timing [5,6]. The current implementation reproduces this by choosing the offset from a normal distribution with the same standard deviation and mean; we do not currently vary the duration of a gesture. The concrete gesture schedule is then created using the timing information returned by the speech-synthesis module.

5   Related and Future Work

Several previous systems have addressed the task of synthesising naturalistic gestures for animated agents. Two such systems are BEAT and Max, both of which use findings on human gesture behaviour to synthesise gestures for full-body avatars.

The BEAT system (Behavior Expression Animation Toolkit) [7] aims to provide animators with capabilities similar to a text-to-speech system: it processes typed text and synthesises appropriate motions for a full-body animated actor. The animation is generated based on linguistic and information-structure features derived from the text, and on studies of human behaviour. For example, based on human findings, BEAT is more likely to generate gestures during the rheme of an utterance (where new information is added to the discussion) than during the theme (which links the utterance to the previous discourse). The library of gestures is designed to be extended by a skilled animator when necessary. Since the input to BEAT is plain text, it must first parse the text and analyse its information structure before creating the animation schedule.

Max [6,8,9] is an animated conversational agent developed by the Artificial Intelligence Group at the University of Bielefeld. Max acts as an assembly expert in an immersive 3D virtual environment for simulated construction and design tasks. In addition to its face, Max can also move its arms, hands, and fingers, which it uses together with speech to demonstrate assembly procedures to users. The goal of the project is to render real-time, lifelike animations from representations of spatio-temporal gesture knowledge. The entries in the gesture lexicon, which are based on annotated recordings of humans, define a mapping from communicative functions to explicit movement descriptions.

It is clear that it is desirable to base the movements of an avatar with a body on human behaviour, as in the two projects described above; similarly, Cunningham and de Ruiter [10] also suggest that facial expressions should be based on reality to be believable. However, it is less obvious that basing deictic gestures with an on-screen pointer on observed human behaviour will be more successful than using a hard-coded planning strategy. For example, will users like the naturalness of the variation in gesture offsets, or would they prefer more fixed, predictable timing?

This issue will be addressed as part of an upcoming evaluation of the COMIC demonstrator. We will compare user satisfaction with, and perceived naturalness of, the output produced by the corpus-based fission module described here against that of one using a baseline configuration that always picks the most frequent option, with no variation. This is not a comparison that has been made in the other systems described above, as they both emphasise creating motions that are as natural as possible for their full-body avatars.

In future versions of the fission module, we would like to move away from stochastic models such as those described here, and toward a more instance-based implementation of fission. Instance-based techniques have been successful in other generation tasks where decisions must be made for which rules are difficult to write directly, but where there are readily available good examples that can be used to guide the search. Such tasks include instance-based natural language generation [11] and unit-selection speech synthesis [12].

To create the instances, we will produce a number of possible system outputs, varying all of the possible parameters systematically, and have users rate them for acceptability. We will then use the most successful multimodal combinations as examples to emulate. We hope to extend this instance-based version to cover output planning in other modalities, including selecting among alternative textual realisations and facial expressions.

6   Conclusions

We have described how a the analysis of a corpus of human-human role-playing dialogues has been used to guide the planning of deictic gestures in the COMIC multimodal dialogue system. As part of the upcoming evaluation of the COMIC system, the success of the corpus-based fission module will be assessed in a user study that compares its output with that of a version that hard-codes all of the relevant choices, with no variation. We have also outlined how we plan to extend the gesture-planning process to use a more instance-based approach in future versions of the module.

Acknowledgements

Thanks to Michael White, Johanna Moore, Jon Oberlander, and the anonymous reviewers for their useful comments on previous versions of this paper. This work was supported by the COMIC project (IST-2001-32311).

References

1. COMIC project: Homepage. http://www.hcrc.ed.ac.uk/comic/
2. den Os, E., Boves, L.: Towards ambient intelligence: Multimodal computers that understand our intentions. In: Proceedings of eChallenges e-2003. (2003)
3. Foster, M.E.: Description of "Wizard of Oz" recordings. Deliverable 6.4, COMIC project (2003)
4. Kipp, M.: Anvil homepage. http://www.dfki.de/~kipp/anvil/
5. de Ruiter, J.P.: The production of gesture and speech. In McNeill, D., ed.: Language and Gesture. Cambridge University Press (2000) 284–311
6. Kranstedt, A., Kühnlein, P., Wachsmuth, I.: Deixis in multimodal human computer interaction: An interdisciplinary approach. In Camurri, A., Volpe, G., eds.: Gesture-Based Communication in Human-Computer Interaction (LNAI 2915). Springer (2004) 112–123
7. Cassell, J., Vilhjálmsson, H., Bickmore, T.: BEAT: the Behavior Expression Animation Toolkit. In: Proceedings of SIGGRAPH'01 (2001) 477–486
8. Wachsmuth, I., Kopp, S.: Lifelike gesture synthesis and timing for conversational agents. In Wachsmuth, I., Sowa, T., eds.: Gesture and Sign Language in Human-Computer Interaction (LNAI 2298). Springer (2002) 120–133
9. Kopp, S., Wachsmuth, I.: Model-based animation of coverbal gesture. In: Proceedings of Computer Animation 2002. (2002) 252–257
10. Cunningham, D.W., de Ruiter, J.P.: Research on modality effects in mutual trust and interactive comfort. Deliverable 2.4, COMIC project (2003)
11. Varges, S., Mellish, C.: Instance-based natural language generation. In: Proceedings of NAACL-01. (2001)
12. Hunt, A.J., Black, A.W.: Unit selection in a concatenative speech synthesis system using a large speech database. In: Proceedings of ICASSP-96. Volume 1. (1996) 373–376

Hybrid NLG in a Generic Dialog System

Martin Klarner

University Erlangen-Nuremberg, Chair for Computer Science 8 (Artificial
Intelligence), Haberstaße 2, D-91058 Erlangen, Germany
`klarner@cs.fau.edu`

Abstract. Natural Language Generation (NLG) systems are increasingly becoming available as "market-ready" products, mainly due to the
now-removed boundary between shallow and deep generation and the
emergence of hybrid systems as a de-facto standard. In this paper, we
present HYPERBUG[1], a novel approach towards hybrid NLG, coupling
shallow and deep processing not only with respect to the resources used
for parsing and generation, but also on the architectural level to increase
the generative power of the shallow generation branch and the processing
efficiency of the whole generation system. The architecture is discussed
both in theory and in practice, using a comprehensive example spanning
the complete output part of our dialog system.

1 Introduction

NLG systems are now becoming available as "market-ready" products, mainly
because the boundary between shallow and deep generation has been overcome
and hybrid systems have emerged as the de-facto standard.

In this paper, we propose a novel variant of hybrid NLG, extending and combining existing approaches. The paper is organized as follows: In the remainder
of this section, we will discuss some aspects of hybrid NLG in general. In Section
2.1, we describe the system core of HYPERBUG, our hybrid NLG system which
couples and interleaves shallow and deep processing not only with respect to
the resources, but also on the architectural level to increase processing efficiency
as well as generative power. The complete system architecture is discussed in
Section 2.2. In Section 3, we will use a comprehensive example to describe our
system at work and address some interesting implementation problems. Finally,
we discuss some relevant work in our context in Section 4.

Not to use hybrid systems is quite out of the question now for NLG researchers: everybody needs them, everybody builds them, and everybody claims
to have one. But there are several notions of hybridism around, including stochastic approaches [1], machine learning (ML) [2], and NLG with XSLT [3]. However,
we want to stick to a definition of hybridism that concentrates on a strategy of
mixing only the two classical approaches, shallow and deep generation. [4] describes two types of such hybrid NLG systems: Type I uses shallow generation

---

[1] The acronym stands for **hy**brid **p**ragmatically **e**mbedded **r**ealization with **b**ottom-**up**
generation

A. Belz et al. (Eds.): INLG 2004, LNAI 3123, pp. 205–211, 2004.

with deep elements, type II the opposite, i.e. deep generation with shallow elements. We add a third type to this typology: Our type III uses separate shallow and deep processing branches and combines the results appropriately, in analogy to the approach taken in VERBMOBIL [5] for language analysis.

2 System Overview

2.1 System Core

Our generation system HYPERBUG integrates all three types of hybrid NLG approaches mentioned in Section 1, i.e. it combines shallow processing with deep elements, deep processing with shallow elements, and concurring shallow and deep processing in a single system, relying on a decision module as front-end and a feedback module from deep to shallow generation as back-end. The system core is displayed in Figure 1.

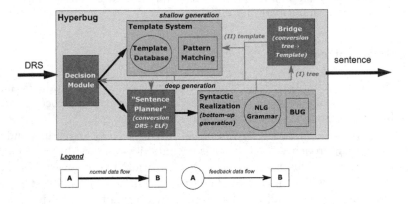

Fig. 1. System Core

A Discourse Representation Structure (DRS) [6] representing the semantic content is fed as input into a **decision module** which determines whether shallow or deep generation is more appropriate to produce the desired output. Its default decision rule is to use deep generation only if shallow generation is unavailable, i.e. if there is no pointer to an appropriate template in its index table.[2] The decision is based on values for certain XPath variables, resulting in an analysis which is only shallow but nevertheless sufficient for the task: We do not want to preoccupy computational resources needed only for deep *or* shallow generation. The XPaths are possibly domain dependent and must be replaced when a domain change is envisaged, but only if the data specifications are modified. Concurring shallow and deep processing branches combined with the decision module result in our system becoming type III in our classification in Section 1.

---

[2] This spares using the somewhat more complex template matching algorithm.

If shallow generation is chosen, a **template system** with an advanced pattern matching technique is invoked, using a database with complex templates[3]: The entries in the template database are recursive and modular, they contain subparts and repeatable sections, syntactic features and pointers to wave files for speech synthesis. Furthermore, access to the NLG lexicon and to the morphology component (linguistic resources normally used only for deep generation) is encoded in our templates. This enriched template system makes our NLG approach one of hybrid type I in our classification as well.

On the other hand, if deep generation is selected, a "**sentence planner**" first converts the input DRS into an Extended Logical Form (ELF). The extensions of a conventional LF include syntactic features like tense and mode, topicalization information, and subordination clause type. Surface forms like proper nouns are also allowed in our ELF; hence our NLG system is also of hybrid type II.

The ELF is then processed by the deep syntactic realization module: As the acronym HYPERBUG already suggests, we have implemented an enhanced version of the **bottom-up generation** algorithm presented in [7] as our deep generation component, using a unification grammar and re-using the system lexicon and morphology component. During the generation process, syntactic information is collected by the unification algorithm and stored in an extended derivation tree. Its leaves represent the surface structures of the words making up the generated sentence, their syntactic categories, and agreement features.

After deep generation has been processed, a "**bridge**" generates a new template out of the derivation tree and feeds it back to the shallow generation branch for further use in the current dialog or in subsequent dialogs. The decision module is also requested to update its index table of available templates, so that utterances of the same type do not have to be processed by the deep generation branch any more. The workload on deep generation is thus consistently reduced at runtime. – In any case, HYPERBUG produces a sentence which is then converted into a wave file and uttered to the user by the speech synthesizer.

2.2   Embedding NLG into Our Dialog System

Our NLG system is not implemented as a stand-alone product, but embedded in a complete generic multi-agent dialog system containing agents for speech analysis, dialog management, speech output, and for the technical system which encapsulates application information and control.

The dialog manager (DM) integrates user and system utterances into the discourse context. It is also responsible for content determination, i.e. it provides the generation module with an output specification, albeit without any linguistic knowledge: The DM is amodal, and from its perspective the language output part of the system is just another application, comparable to the technical system. In our dialog system, this desired output is represented as a DRS and encoded in XML, which is in turn used as the content part of a message in the agent communication language KQML from the DM to HYPERBUG.

---

[3] We will provide an example in Section 3.

The DM also decides which speech act is adequate to integrate the utterance to be generated into the current dialog context[4]. For planning, the utterance in detail, all this information is handed over to the generation module which has to decide how the speech act and the content of the utterance can be verbalized.

3   A Comprehensive Example

In this section, we want to give an overview of our system at work, using an example in a home A/V management domain which is relatively simple but still demonstrates some interesting linguistic issues and implementation problems.

Dialog Manager. Suppose the user has just requested a VCR recording of the program "Tatort" tonight at 08:15 PM and the system wants to inform the user that the request has been processed successfully. In a situation like this, the DM receives a message from the technical system (the A/V management application) whose content is shown in Figure 2.[5]

$$\left[\begin{array}{l} a\ t\ s\ e\ p\ c\ ts\ m\ i\ l\ id\ at\ as \\ \hline [\ldots], \text{has-StartTimeValue}(s, 2004\text{-}03\text{-}28\ 20\text{:}15\text{:}00), \\ [\ldots], \text{has-AVLocationIDValue}(l, \text{ARD}), \\ [\ldots], \text{has-ActionTypeValue}(at, \text{RECORD}), \\ [\ldots], \text{has-ActionStatusValue}(a, \text{WAITING}) \end{array}\right]$$

Fig. 2. DRS representation of the system response

The DRS is accompanied by the information that the message is a response to a request, that a reaction to the request has taken place (the request has been satisfied), and that the effects of the reaction are described in the content of the message. From this information, the DM concludes that it can update the dialog situation: On the one hand, the pending user request needs a response about the successful outcome of the related system activities, and on the other hand, the information in the system message must be communicated to the user.

Therefore, the DM initiates the generation of the German sentence "Ich werde um 20:15 h 'Tatort' aufnehmen." ("I'm going to record 'Tatort' at 08:15 PM.").[6] The DRS in Figure 2 is thus transformed into the XML structure displayed in Figure 3 which serves as input for our generation system.

Preprocessing: The decision module. At first, the XML input is analyzed and information relevant to determining the appropriate generation branch is extracted. This is done using XPath expressions.

In our example, the XML input indicates that the desired action is of the `Record` type. Suppose we have not yet generated a sentence of this type before

---

[4] This decision procedure is described in more detail in [8].

[5] For the reader's convenience, only the parts which are relevant for processing the example are printed out in Figure 2.

[6] From the linguistic point of view, this example is straightforward in several ways: It is just a single main sentence in normal word-order (no topicalization), the verb form is not separated, and there are no complex noun phrases. However, we have an analytical tense form (future tense) and a proper noun which has to be realized without any article here.

```
<SystemDialogAct status="ok" speechact="message_inform" ID="1701">
<Information><ApplicationStatusInfo><TimeInterval>
   <StartTime><StartTimeValue>2004-03-28 20:15:00</StartTimeValue></StartTime>
   <EndTime><EndTimeValue>2004-03-28 21:45:00</EndTimeValue></EndTime>
</TimeInterval>
<AVProgram><AVContentInfo><TitleSpec><MainTitle>
   <MainTitleValue>Tatort</MainTitleValue><ValueLang>de</ValueLang>
</MainTitle></TitleSpec></AVContentInfo>
<AVInstanceInfo><AVLocation>
   <AVLocationID><AVLocationIDValue>ARD</AVLocationIDValue></AVLocationID>
</AVLocation></AVInstanceInfo></AVProgram>
   <ActionType><ActionTypeValue>RECORD</ActionTypeValue></ActionType>
   <ActionStatus><ActionStatusValue>WAITING</ActionStatusValue></ActionStatus>
</ApplicationStatusInfo></Information></SystemDialogAct>
```

Fig. 3. XML input structure for the system response

in our dialog history. Therefore, the decision module cannot find an appropriate entry in its index table of templates and must pass the task of generating the sentence to the deep generation branch.

Deep generation. The "sentence planner" converts the DRS encoded in the XML structure in Figure 3 into the following ELF:

$$\text{(AT (20:15 (FUT (RECORD SYSTEM TATORT))))}$$

To this end, it completes the analysis performed by the decision module and extracts the relevant XPaths needed for conversion. These paths are stored for further use. The ELF contains a proper noun (TATORT) which is normally not allowed in a semantic representation for deep generation but is valid in our type II hybrid NLG system. After processing the ELF input, the deep generation branch produces the derivation tree displayed in Figure 4.

```
[MAIN, [NP, [[PRON [case nom, number sg, person 1]], ich]],
       [VO, [[AUX [number sg, person 1, type FIN]], werde]],
          [S, [VP, [PP, [P, um], [NP, [20:15 uhr]]],
                   [VP, [NP, [[EN [case akk, number sg, person 3]], tatort]],
                        [V1, [V, VGAP], [[VO [type INF]], aufnehmen]]]]],
       [INTPKT, .]]
```

Fig. 4. Derivation tree for our example

Post-processing: The "bridge". Coupling deep and shallow generation in our NLG system is completed by the "bridge" between these two processing branches. The "bridge" uses the deep generation output to generate the template shown in Figure 5. This template is then passed on to the shallow generation branch where it is stored and can be used later for similar sentences.

The dialog act for the generated template is taken from the initial input structure as well as the relevant XPath entries which were stored by the "sentence planner" before. The resulting entry in our template database contains tokens with XPaths and syntactic features (category and agreements), several constant

```
DialogAct: message_inform
Token #1:  ".//TimeInterval/StartTime/StartTimeValue/text()"
Token #2:  ".//AvContentinfo/TitleSpec/MainTitle/MainTitleValue/text()"#N.case_ACC_number_SG
Token #3:  ".//ActionType/ActionTypeValue/text()"
Template #1:
  TempStr: "Ich werde (um %1 %2) %3."
  TempPart #1: "Ich werde (um"
  TempPart #2: "%1"  // reference to token #1 (StartTime)
  TempPart #3: "%2)" // reference to token #2 (MainTitleValue)
  TempPart #4: "%3." // reference to token #3 (ActionType)
```

Fig. 5. Generated template for our example

and variable parts,[7] and an interesting generalization feature: The brackets ()
indicate a potential enumeration (in our example, this is useful if more than one
program will be recorded).

Shallow generation. Hence, the next time a sentence of the type described
in our example has to be generated, the decision module is now able to find an
appropriate entry in its index table. Therefore the shallow generation branch is
invoked. A matching template like the one depicted in Figure 5 is found and
instantiated, producing the sentence mentioned above.

Speech synthesis. Finally, the generated sentence is sent to the speech
synthesis module which is essentially a wrapper agent around the open-source
synthesizer MBROLA. The agent checks for each constant part of the sentence
whether it has already been synthesized before. If so, it uses a pointer to previously stored wave files; if not, the newly synthesized constant parts are stored
for further use. After that, the variable parts are synthesized as well, and the
wave file is concatenated and uttered to the user.

4   Related Work

In [9], the author applies Conversation Acts Theory to NLG, namely to the text
planning part. In our system, we extend this application to linguistic realization
by identifying appropriate realization methods for each conversation act type.

Explanation-based generalization or explanation-based learning (EBL), an
approach known from ML, contains ideas similar to the ones described here and
has already been applied to NLG: In [10], templates for sub-grammars are generated from a corpus using EBL methods. However, normally a training phase,
a running phase, and a separate training corpus are needed in EBL, which is not
the case in our approach.

As we use XML as input structure, generation from XSLT [3] can be seen as
an alternative to our approach, albeit without ML ideas and deep processing.
Therefore XSLT generation is rather shallow and static in our point of view.

---

[7] The distinction between constant and variable parts is important for our speech
synthesis agent, see below.

5   Conclusion and Further Work

We have presented a hybrid approach to linguistic realization embedded in a natural language dialog system. The NLG system is fully implemented in Java and currently used in three different domains, namely home A/V management, model train controlling, and B2B e-procurement. The required domain shifts were carried out without major problems, but admittedly not completely automatically.

We are going to introduce deep processing into our "sentence planner" in the near future using the DL inference engine RACER [11]. Furthermore, we want to improve the decision module by implementing a planning procedure which makes use of the speech act, the discourse situation, and the user model to ensure that the most appropriate processing branch is selected.

Acknowledgements

The author would like to thank Peter Reiß for fruitful discussions and Bernd Ludwig for some very helpful comments on this paper.

References

1. Oh, A., Rudnicky, A.: Stochastic language generation for spoken dialogue systems. In: Proc. ANLP/NAACL 2000 Workshop on Conversational Systems, Seattle (2000)
2. Corston-Oliver, S.: An overview of amalgam: A machine-learned generation module. In: Proc. INLG-2002, New York (2002)
3. Wilcock, G.: Integrating natural language generation with xml web technology. In: Proc. EACL-2003 Demo Sessions, Budapest (2003)
4. Busemann, S.: A shallow formalism for defining personalized text. In: Proc. KI-98 Workshop, Bremen (1998)
5. Wahlster, W.: Verbmobil: Foundations of Speech-to-Speech Translation. Berlin, Heidelberg, New York (2000)
6. Kamp, H., Reyle, U.: From Disourse To Logic. Dordrecht (1993)
7. van Noord, G.: An overview of head-driven bottom-up generation. In Dale, R., Mellish, C., Zock, M., eds.: Current Research in Natural Language Generation, Berlin, Heidelberg, New York (1990)
8. Ludwig, B.: Dialogue understanding in dynamic domains. In Kühnlein, P., Rieser, H., Zevat, H., eds.: Perspectives on Dialogue in the New Millennium. John Benjamins Publishing Company (2003)
9. Stent, A.J.: Dialogue Systems as Conversational Partners: Applying Conversation Acts Theory to Natural Language Generation for Task-Oriented Mixed-Initiative Spoken Dialogue. PhD thesis, University of Massachusetts Amherst (2001)
10. Neumann, G.: Applying explanation-based learning to control and speeding-up natural language generation. In: Proc. ACL/EACL-97, Madrid (1997)
11. Möller, R., Haarslev, V.: Description logics for the semantic web: Racer as a basis for building agent systems. KI - Zeitschrift für Künstliche Intelligenz (special issue on Semantic Web), No. 3 (2003)

Two Kinds of Alternative Sets and a Marking Principle – When to Say *Also*

Kristina Striegnitz

Computational Linguistics, Saarland University
kris@coli.uni-sb.de

Abstract. Discourse anaphora other than definite NPs have not received much attention in generation. This paper proposes a strategy for generating the additive particle *also*, a non-nominal discourse anaphor. The strategy is based on a treatment of additive particles as markers rather than presupposition triggers (following [14]) and two sorts of contextually given alternative sets.

1 Introduction

Discourse anaphora are important devices for achieving cohesion in discourse [3]. In generation, work on anaphoric expressions has mainly concentrated on definite descriptions and pronouns. Other kinds of discourse anaphora, and in particular anaphoric discourse adverbials [13], have not received a systematic treatment as anaphoric expressions. Based on the assumption that being able to generate a wider variety of anaphora will allow us to build generation systems that produce more cohesive output, this paper presents a first step toward an approach to the generation of anaphoric adverbials. It proposes a strategy for deciding when to use additive particles, such as *also* or *too*, which establish an anaphoric link to an event previously mentioned in the discourse. While the paper discusses the special case of additive particles, I think that the concepts and mechanisms proposed will also be useful for other anaphoric expressions.

Section 2 reviews the basic properties of additive particles. Section 3 then characterizes the conditions under which additive particles are used. Following work in theoretical semantics, this characterization is based on sets of alternative entities. I further distinguish two kinds of alternative sets that play a role: sets which group entities due to their ontological category and sets which are induced by discourse structure. In Section 4, I introduce the general generation strategy which is based on a treatment of additive particles as context markers as proposed in [14]. I argue that this view is better suited from a generation point of view than the traditional view of additive particles as presupposition triggers. Section 5 describes an implementation of the suggested strategy in an application that in particular requires the generation of object descriptions. Section 6 concludes the paper.

A. Belz et al. (Eds.): INLG 2004, LNAI 3123, pp. 212–218, 2004.

2   Additive Particles

Additive particles, such as *also, too, either, associate* with a constituent of the sentence they are used in (the *associated constituent*) and express that whatever is said about the referent of this constituent also holds of some *alternative* entity (see, e.g., [4,5,9,7]). In (1a), e.g., *also* associates with *Antonia* and expresses that besides Antonia somebody else gave a book to Norbert. In (1b) and (1c), *also* associates with *a book* and *Norbert* respectively, and the alternative entities are some chocolate and Charlie.

(1) a. *Charlie gave a book to Norbert. Antonia **also** gave a book to Norbert.*
     b. *Antonia gave some chocolate to Norbert. She **also** gave a book to Norbert.*

     c. *Antonia gave a book to Charlie. She **also** gave a book to Norbert.*

This paper aims at determining when to use an additive particle. It will not discuss issues pertaining to the realization, such as the choice between different additive particles or the position of them in a sentence. Therefore, all of my examples use the additive particle *also*, which is the most frequently used and the most flexible.

In order to devise a generation strategy two questions have to be answered: First, what characterizes the situations in which the use of an additive particle is licensed. In particular, we have to know when two entities count as alternatives. Second, how is the use of an additive particle triggered? The next two sections address each of these questions in turn.

3   Two Kinds of Alternative Sets

Above I said that *also* expresses that there is an entity which a) is an alternative of the entity referred to by the associated constituent and of which b) the property attributed to the associated constituent holds as well. So, in a generation system we will have to be able to decide whether an entity has alternatives, i.e., whether two entities belong to the same *alternative set*. Alternative sets are formed according to ontological and contextual restrictions [5,11], but what exactly that means is usually not specified any further. I now show that there are two different types of alternative sets that play a role. Consider the following example.

(2) (a) *Antonia invited friends for a Japanese dinner.* (b) *She prepared miso soup, sushi, and tempura.* (c) *She **also** made some green tea ice cream.*

The associated constituent of *also* is *green tea ice cream*. So, the relevant alternative set has to contain green tea ice cream as well as miso soup, sushi and tempura. There are two possible explanations. First, the alternative set in question could be the ontologically defined set of (Japanese) dishes. Second, the alternative set could be evoked by discourse structure. The *question under discussion* [8,2,12] for sentences (a) and (b) is what Antonia prepared for dinner.

Green tea ice cream, miso soup etc. all belong to the alternative set of all those things that Antonia prepared.

Example (2) does not let us decide which of the two possible alternative sets triggered the use of *also*, but here is an example which can only be explained with the help of structurally evoked sets.

(3) (a) *Antonia hit Norbert* (b) *because he had stolen her bicycle.* (c) *He had* **also** *called her a monkey.*

The associated constituent of *also* in the last sentence is *has called her a monkey.* The use of *also* marks that the event of Norbert calling Antonia a monkey (let's call it e_1) as well as the event of Norbert stealing Antonia's bicycle (let's call it e_2) are reasons for Antonia's hitting Norbert. So, the relevant alternative set has to be a set of events including both e_1 and e_2. It is not plausible to assume an ontological category that subsumes both of these events. Discourse structure, on the other hand, does allow us to group e_1 and e_2 into one set. The question under discussion for sentences (b) and (c) is *Why did Antonia hit Norbert?*, i.e., $\lambda x[reason(x, e)]$ with e being the event of Antonia hitting Norbert. The events e_1 and e_2 both fit this description and are therefore alternatives.

Example (4) shows that ontologically defined alternative sets are also important. In this example, *also* expresses that Charlie, besides Norbert, likes cake. So, the relevant alternative set contains at least Charlie and Norbert. The set of all human beings would be a possibility. Discourse structure, on the other hand, does not provide an appropriate alternative set. The issue addressed by sentence (b) is why Norbert ate all the cake, while the question under discussion that sentence (e) is answering is why Antonia scolded Norbert.

(4) (a) *Antonia baked a cake.* (b) *Norbert really likes cake* (c) *and ate it all.* (d) *Antonia scolded him* (e) *because Charlie* **also** *likes cake.*

To sum up, I call two entities *alternatives* if they both belong to the same alternative set $\{x|P(x)\}$ where P is either an ontological category or the question under discussion. I will furthermore say that a sentence describing the event e and attributing property $\varphi(e)$ to an entity a is *also-parallel* with regard to the context if there is an alternative b of a such that the discourse context entails that $\varphi(e')$ also holds of b for some discourse old event e'. Additive particles are used to express that a sentence is also-parallel with regard to the context.

The distinction between ontology based and discourse structure based alternative sets is based on an exploratory corpus study of 167 cases of *also* found in the Wall Street Journal and the Brown Corpus. 60% of the 62 cases examined in the Brown Corpus involved discourse structure based alternatives and 32% ontologically defined alternatives. In the remaining cases it was either not possible to decide between the two options (3%) or to analyze the example at all (6%).

4   Additive Particles as Context Markers

Traditionally, *also* is taken to trigger a presupposition. According to [4], e.g., *also* triggers the following presupposition: "There are other x under consideration besides the entity *e* described by the associated constituent, such that what is said about *e* also holds of *x*." Zeevat [14], however, points out that many particles (among them additive particles) have a number of characteristics which are untypical for presupposition triggers. He argues that the behavior of these particles can be explained better if a *marking principle* is assumed and they are treated as *context markers*, i.e., expressions that mark that the content of the current sentence is in a certain relation to the discourse context. The *additive marking principle* relevant here would look as follows: If a sentence is also-parallel with regard to the context, then this has to be marked by an appropriate marker.

Zeevat's approach is useful from a generation point of view because it predicts that an also-parallel sentence not containing an appropriate marker is infelicitous. Purely presuppositional analyses do not make such predictions. Assume that a generation system has to describe the eventuality *like(antonia,cake)* in a context in which *like(antonia,ice_cream)* holds. The sentence *Antonia likes cake* and the sentence *Antonia also likes cake* both express this content. The second version additionally carries a presupposition which is satisfied in the given context. This presupposition, however, is coupled to the use of the lexical item *also*. It imposes a restriction on the contexts the second sentence can be used in; it does not have any impact on the appropriateness of the version without *also*.

Marking principles impose well-formedness constraints on linguistic expressions. But for generation purposes they can also be viewed as rules licensing the introduction of markers. The next section describes an example of how to integrate a treatment of marking principles into a sentence planner.

5 An Implementation

A strategy for generating additive particles based on the notions described so far is currently being implemented in the generation module of a text-based computer game. One of the main generation tasks in this application is the description of rooms and objects.

The system has access to the following knowledge bases: the state of the game world, what the user knows about the game world, and information about the discourse history, such as salience of entities. In the first step schemata are used to plan the text structure. The output of this text is a tree with communicative goals for individual sentences at the leaves. A SPUD-like module [10] is then used to plan and realize these sentences.

5.1 Detecting Alternative Sets

For detecting ontologically defined alternatives I follow previous approaches, such as [6], which uses ontology based alternative sets for generating contrastive intonation, and assume that all entities with the same parent class (the most specific class they belong to) are alternatives. For applications with small, shallow ontologies this seems to work quite well. For bigger ontologies, however, it might be problematic that the design of the ontology directly influences what

user: *Look at the green frog.* The frog is ugly and slimy. It is wearing a small crown user: *Look at the brown frog.* The brown frog also is ugly. It is carrying a tiny sword.	user: *Look at the sword and the crown.* The sword is old and rusty. It has an inscription. The crown is golden. It also has an inscription.

user: *Look at the frog.* The frog is green. It is wearing a small crown. It is also carrying a tiny sword.

Fig. 1. Example interactions involving also-parallelism.

counts as alternatives. I furthermore consider entities alternatives if the user explicitly introduced them as a group by using a coordinated or plural NP. The examples at the top of Figure 1 involve ontologically defined alternatives. The green frog and the brown frog are alternatives because they both have the parent class *frog*. The sword and the crown are alternatives because the user introduced them as a group.

Discourse structure based alternative sets are determined during document planning. The document planning module is based on schemata providing templates for how to structure the information in the description. Schemata can be viewed as specifying which questions have to be raised (implicitly) to fulfill a particular communicative goal. Under this view, the steps of a schema (calls of sub-schemata or instructions to retrieve information from the knowledge base) correspond to questions under discussion. So, whenever a query to the knowledge base (corresponding to a question under discussion) yields more than one answer, these answers form an alternative set. The crown and the sword mentioned at the bottom of Figure 1 are alternatives evoked by discourse structure. The schema used for generating this description first presents the physical appearance of the object and then its accessory. The knowledge base query for retrieving the accessory returns several answers (the crown and the sword) which are taken to constitute an alternative set.

5.2   The Sentence Planner and Surface Realizer

SPUD [10] starts from communicative goals of the form $\langle Cat, a, \Gamma \rangle$ where Cat is the syntactic category of the linguistic structure that has to be built, a is the main discourse entity described by that structure (e.g., sentences describe events or states), and Γ is a set of facts that the output should convey. SPUD then simultaneously assembles the semantic content and syntactic structure of an utterance achieving this goal. This is done as follows: Starting from a tree consisting of one node (with label Cat), TAG (Tree Adjoining Grammar) elementary trees are added incrementally until a) the tree is syntactically complete, b) all references to entities known to the hearer are unambiguous, and c) all facts specified in Γ are conveyed. In each search step, SPUD computes all possible ways of extending the current tree, the possibilities are ranked according to heuristics evaluating the progress toward the goal, and the best one is retained. In SPUD's grammar, elementary trees are associated with a representation of their assertions and presuppositions. The addition of an elementary tree is licensed if the asserted part of its semantics is supported by the system's knowledge and the presupposed part is supported by the shared knowledge.

Marking principles constitute additional constraints on the tree being built. The final tree therefore has to satisfy the following additional constraint: if a marking principle applies, the structure has to contain an appropriate marker, and vice versa. In each search step, all elementary trees for markers contributing information that is satisfying a requirement issued by a marking principle are licensed to be added. They are competing with all other possible extensions.

Elementary trees for markers are licensed to be added if their contribution satisfies a requirement issued by a marking principle. That means marking principles are checked in each search step.

The additive marking principle is defined to only apply to syntactically complete sentences. It checks whether the sentence refers to an entity a for which an alternative b is available. If this is the case, it checks whether replacing the reference to a with one to b yields a formula that follows from the shared knowledge. This is best illustrated by means of an example. Assume that the expression built so far is *the frog has a crown*. The grammar associates the presupposition $frog(X)$ and the assertion $have(Z, X, Y) \land crown(Y)$ with this sentence. The variables Z, X, and Y are bound to domain entities when choosing the corresponding elementary trees. Let's assume that the intended binding is $\sigma = \{Z \leftarrow e,\ X \leftarrow f_1,\ Y \leftarrow c_1\}$, and let's furthermore assume that the hearer can correctly resolve the presupposition, so that the information conveyed to the hearer is $have(Z, f_1, Y) \land crown(Y)$. Z and Y are two entities which are new to the hearer.

Let's say entity f_2 is an alternative of f_1. If there is a variable binding σ' such that $\sigma'(have(Z, f_2, Y) \land crown(Y))$ follows from the shared knowledge, then the sentence is also-parallel. Markers with the contribution $also\text{-}parallel(\sigma(Z), \sigma'(Z))$ are licensed to be added. The pragmatic constraints associated with additive markers furthermore require that $\sigma'(Z)$ be discourse old.

If instead of entity f_1, entity c_1 has an alternative, e.g., c_2, then we have to check for a variable binding σ' such that $\sigma'(have(Z, F_1, c_2))$ follows from the shared knowledge.

6   Conclusions

I have proposed a strategy for generating sentences containing the additive particle additive particles. I assume that the use of additive particles is triggered by a marking principle along the lines of [14] requiring that a sentence be marked if it is also-parallel with regard to the context. I believe that this view is useful for generating other kinds of anaphoric expression as well, such as other discourse particles, but also, e.g., NPs with the determiner *another*. Also-parallelism is defined in terms of alternative sets. To make the notion of alternative sets useful for generation, we have to make more precise according to which properties entities are grouped in alternative sets. I argue that there are two kinds of alternative sets which play a role in the analysis of *also*: sets which group entities due to their ontological category and sets which are induced by the implicit questions structuring discourse [12].

This paper has concentrated on characterizing the conditions under which additive markers are used. Further investigation addressing the realization and the influence of salience is needed. However, I believe that the proposed strategy is a starting point for investigating the generation of other focus particles and, more generally, other expressions involving alternative sets, such as the alternative markers studied in [1].

References

1. Gann Bierner. *Alternative Phrases – Theoretical Analysis and Practical Application*. PhD thesis, University of Edinburgh, 2001.
2. Jonathan Ginzburg. Dynamics and the Semantics of Dialogue. In Jerry Seligman and Dag Westerstahl, editors, *Logic, Language and Computation*. CSLI Lecture Notes, 1996.
3. M.A.K. Halliday and Ruqaiya Hasan. *Cohesion in English*. Longman, London, 1976.
4. Lauri Karttunen and Stanley Peters. Conventional Implicature. In Choon-Kyu Oh and David A. Dinneen, editors, *Presupposition*. Academic Press, 1979.
5. Manfred Krifka. Compositional Semantics for Multiple Focus Constructions. In Joachim Jacobs, editor, *Informationsstruktur und Grammatik*. Westdeutscher Verlag, 1992.
6. Scott Prevost. *A Semantics of Contrast and Information Structure for Specifying Intonation in Spoken Language Generation*. PhD thesis, University of Pennsylvania, 1995.
7. Marga Reis and Inger Rosengren. A Modular Approach to the Grammar of Additive Particles: the Case of German *Auch*. *Journal of Semantics*, 14, 1997.
8. Craige Roberts. Information Structure in Discourse: Towards an Integrated Formal Theory of Pragmatics. In Jae-Hak Yoon and Andreas Kathol, editors, *Papers in Semantics*, volume 49 of *OSU Working Papers in Linguistics*. Ohio State University, 1996.
9. Mats Rooth. *Association with Focus*. PhD thesis, University of Massachusetts, Amherst, 1985.
10. Matthew Stone, Christine Doran, Bonnie Webber, Tonia Bleam, and Martha Palmer. Microplanning with Communicative Intentions: The SPUD System. *Computational Intelligence*, 19:311–381, 2003.
11. Enric Vallduví and Maria Vilkuna. On Rheme and Kontrast. In *The Limits of Syntax*, volume 29 of *Syntax and Semantics*. Academic Press, 1998.
12. Jan van Kuppevelt. Discourse structure, topicality and questioning. *Journal of Linguistics*, 31, 1995.
13. Bonnie Webber, Matthew Stone, Aravind Joshi, and Alistair Knott. Anaphora and Discourse Structure. *Computational Linguistics*, 29, 2003.
14. Henk Zeevat. Particles: Presupposition Triggers, Context Markers or Speech Act Markers. In Reinhard Blutner and Henk Zeevat, editors, *Optimality Theory and Pragmatics*. Palgrave-McMillan, 2003.

Author Index